MOSCOW'S CITY GOVERNMENT

MOSCOW'S CITY GOVERNMENT

E.S. Savas and J.A. Kaiser

PRAEGER

PRAEGER SPECIAL STUDIES • PRAEGER SCIENTIFIC

New York • Philadelphia • Eastbourne, UK
Toronto • Hong Kong • Tokyo • Sydney

Library of Congress Cataloging in Publication Data

Savas, Emanuel S.
    Moscow's city government.

    Bibliography: p.
    Includes index.
    1. Moscow (R.S.F.S.R.)—Politics and government.
I. Kaiser, J. A. II. Title.
JS6082.S38   1985   352.047'312   84-26308
ISBN 0-03-000114-5

JS
6082
.S38
1985

Published in 1985 by Praeger Publishers
CBS Educational and Professional Publishing
a Division of CBS Inc.
521 Fifth Avenue, New York, NY 10175 USA

© 1985 by Praeger Publishers

56789 052 987654321

Printed in the United States of America
on acid-free paper

To our wives and children:
Helen, Jonathan, and Stephen
Kay, Shannon, Matthew, Daniel, and Meghan

PREFACE

This volume is the result of a collaborative effort by U.S. and Soviet coauthors under the 1973 U.S.-U.S.S.R. Agreement on Scientific and Technical Cooperation. Specifically, it is a product of a joint project on the management of large cities, of which Dr. E. S. Savas was the U.S. director, and which had Soviet directors as well. This book has a counterpart volume on the government of New York City, published in the Soviet Union.

An unprecedented effort of this sort was not without difficulties. It took time, effort, and goodwill to overcome communication problems, problems that were not due to language but to the episodic nature of contacts and to the vast—and initially bewildering—difference between the two societies with respect to the role of city government. The magnitude of the difference became evident to Dr. Savas on his first visit to the Soviet Union in this context, shortly after the so-called détente agreement created the opportunity to study Soviet cities. This visit came at a time when U.S. cities began experiencing fiscal stress that was a symptom of shortcomings in their strategic management. There was a clear need for a book that would describe the basic organization and functions of U.S. and Soviet city governments so that, with this as a foundation, more substantive collaborative work might subsequently take place in numerous practical areas of mutual interest, such as productivity, decentralization, neighborhood governance, urban development, mass transit, traffic control, and environmental protection. Therefore, this book was proposed by Dr. Savas as part of a joint undertaking, and the Soviet side agreed.

The basic idea is that exposure to the practices of other cities is valuable for managing one's own city. Indeed, the greater the differences between cities and the societies in which they are embedded, the more likely it is that revealing insights will be gained. Studying municipal management in Soviet cities casts an oblique light on U.S. practices that enhances perspective.

The original, ambitious plans called for the Soviet side to prepare materials for Moscow and Leningrad while analogous materials for New York and Los Angeles were to be written by the U.S. authors, all following a common outline. However, the Soviet authors, who were located in the Moscow city government, found it difficult to secure the cooperation of city officials in Leningrad; the professional collegiality that we take for granted in the United States under such circumstances is by no means a universal attitude. Ultimately, to save time and to keep the size of the resulting book within reason, it was jointly decided to include only New York and Moscow in the work.

There were institutional barriers also, as is suggested by the recurring use of the term "Soviet side" in the preceding paragraphs. Whereas the U.S. half of the work was undertaken by us as scholars with municipal expertise acting entirely without government supervision, as is perfectly normal in the United States, the Soviet half of the work was undertaken as an authorized and controlled activity of the Moscow city government. Consequently, the initial Soviet product resembled a bureaucratic committee report with several anonymous contributors.

After several exchanges of materials, requests for additional materials, and meetings to clarify the many confusing and arcane features of each other's cities, each side submitted a report on its city to the other side. The text that was prepared by the Soviet authors was translated in the United States, edited extensively by the U.S. authors, and, inasmuch as it had some significant gaps, was supplemented by these authors with information obtained in discussions with knowledgeable and responsible Moscow authorities. (This was no easy task, for city budget documents are classified "secret" and were not available to us.) The material developed in this manner by the U.S. authors is clearly labeled as such wherever feasible.

The initial overview chapter was written primarily by Dr. Savas. In a number of other places throughout the book, the U.S. authors make some asides or explanatory comments; these are set off in brackets. Nevertheless, one should note that the process of editing inevitably results in changes in emphasis, and hence editorializing, which may have altered the intention of the Soviet authors. The U.S. authors, as editors of the Soviet-prepared materials, can honestly say that they made a sincere effort to be faithful to the facts as they know them while editing out some propagandistic phrases and overtones that almost inevitably, it seems, find their way into authoritative Soviet reports. However, in some cases, the U.S. authors left an accurate translation intact, however stilted or embarrassing the thought, in order to convey more accurately the (sometimes chilling) view of society that the Soviet authors reflect.

It should be stressed that most of the original material was prepared for us by Moscow city employees, and, with relatively few exceptions, it does not represent original research by the U.S. authors and therefore cannot be described as material that we developed independently and could stake our professional reputations upon.

Despite the obstacles and difficulties, both sides exhibited patience and a common desire to achieve the objective originally set forth. Perseverance prevailed. While other western authors, notably Cattell,[1] Frolich,[2] Taubman,[3] and Lewis and Sternheimer,[4] have written about Soviet cities, primarily from a political science viewpoint, to the best of our knowledge this is the first time that municipal management in Moscow has been described in detail, in English, in a form readily accessible to scholars and practitioners in the field.

The data were obtained over a prolonged period in the late 1970s. Given the great difficulty involved in collecting this information, subsequent updating was deemed by us to be impractical. The principal value of the information lies in its uniqueness rather than its timeliness.

This was intended to be only a first and imperfect step along the road to fruitful joint U.S.-Soviet research on urban problems, with the ultimate goal being to enable city officials to learn and benefit from the insights and experiences of the other country, so that urban dwellers in both lands might enjoy a better life. Unfortunately, the Soviet invasion of Afghanistan dashed these and many other hopes as well.

NOTES

1. David Cattell, *Leningrad: A Case Study of Soviet Urban Government*, Praeger, New York, 1968.

2. B. M. Frolich, *Soviet Urban Politics*, Unpublished doctoral thesis, York University, Toronto, 1970.

3. William Taubman, *Governing Soviet Cities: Bureaucratic Politics and Urban Development in the U.S.S.R.*, Praeger, New York, 1973.

4. Carol W. Lewis and Stephen Sternheimer, *Soviet Urban Management: With Comparison to the United States*, Praeger, New York, 1979.

ACKNOWLEDGMENTS

The authors are indebted to many people in the United States and in the Soviet Union, too numerous to mention, for both the opportunity to see and study city governments in the latter country and for providing the information and framework that are reflected in this volume. Special thanks, however, must go to Don Aufenkamp, David Cattell, and Peter Tropp, and to the National Science Foundation, which supported this work. An award for patience and diligence must go to Mrs. Blanche Winikoff, who typed this manuscript and numerous earlier drafts.

CONTENTS

Preface   vii

Acknowledgments   xi

Introduction   xix

1. URBAN DEVELOPMENT   1

2. BASIC FACTS ABOUT MOSCOW   5
      History   5
      Physical Features   5
      Climate   6
      Political Geography   6
      Demography   8
      Economy   11
      Transportation   13
      Housing and Utilities   14
      Education   16
      Environmental Protection   17
      Parks and Recreation   17

3. ORGANIZATION OF THE CITY GOVERNMENT   19
      Legal Basis of the Authority of the City Soviets   19
      Rights and Powers of the Local Soviets   22
      Structure of the Municipal Government   28
      Structure of the Raion (District) Government   34
      Functions of the City and Raion Soviets   36
      Functions of the City (or Raion) Soviet Executive Committee   36
      Standing Committees, Deputies, Deputy Groups, and
         Public Organizations   44
      Role of the Communist Party   47
      Appendix   49

4. LONG-TERM PLANNING AND ECONOMIC DEVELOPMENT   54
      Basic Planning Procedure   54
      General Plan for Municipal Development   56

5. SHORT-TERM PLANNING AND BUDGETING   60
      Budgeting Procedures   60
      Revenue Sources   65

	City and Raion Revenues	67
	Budget Expenditures	71
	Modern Management Efforts	79
6.	PERSONNEL	85
	Administration for Personnel and Training	87
	Evaluation of Specialists and Technical Managers	90
7.	MUNICIPAL SERVICES	92
	Housing	92
	Health Care	115
	Education	121
	Preschool Children's Institutions	127
	Transportation	130
	Public Services	142
	Water and Waste Water	166
	Parks	170
	Public Safety	174
	Trade and Public Food Services	177
	Everyday and Communal Services	187
	Appendix	198
Bibliography		201
Index		202
About the Authors		206

LIST OF TABLES AND FIGURES

TABLES

2.1	The Raions of Moscow	7
2.2	Population Growth in Moscow	8
2.3	Distribution of Moscow's Inhabitants by Age	9
2.4	Illustrative Measures of Production in Moscow, 1973-77	12
2.5	Outputs of Selected Industries in Moscow, 1971	13
2.6	Railway Activity in Moscow, 1972-77	14
2.7	Educational Level of the Population of Moscow, 1970	16
3.1	City Agencies Under Dual Subordination	35
5.1	Sources of Actual Revenue, 1975	68
5.2	Fixed and Other Income in City Revenues, 1975	69
5.3	Actual Budget Expenditures, 1975	72
5.4	Expenditures for Capital Investments, 1975	72
6.1	Estimated Number of Moscow City Employees	86
7.1	Moscow Housing Statistics	93
7.2	Planning Norms for Housing	93
7.3	Expenditure for Housing	94
7.4	Growth of Housing Stock in Moscow	95
7.5	Staffing Norms for Administrative and Management Personnel in a Zhek	106
7.6	Work Expenditure Norms for Current Repairs	110
7.7	Rates for Converting Other Activities into an Equivalent Area Cleaned	111
7.8	Selected Norms for Complex Capital Repairs	112
7.9	Selected Norms for Optional Capital Repairs	113
7.10	Selected Norms for the Improvement of Facilities	114
7.11	Selected Material Expenditure Norms for Repairs	114
7.12	Statistics of the Moscow Public Health System	115
7.13	Hospital Centers in Moscow, 1970	117
7.14	Growth of Health Services in Moscow	122
7.15	Education Statistics, 1970	125
7.16	Number of Schools by Raion, 1970	126
7.17	Recent Preschool Enrollment	128

7.18   Distribution of Preschool Children's Institutions
            Among the Raions of Moscow, 1977   129
7.19   Growth of the Moscow Public Transport System   135
7.20   Changing Patterns of Public Transport Usage   136
7.21   Metro Operating Statistics, 1974   138
7.22   Profits from Metro Operations   138
7.23   Profits from Surface Transit Operations   139
7.24   The Moscow Street and Public Works System   147
7.25   Recent and Planned Street Services   148
7.26   Work Measures for a Recent Winter Quarter
            in Moscow, January to March   149
7.27   Road Construction Material per 1,000 Square Meters
            of Paved Roads and Streets   149
7.28   Standard Use of Materials for the Repair and
            Maintenance of 1,000 Square Meters of City Streets   150
7.29   Volume of Work for Street Cleaning   152
7.30   Types of Vehicles Used in Snow Removal   153
7.31   Cost Structure of the Moscow Refuse Collection Enterprises   159
7.32   Refuse Collection Measures   164
7.33   Illustrative Activity Measures for the Road and Public
            Service Administration, January to March 1975   164
7.34   The Moscow Water Supply System, 1970   168
7.35   The Moscow Waste Water Treatment System, 1970   169
7.36   Growth of Water Supply and Waste Water Systems in Moscow   170
7.37   The Moscow Park System   172
7.38   Selected Municipal Expenditures for Parks and Greenery   174
7.39   The Moscow Emergency Ambulance System, 1975   177
7.40   Trade and Food Enterprises in Moscow   184
7.41   Data on Equipment Used in the Retail System   185
7.42   Growth of Retail Trade Turnover   185
7.43   Growth Turnover in Public Eating Places   185
7.44   Growth of the Trade and Food Service System   186
7.45   The Moscow Service Network and Its Output   197

FIGURES

2.1   Effect of Natural Growth and Migration on the
            Population of Moscow, 1960-74   10
3.1   Organizational Structure of the Moscow City Government   30
3.2   Organizational Chart of the Moscow Soviet Executive
            Committee and the City Planning Commission (Gorplan)   32
3.3   Distribution of Responsibilities on the Moscow Soviet
            Executive Committee   33
3.4   Structure of a Raion (District) Soviet of Worker's Deputies   37

7.1	Administrative Bodies for the Design, Construction, Allocation, and Operation of Housing in Moscow	97
7.2	Organization of Housing Management in Moscow	101
7.3	Typical Organizational Structure of a Raion Administration of Housing in Moscow	102
7.4	Typical Organizational Structure of a Housing Operations Office (Zhek) in Moscow	104
7.5	Organization of the System of Public Health in Moscow	116
7.6	Organizational Structure of the Main Moscow Administration for Public Health	119
7.7	Organizational Structure of a Sanitary-Epidemiologic Station	120
7.8	Organizational Structure of the Moscow Main Administration of Public Education	124
7.9	Organizational Structure of the Passenger Transport Administration	131
7.10	Organizational Structure of the Administration of Taxi and Automobile Transport	133
7.11	Organizational Structure of the Main Moscow Administration of Auto Transport (Glavmosavtotrans)	134
7.12	System Map of the Moscow Metro	137
7.13	Organizational Structure of the Moscow Administration of Roads and Public Services	143
7.14	Subordinate Enterprises of the Moscow Administration of Roads and Public Services	145
7.15	Organizations That Provide and Receive Sanitation Services	158
7.16	Organizational Structure of the Administration of Water and Sewers	167
7.17	Organization of the Moscow Main Administration of Culture	171
7.18	Organization of the Moscow Administration of Forests and Parks	173
7.19	Organizational Structure of the Trade and Public Food Service System in Moscow	179
7.20	Organizational Structure of Everyday Services in Moscow	190
7.21	The System of Planning for the Everyday Services of Moscow	191
7.22	Labor Time of Workers in Different Sections of a Laundry Enterprise	193

INTRODUCTION

A U.S. citizen studying Soviet cities is struck first of all by the vast difference between the functions of municipal governments in the two countries. In the United States, the city governments are engaged in cleaning streets, putting out fires, running schools, providing social services, and so forth. In the Soviet Union, the city governments not only do most of these same things, but in addition they operate hotels, restaurants, retail stores, department stores, bakeries, breweries, tailor shops, ice cream carts, beauty parlors, and factories that produce household goods. They deliver virtually all goods, including bread, boots, and bricks. They build and operate most of the housing in the city, and administer the pension system for retirees. In fact, so large are these responsibilities that the services traditionally considered to be municipal in the United States constitute a rather minor activity of city governments in the Soviet Union.

The feeling of disorientation is heightened when one peruses the list of Moscow city agencies in Chapter 3. What is one to make of the Commission for the Preparation of Propositions Concerning the Distribution of Space in the First Stories of Houses? Or of the Supervisory Society of Ornamental Dog Breeding, the Office of Issues Related to the All-Union Voluntary Society for the Assistance to the Army, Air Force, and Navy of the Soviet Union, and the Office of the Study to Organize Workers' Recreation?

But then again a Moscow city official would no doubt be equally bewildered by New York's Firearms Control Board, the Vacancy Control Board (for city jobs, not housing), the Board of Ethics, the Commission on Human Rights, the Mayor's Committee on Judiciary, the Board of Revision of Awards, the Subway Service Watchdog Commission, the New York State Board of Masseur Examiners, and, in 1970, the Temporary State Commission to Study Transplantation of Vital Organs of Human Beings.

When one talks to Soviet city officials and reads what they write about city government, it becomes very clear that they view the city as a production unit; that is, it is a machine or a factory for producing goods, and the principal role of city government is to feed, clothe, and house the workers and their families, and provide harmless recreation between work periods. The city is a company town, where the company is the state and the city government is simply the local agent of the state. The subjective feeling of this observer was a negative one: The notion of a city as the soaring achievement of civilization, the stage on which the dreams and ambitions of creative and talented individuals come together, does not apply here. The Soviet city is simply an organized engine of production, a work station whose monuments and cultural attractions—impressive though they are—now have a primarily utilitarian function, namely, to enrich the work break. The city is an economic engine where production is the power stroke and sociocultural activities represent the recovery stroke.

Indeed, there is even a caste system within this unit of production. There is real production and then there is the service sector. The latter has long been considered a decidedly inferior activity—the emphasis has been on the production of tangible, material goods. (However, there is growing official recognition of the shortage and inadequacy of services, including retail clerks and waitresses, and it is planned to transform 350,000 jobs from the production to the service sector.)

Having said all this, the virtues of such a view of the city should not be entirely overlooked. Consider the case of New York where the city government plays a relatively indirect role in the city's economy. For many years, elected officials treated local business and industry as a convenient cow to be milked, providing cream for the city's coffers, and they paid relatively little attention to what was needed to maintain a healthy local economy. In other words, compared with their Moscow counterparts, the officials did not look at the city as an integrated economic entity that provided a livelihood for its residents in exchange for the latter's productive labor. Their view of the city was narrow and circumscribed, for their formal responsibilities were limited compared with the all-encompassing authority of their Soviet city counterparts. Their short-sighted policies cost New York dearly, as jobs and jobholders left the city to seek a higher quality of life elsewhere.

PLANNING

Planning is the official religion of the state. The plan is pervasive, all embracing, and sacrosanct. It is cited as the ultimate authority and, in effect, has the force of law.

An action in accordance with the plan is justifiable, and failure to do something not in the plan is excusable. Whereas in the United States the chief virtue of planning, such as it is, is generally considered to be the process, in the Soviet Union it is the product that reigns supreme.

The size of the planning bureaucracy is awesome. Noting its rapid growth, Kruschchev is said to have remarked with resignation that by the year 2000, every man, woman, and child in the Soviet Union would be a planner. Impressionistically, staff agencies seem bloated, whereas line agencies, which are supposed to do the actual work, seem starved by comparison. Informed visitors who look out their hotel window and watch a solitary sweeper at work can readily visualize the vast assemblage of planners, directors, chiefs, section heads, planners, liaison personnel, coordinators, expediters, planners, norm setters, controllers, inspectors, committee members, and planners, all overseeing and supervising the one little old dvornik (porter) who, with her worn twig broom, humbly sweeps the little dvor (courtyard) to which she has been assigned.

The faithful emphasis on plans is abundantly evident in this text, where the Soviet contributors constantly use the future tense. After a while, it seems indistinguishable from the laconic, stereotypical, Latin American reference to manana. Tomorrow never seems to arrive.

Despite the apotheosis of the plan, its shortcomings are legion. For example, the formal plans for Moscow have always included rigid limits on population size. These limits are enforceable because there are strong controls on internal migration, and one needs permission to live in any particular city. Yet, in spite of these controls, the population limit for Moscow has been raised repeatedly, after the fact, to legitimize the inexorable in-migration that occurs because so many officials want more workers for their unproductive agencies. The deputy mayor of Moscow complained that his municipal work force of 1.4 million employees (!) was not enough and that he needed another 300,000 workers. (Genghis Kahn conquered Asia with an army of less than 200,000 men.)

Planning is the butt of many jokes. "Comrade, if we established a Planning Committee for the Gobi Desert, in five years there would be a shortage of sand." Apocryphal stories abound, about the shoe factory that produced a record number of shoes from a given quantity of leather—by making only small sizes. The same is said of a brassiere factory and a nail-making foundry. In each case, exceeding the plan brings bonuses.

The plan reigns supreme and is irresistible. This leads to unanticipated actions, as is illustrated by a report from an investigative journalist. (Freedom of the press is an unimaginable concept, but approved newspaper stories are used extensively to spotlight "antisocial behavior" and the baleful consequences thereof. Such articles are similar to those by U.S. reporters who uncover municipal scandals.) The journalist hung around a gas station on the outskirts of Moscow, and in several hours, for the equivalent of less than 20 dollars, he was able to purchase (illegally) enough gasoline coupons to drive from Moscow to Vladivostok and back, a distance of almost 10,000 miles. He bought them from truck drivers who had extra fuel coupons. Why the surplus? The explanation was very simple. The annual plan called for the state trucking enterprise to drive a certain number of miles that year delivering goods, and the enterprise was issued enough fuel coupons to fulfill the plan. In fact, the plan was overambitious and far fewer miles were actually driven. Therefore, the truck drivers were awash in extra coupons, which they sold on the black market.

But having poked fun at the excesses of planning, there are some positive things to be said as well. It is refreshing to visit a big city where the officials know the total area of the streets and of the sidewalks, so they can calculate the resources needed to clean and wash them; there is not a city in the United States where the officials know this. It is impressive that reasonable targets, or norms, have been established for such things as the number of residents per ambulance (10,000), park area per capita (about 250 square feet), and door-to-door commuting times (no more than 40 minutes for at least 80 percent of the work force). Even though these goals may not have been reached yet, and may never be, their very existence suggests that some basic thinking has been done about what is needed in the way of public services to ensure a satisfactory quality of life.

Unfortunately, this admirable feature is quickly swallowed up in the vast sea of norms as the full dimension of the latter comes into view. There are norms for the number of movie seats per thousand population (23.5) and for the number of seats in eating places per thousand (150). There are norms for the number of square meters of living space per capita in 1990 (15, or 161 square feet) and for the number of shoe repair shops (of a standard size) per thousand of population. There are norms for the number of food service employees per thousand of population (6) and per hundred square meters of area of food service establishments (5).

It all seems so relentlessly preprogrammed, overplanned, and underachieved. There is no room for change or chance. Stability, or stolidity, is more highly valued than dynamism. The notion of a spontaneous new idea—that is, change originating from below—followed by adaptation seems utterly alien; it would not be in accordance with the plan. It is impossible for a fast food business—a Colonel Sanderov's Chicken Kiev or a Burger Czar—to be created in Moscow, and "it is not within the realm of possibility" for an ambitious young chef to open up an appealing little restaurant on a side street. The whole place is run like one of Frank Perdue's chicken-producing factories. Where is the ferment, excitement, and innovation that a great city should generate? How can a society evolve, advance, and grow, and if not in a big city, where?

The stultifying effect of planning in the Soviet Union is further illustrated by the experience one of the authors had in describing to a group of educated middle managers in Moscow how a friend of his had recently gone into the plastics business in New York. The explanation was completely incomprehensible to them. How could your friend get factory space? How many years did he have to wait for the state to build it? What do you mean he rented an available building—how could it be that there was empty space? Where did he get his raw materials and equipment if their production and delivery were not in the plan? How did he arrange to have workers assigned to his plant? To whom did he ship his product, that is, how did he succeed in getting the plan changed so that his output would be accommodated? The discussion ended in total disbelief when the speaker, responding to a question, reported that it took six months from the time his friend made the decision to start the business until the day the first units of product were shipped to a customer.

The pitiful aspect of this vignette is that this group from the intellectual elite in management positions of the Moscow city government had no framework whatsoever within which to place this simple example of a market economy. Although they had been exposed to farmers' markets in Moscow, they were incapable of extending that concept to a more complex economic activity.

Another example must be cited. One of the authors stayed for several days in a new hotel as a guest of a Soviet institution. His three-room suite was well equipped with imported furniture, TV, bar, fully supplied dining room, short-wave radio, two bathrooms, and a piano. (Both toilets leaked, there were no shower curtains, the suite slept only two people, and one room was so stuffed with furniture that the door would open only wide enough to permit someone to slip in sideways—but these are aside from the main point.) Now it is important to remember that each of these features involves an extra charge, such as a ruble per day for the TV, and so forth. The visitor, ignoring the negative points, made a complimentary remark about the suite's opulence to a chance Soviet acquaintance, who turned out to be remarkably uninhibited and cynical about the system. Responding to the visitor's ingratiating comment that he never before had a hotel room with a piano in it, the Russian asked, slowly, as though speaking to a dullwitted child, "Don't you know why there is a piano in your hotel room?" The visitor admitted that he did not, whereupon it was patiently explained to him: "Right after the war, there was a serious shortage of musical instruments. Later, we started up some factories to produce them, and gradually enough instruments were made. But in our system there is no way to stop factories. They keep turning out more and more pianos, violins, trumpets, and everything else, and we don't know what to do with them. Finally, some genius in Gosplan [the State Planning Committee] said, 'I know what to do with all those pianos; let's put them in hotel rooms and let the tourists pay for them!'." Then he closed with a triumphant flourish, "Come back next year and you'll find a farm tractor in your hotel room!"

A final personal experience involving hotels and the consequences of Soviet planning: One of the authors was staying in a hotel in Leningrad in late June, during the "White Nights," when it is light throughout the short night. The windows had neither curtains nor drapes, however, and repeated requests brought nothing but helpless shrugs and the explanation that none were available. While prowling the corridors in search of extra sheets to cover the windows, the author found a storeroom filled with drapes. More diligent inquiry revealed the real underlying problem: There were plenty of curtains and drapes, but there were no hooks to hang them! It appeared that the curtains were planned for one year and the corresponding hooks for another. In a second hotel, there were no hooks in the shower stall to hang up the telephone-style shower head, and in a third hotel there were hooks but no shower curtains. After a while, a visitor just assumes that the Soviet economic system cannot get all the parts to the right place at the right time, and, like the Soviet people themselves, becomes both inured and resigned to the situation.

THE HIERARCHICAL MACHINE

Hierarchy and formalism dominate the system. Edicts will work. There is no such phenomenon as organizational behavior to worry about, and human resources are taken for granted. Organizations are machines to be controlled by operators from above. Workers are little more than programmable robots, with certain maintenance needs; they can be moved around and assigned to jobs and apartments. The entire system seems trapped in a time warp—mired in turn-of-the-century "scientific management" mode of thought, almost 100 years out of date. No wonder productivity is low and alcoholism is high.

A mechanistic view of society prevails. When the author expounded on the virtues of decentralized decision making in complex organizations to a senior city official in Moscow, the latter thought for a moment and ended the discussion with finality: "You cannot have each stationmaster making up his own timetable for the railroad." What a shockingly simplistic view of industrial, urban society! Just to think of a city as a linear system in which events proceed sequentially, unidimensionally, and predictably is astonishing and depressing.

Was this the anomalous view of an aging bureaucrat? Not at all. A dynamic young manager, infatuated with computers and running a large city agency responsible for computing everything in sight, was no different. In a meeting in the United States, he exuberantly described his big project. He was constructing a large-scale, computerized, mathematical model of Moscow's economy and activities. It would comprise tens of thousands of equations and hundreds of thousands of parameters. When completed, one would enter into the computer information about the population of Moscow, the life expectancies of different demographic groups, desired levels for the quality of life, etc., and the model would proceed to calculate exactly how many people would be needed to work in each of the activities in the city, and how large a budget should be allocated to each agency in order to achieve the desired objective. Moreover, the model would be able to calculate the optimal city budget in this manner for one-, five-, and ten-year periods, permitting Moscow to become a showplace of the best in superior city management and guidance of the economy. The project would absorb all the resources of his thousand-person unit for 20 years, but the results would surely be worth it. He closed his enthusiastic presentation with a genuine offer to permit U.S. experts to participate in his ambitious endeavor.

The U.S. author, dependent on a translater, doubted the latter's competence as this grandiose scheme was unfolded. However, polite but persistent questioning, with carefully concealed incredulity, resulted in naught but confirmation of the initial translation. Then the author delicately inquired about what the mayor of Moscow thought of the novel idea, and whether he was prepared to wait for 20 years and to expend 20,000 person-years for this wonderful planning tool.

The response, quite icy by now, was, "That question is outside the bounds of discussion," and he announced his intention to proceed with or without U.S. involvement.

When the author visited Moscow a few months later, he learned that the fellow had been reassigned to Minsk, no doubt to practice on the presumably more gullible country cousins in Byelorussia.

Consistent with the obeisance to hierarchy and the mechanistic, preprogrammable view of society is a reliance on control. This was evident in four different major cities where the highest priority for the municipal data-processing department was to develop a computer system that would monitor and follow up to ensure timely execution of decisions of the executive committee of the city soviet. The description of the systems were virtually identical, and indeed all were modeled on Moscow's prototype.

A word is in order about computers in the Soviet Union. In the 1950s, when the first commercial computers were introduced in the United States and were gaining rapid acceptance, the Soviet Union under Stalin was deeply suspicious of them and initially considered them an exploitative capitalist tool. By 1970, however, the Soviet attitude had changed to one of uncritical and unbridled enthusiasm for computers, which were hailed as the key to socialist salvation; at long last, here was a tool that would make their frustrating system work. The five-year plan promulgated in 1971 explicitly called for a major effort to introduce computers and exploit their capabilities to the utmost: "The plan for development of the national economy of the U.S.S.R. for 1971 envisages a large volume of work on the introduction of automated systems for controlling complex industrial processes, enterprises, and branches of the national economy, with the application of computers." The directives of the Twenty-Fourth Congress of the Communist Party decreed that the number of automated systems of management be increased by a factor of four. Premier Kosygin stated that "the creation and introduction of more than 1,600 automated systems of planning and management of branches of the economy, associations, and enterprises using econometric methods based on technology is intended in the five-year plan."

The terminology used is itself revealing. In the United States, we speak of "management information systems," but in the Soviet Union, they refer to "automated systems of management," a term that implies that management itself is a rigid, mechanical activity that can be controlled and automated like a machine or an assembly line.

Some of the techniques used to control the bureaucracy may well be worthy of emulation. For example, just as U.S. government agencies have inspector generals and departments of investigation, Moscow has a multiplicity of inspectorates, but they have the authority to impose direct penalties for infractions of various kinds by agencies and their employees. Indeed, in a recent six-month period, they had levied penalties in 8,500 instances.

The emphasis on hierarchy and control is very strong in Soviet cities, in contrast to the United States. Here, the concern of the founding fathers about an overly strong central government produced a Constitution that separated and balanced power among the executive, legislative, and judicial branches. Moreover, cities and states are separate legal entities from the national government. Mayors and governors (and even presidents) do mutual battle and bargain quite publicly. Not so in the Soviet Union. There, each city is a subunit of a larger entity, and a city's budget is an integral part of the republic budget, which in turn is an integral part of the national budget.

An additional chain of control exists in the system of dual subordination; that is, an agency of the city government, say a health care unit, is subordinate not only to the city government but also to the corresponding health unit of the republic government. Of course, this leads to a lot of duplication, delay, and problems of coordination, but presumably when all is finally agreed upon, the consensus ensures smooth functioning.

There is yet another chain of control in the system, one exercised by the Communist Party. In parallel with each unit of government, down to quite small agencies and subagencies, there is a Communist Party organization. The head of the Party unit that mirrors the bus transportation agency is usually not the head of the latter, although many of the members of the Party unit will work in the agency. In other words, the Party structure parallels the government structure at all levels. At the very top, the secretary of the Communist Party is the party leader, while the chairman of the presidium of the Council of Ministers heads the government. Under Brezhnev, Andropov, and Chernenko, the same individual held both positions. At lower levels, the parallelism prevails, but the head of the government unit may not be the same as the head of the corresponding Party cell. The role of the Party unit with respect to its counterpart government unit is to ensure that the Party's interests are served.

In addition to this parallel power hierarchy, the Party directly shapes the agencies by filling what are, in effect, specific patronage positions set aside for it in each agency. The nomenklatura is the list of such positions. To translate this into somewhat analogous U.S. terms, it is like the list of positions exempt from the civil service, or the so-called "plum list," which incoming presidents have in order to identify the positions they can fill by appointment without reference to civil service examinations, seniority lists, etc.

One suspects that Boss Tweed would have felt very much at home in Soviet cities. Local officials may have been elected and appointed in the boss-controlled U.S. cities of yore, but political leaders placed their people in all the agencies and exercised enormous power over their activities.

A stark passage in Chapter 6 identifies the most important criterion for evaluating professionals, that is, technical specialists and managers, in city government: their ideological-political qualities. These are measured by political maturity, ideological conviction, comprehension of the basic goals of Soviet society, vigor in pursuit of those goals, and subservience to societal interests. Distinctly secondary in the evaluation are such things as professional competence, the ability to work well with others, creativity, and work performance. Whereas high-level city officials in the United States may seek some of these qualities in some of their policy-making subordinates, at least there is party rivalry, and there is a large private sector that tends to reward competence in commerce and industry. The transcendent role of one-party city government in Soviet cities means that competence is a secondary consideration in addressing large areas of public need.

On the other hand, it is worth noting that most of the mayors encountered had previously served as heads of their city's housing construction agency. (Another was an engineer who had directed the city's rapidly growing transportation system.) This is generally the largest agency; it spends the most money, and its work has the highest priority. Thus, the mayors of Soviet cities generally have acquired considerable executive experience running large and highly visible agencies. These backgrounds are in sharp contrast to the typical experience of U.S. mayors, who have generally served in legislatures and whose executive experience often consists of nothing more than running a small law office.

To summarize the pattern of hierarchy and control from the perspective of a city agency: Its budget is part of the city budget, which is part of the national budget; it is subordinate to higher levels of the city government, and also to a corresponding agency of the republic; principal positions in the agency are reserved for the Party; and a shadow agency within the Party hierarchy monitors and influences the daily operations of the agency.

A noteworthy feature of city government is the extensive system of decentralization. In that respect, Moscow is more like London than New York. The city is divided into 32 raions (the same as the number of London boroughs), each with an elected council and budget, its own tax sources, and its own employees who perform local municipal services. Raions in turn are divided into mikroraions, analogous to neighborhoods. Even smaller units with quasi-governmental duties are the zheks, the organizations that operate large housing projects, which may have thousands of dwelling units in high-rise buildings.

Zheks and mikroraions emphasize citizen involvement on a cooperative, voluntary basis. They organize street patrols, social activities, hobby groups, and recycling efforts. They work with police agencies and school authorities to supervise and rehabilitate juvenile delinquents. While some may consider such efforts as merely another means of exercising control over the population, U.S. cities could benefit by encouraging a greater scope for informal, cooperative neighborhood efforts aimed at improving citizens' behavior. This impossible task has been left to higher-level government agencies such as the police and the courts in the United States. These are most ineffective at addressing problems of delinquency, family disputes, graffiti, boisterous and menacing actions, noise, drunkenness, neighborhood arguments, public lewdness, coarse and vulgar public behavior, and other quality-of-life offenses. Appropriate neighborhood institutions offer the promise of being much more effective in handling such troublesome problems.

PUBLIC SERVICES AND THE QUALITY OF LIFE

Lines and shortages are endemic in the Soviet Union, as is well known. This is true for food, clothing, shelter, and consumer goods of all kinds. People wait on line for hours for hideous and shoddy goods, and it is no wonder that Soviet citizens visiting the West buy potato peelers, tape measures, panty hose, and other mundane goods, although clothing is most highly prized. Sanitary napkins are virtually nonexistent, and so the modern Soviet woman makes do with rags and cotton. Scientists and engineers covet calculators, and everyone wants blue jeans and portable radios.

A sad yet amusing example of the lengths that natives will go to in order to enjoy the material privileges of foreigners was witnessed in the Berioska Shop (where goods are sold only for Western currency— the possession of which is illegal for Soviets) in the Ukrainia Hotel in

Moscow. A man who was obviously Russian, judging from his accent and dress, was attempting to purchase a high-quality, traditional Russian fur hat (which is difficult for natives to get) by masquerading as a foreigner. He spoke in very broken English to a salesgirl who responded with equally broken English. As long as neither acknowledged the charade by lapsing into their native Russian, the labored pretense could continue to a mutually successful conclusion.

Russians who speak Western languages routinely pretend to be foreigners in order to get preferential treatment in restaurants, theatres, and special museum exhibits. Understandably, however, they are outraged at having to resort to this humiliating practice in their native land.

In marked constrast to consumer goods, conventional municipal services are very good. The streets are clean, street crime is low, and mass transit is excellent, with clean subways, stations, and buses, and frequent, dependable service. When the author ran and just missed a subway train near midnight one evening, he saw an electric sign on the platform indicating that the next train would arrive in four minutes. Sure enough, it did. What he found remarkable compared with subways in the United States was that (1) there was an indicator, (2) it was functioning, (3) it proved to be correct, and (4) trains ran that frequently so late at night.

The emphasis on community and cooperation pays off. On buses and trains, the driver merely operates the vehicle and does not collect fares or even watch passengers pay. Nor is there a fare collector aboard. Instead, passengers are expected to work their way to the midpoint of the vehicle and deposit the exact fare into a simple, wall-mounted coin box. Then they tear a paper ticket from a roll of tickets that hangs next to the fare box. Fellow passengers cooperate in making change and passing coins and tickets from hand to hand when it is crowded. The passenger seated nearest to the fare box often assumes a quasi-official, sometimes gravely officious, interest in the proper functioning of the system and diligently assumes and discharges his or her civic responsibility. It is said that occasionally an inspector will board the vehicle and check to see that all passengers have tickets, and if they do it is assumed that the ticket has been paid for; it is unthinkable that someone would dare take a ticket without paying. The system is breathtakingly simple and remarkably effective. The U.S. visitor is embarrassed even to contemplate how such an honor system would work in the United States. It just would not. The visitor seeks chauvinistic comfort by imagining that the penalty for being caught without a ticket is death.

Transgressions elsewhere are plentiful. With much curiosity, a visiting VIP noted that the drivers of official limosines remove the windshield wiper blades and place them in the glove compartments when they park. The explanation was simple enough: Wiper blades are scarce and commonly stolen, as are exterior mirrors, hub caps, and anything else.

The visitor is astonished to see modern, imported U.S. burglar alarm systems installed in vegetable stores that at night seem to have nothing but a few half-rotten cabbages and turnips left in their bins. Bars on ground-floor windows are commonplace, and so are closed-circuit TV cameras monitoring walks and entrances of housing projects. Burglary is clearly a problem; however, crime statistics are not revealed. In fact, it is an insult to one's intelligence to be told officially that there are virtually no fires in Moscow. Like crime statistics, fire statistics are a state secret, and like airplane disasters, they are not reported. Perhaps in the United States, reports of crimes, fires, and various disasters and misfortunes are overreported, but the other extreme is not satisfactory either.

A major fire in the huge Rossiya Hotel in Moscow in the late 1970s resulted in the deaths of several dozen foreigners, and therefore could not be hidden. A visit to the hotel a few months later showed the precautions taken subsequently: A fire engine (a pumper, not a ladder truck) was parked outside, with two crew members asleep in the cab. Stationing the pumper there seemed to be a symbolic gesture and utterly ineffective. Hotels in the Soviet Union are dangerous because the standard practice is to keep all the exits locked except the main one; this is to prevent Soviet citizens from meeting with Westerners. Guards at the main entrance screen all who enter to make sure they are registered guests.

As in the United States, there are many unnecessary calls for emergency ambulances. About 20 percent of the requests are so classified, and doctors are used to screen out calls. New York City does much the same thing.

An interesting organization that has no U.S. counterpart is the Institute for Municipal Research, commonly known as the Pamfilov Academy. This center is engaged primarily in developing technical approaches to public works problems—water, streets, snow removal, etc. One of their inventions for snow removal is a fascinating, ramplike contraption with moving arms that serves as a conveyor belt, moving a plowed mound of snow from the ground into a dump truck. (Its function, however, would be better served by a front-end loader, which is more versatile.)

Repair of private automobiles is a serious problem in the Soviet Union. Official repair stations are huge and centralized, and have very long delays. Weeks can elapse before they will accept a vehicle for repair, and months can go by while waiting for parts. As a result, a brisk black market operates in both parts and labor.

Further evidence that the Soviet Union has not yet become an automobile society—for better and for worse—is to be found in the relations between drivers and pedestrians: They have not yet reached a state of peaceful coexistence. Drivers are openly contemptuous of pedestrians, and the latter seem unaware of themselves and ignorant of driver behavior, no doubt because so few of them are drivers. Even simple humanity seemed absent when the authors saw an elderly woman moaning and dying in the street after being struck by an auto. No one tried to comfort her or indeed paid any attention to her, while a traffic policeman laconically directed traffic around her.

Considering the decades of propaganda about the role of women in Soviet society, a visitor is surprised to discover how subservient women are, and how dominant male chauvinism is. Much is made of the fact that almost half the elected members of the Moscow City Council (City Soviet) are women; however, the council is a rubber stamp that is all but irrelevant in municipal decision making. Most doctors are women, but in the Soviet Union that is a relatively low-paid and low-status occupation. Women are treated the same as men when it comes to being assigned grueling manual labor, but in offices they are expected to make and serve tea, regardless of rank. In one meeting with city officials, the lone woman participating as a peer automatically got up to help the (female) secretaries when it came time to serve tea and coffee.

Women lead a dog's life in the Soviet Union. The low productivity engendered by their economic system is perceived as a labor shortage, and so the government urges all able-bodied women to work. Toward that end, day schools have been extended to accommodate the children of working couples until 6 p.m. Nevertheless, women are expected to do the shopping and keep house. The result is dismal home lives, a high divorce rate, and a low birth rate—which paradoxically is exactly the opposite of what would be needed to remedy the labor shortage. The foregoing does not apply to the Central Asian Republics—Kazakhistan, Uzbekistan, Turkmenistan, Tadzhikistan, and Khirghizia—where women serve in more traditional Moslem roles and birth rates are very high.

Just as there are norms or planning standards for numerous services, as noted above, there are work standards for municipal employees. While these may be honored more in the breach than in the observance, they constitute a superior system to those in most U.S. cities, which generally lack such standards. It is also instructive to compare work practices in Moscow and New York: Many municipal employees in the former work approximately 300 days a year, whereas for many in New York, the work year is only about 210 days. As for welfare, Lenin once said, "He who will not work shall not eat." Note that he refers to those who will not work, not those who cannot work. This elegantly simple principle seems to be followed quite literally, and only 3.5 percent of the able-bodied population is "not engaged in socialist industry." Those attending school or caring for young children are considered to be suitably engaged.

It is well known that intoxication is a serious problem in the Soviet Union. How serious is revealed by the fact that in a big city bus depot, each of the 1,000 drivers is examined for sobriety every morning before being permitted to go out on his route.

Considerable concern is manifested about the condition of the environment. There is a concerted effort to guard against suburban sprawl, through land use planning. High priority is given to retaining the forest protective belt—referred to as "the lungs of the city"—and preventing the physical merger of settlements. Heavy fines are levied for damaging trees and shrubs: up to ten times the cost of replacement or up to half the vandal's monthly salary.

Large enterprises provide for the recreational needs of their workers by establishing vacation sites in the green belt outside Moscow and elsewhere, at the Black Sea, for example. Often the facilities are built by the workers themselves, on what is said to be a volunteer basis. They may be somewhat primitive affairs, but they satisfy the Muscovites' need for a change of pace, and the prices charged to workers and their families are modest in comparison to wages. At times, the practice takes on the aspect of a Fresh Air Fund for deprived urbanites, and U.S. citizens may not appreciate spending their leisure time as well as their working time with their fellow workers on their employer's premises. This feature adds to the feeling that Moscow is a company town, with the company taking care of housing, recreation, and work breaks. This feeling is accentuated by the practice of reserving the most desirable time periods at the resorts as rewards for the best workers.

For a U.S. citizen, one of the more disorienting features of the Soviet Union is the implicit classification scheme that applies to human activities. It seems that all activities fall into one or the other half of an all-embracing dichotomy: Things are either in the economic sphere or the sociocultural sphere. There is nothing else. The very concept of private actions is an alien one, and indeed the Russians have no word for privacy.

U.S. citizens on an official visit to the Soviet Union, particularly those who are the heads of delegations, are alerted before leaving the United States that their hotel rooms may be bugged. Ample evidence confirms that this often occurs. The author noted with amusement that when he changed to a second and then to a third hotel room on the first day of a visit, a handyman followed shortly behind him to tinker with the innards of the TV set—although both sets had been tested by the visitor and were working fine. (On the other hand, complaints about malfunctioning plumbing, telephone, TV, or anything else generally bring no response. Even soap is hard to get.)

It may be possible to turn any eavesdropping to one's advantage. Herewith is a description of a tactic devised by the authors that, so far as they know, is original and has never been reported:

After a particularly frustrating day spent with a notable obnoxious and stupid bureaucrat named Ivan, the two authors sat in their hotel room and reviewed the day's annoying events. In a burst of inspiration, the following creative exchange took place:

Kaiser: "Say, isn't that fellow Ivan really clever!"
Savas: "What do you mean?"
Kaiser: "Having that Swiss bank account."
Savas: "Huh?"
Kaiser (gesticulating): "Do you know how hard it must be for a Russian to set up a Swiss bank account?"
Savas (catching on): "Yeah, that's incredible. They must have a million controls. He must be a lot shrewder than he appears."
Kaiser: "I don't know how he's going to get out of the Soviet Union, but he sure is set when he does."

We never saw Ivan again. It is probably wishful thinking to assume that our conversation was responsible for our good fortune, but others in similar circumstances may find it worth trying. At least there is a certain euphoric delight in mischievously using the ponderous Soviet apparatus against itself, a form of intellectual jujitsu. We commend this approach to all who may feel frustrated in their dealings with Soviet officials. However unlikely a real impact may be, at least it feels good and affords cathartic relief. Embroidery and embellishment can be suited to taste. In the (unlikely) event that we did indeed hasten Ivan's departure from his position, we would be guilty only of having thereby enhanced the efficiency of his government unit.

1

URBAN DEVELOPMENT

In the Soviet Union, a city is viewed as a social, territorial, and economic unit. It is subject to and an object of planned management and development in accordance with established goals. The Communist Party program states that "cities and settlements must represent a rational complex organization of productive zones, residential areas, networks of public and cultural enterprises, utility enterprises, transportation, engineering equipment and energy sources, such that the best condition for the work, the life and recreation of the population should be attained."

The most important functions associated with a city are territorial planning, production, housing, personal and professional services, regulation of the population, information and learning, ecology, and management.

The territory-planning function intends to achieve a stable relationship between the interdependent spheres of production, housing, service enterprises, transportation and energy networks, recreation areas, etc., such that the best conditions for work, life, and rest are realized.

The production function implies the formation of a stable and consistent system of the interdependent, developing, productive units of the national economy (industry, agriculture, construction, transportation, etc.) that are established there. This system must be properly linked with the appropriate external units.

1

The housing function is represented by the establishment of an interrelated and interdependent system of residential blocks and the concomitant distribution of population groups.

The service function is characterized by the formation of systems of cultural centers and utilities that provide the entire complex of services of all types for the population.

The population regulation function is defined as the control of the population structure, both demographic and occupational, and the allocation of workers to jobs.

The information and learning function includes the stimulation and coordination of scientific research and the dissemination of information that is to contribute over the long term to scientific and technological progress in all areas of the national economy.

The ecological function involves the preservation and improvement of the environment of the settlement.

The management function is responsible for the development of the settlement, with proper consideration of the structure, relationships, dependencies, and interactions of its parts.

A city is officially defined as a settlement of more than 12,000 in which workers and office employees, together with their families, constitute at least 85 percent of the population. (This definition excludes places that have sizable military encampments.) The State Construction Committee of the Soviet Union classifies cities according to population size: largest cities, over 1 million; large, 250,000 to 1 million; big, 100,000 to 250,000; average, 50,000 to 100,000; small, less than 50,000. The cities larger than 100,000 in population contain the bulk of the economic and cultural potential of society, that is, the most important enterprises, scientific centers, institutes of higher education, cultural centers, certain unique enterprises, management centers, etc.

A study of cities, if limited to their formal boundaries, would not yield a complete image of urban growth and the structural changes recently introduced into city development. As a result of suburban development, a wide area has been formed outside the city limits (often under its own jurisdiction) that is closely related to the city, both economically and culturally (e.g., industrial interactions, commuting, cultural and ethnic relations).

The people in these areas are only technically separated from the city. In actuality, they are indistinguishable from the city's residents, and therefore a census of only the population living within the city limits would lead to gross distortions of the real situation. From the viewpoint of both the continuity of relationships and the density of development, the city as an economic and social unit is not restricted to the "central city" alone, but also includes parts of the suburbs, in other words, the entire city agglomeration or metropolitan area. In fact, the current trend is to incorporate these areas into the city.

The large and especially the largest cities frequently act as metropolitan centers. Compared with other cities, such centers are distinguished by a higher concentration of people and facilities, more interdependent industrial production, stronger interrelationships between production and science, a greater proportion of the work force allocated to the national rather than the local economy, and better-developed transportation, engineering, municipal, and information infrastructures.

Within the boundaries of a metropolitan area, small- and medium-sized cities can develop and can themselves become relatively complete economic units. Thus, the largest cities can gradually transfer a portion of their functions to other cities in the metropolitan area, thus lightening their economic burden and, to a degree, decentralizing the population.

For instance, the intensive concentration of production activities within a radius of 50 kilometers from Moscow has oversaturated this zone and threatens the protective forest belt around the city that serves as the basic health resort area of the capital. At the same time, the population density in a number of peripheral regions is insufficient. This is why limiting the further concentration of production and population in Moscow and its nearest suburbs and giving high priority to the development of the peripheral regions are the most important tasks facing those who must manage the development of the Moscow area. These actions will result in the increased growth of the other cities in the area, and improvements in their environment, architecture, and natural surroundings.

The creation of systems of settlements with relatively uniform economic, social, and cultural characteristics contributes to the achievement of the goal formulated by the Twenty-Fourth Congress of the Party: ". . . an unyielding policy of limiting the growth of large cities; banning, as a rule, the construction of new industrial enterprises in the cities, with the exception of enterprises to provide services to the public and the city economy. Small, specialized enterprises and branches of the factories and the plants of the large cities are to be opened in the small cities and settlements."

City dwelling is becoming a way of life for an increasing number of people. Consequently, the problem of city development and city management are growing. For example, the most urgent problems of the city of Moscow can be summarized as follows:

1. There is a need to improve the welfare of the people, including raising the level of the municipal and everyday services rendered to them. There are not enough multipurpose service establishments, for example, and those that do exist are not of a high enough quality.
2. Closely related to the above problem is the fact that Moscow has a high percentage of elderly residents, and this figure continues to increase. In general, this segment of the population requires more services per capita than other age groups, thus aggravating the service deficit mentioned above.
3. There is a continuing need for a concentrated program of housing construction to upgrade the existing housing stock and provide for the continuing population growth. [Note the implied expectation of failure of the "unyielding policy of limiting the growth of large cities" cited above.]
4. There is a need to improve preschool, school, and especially vocational education and training. During the 1960s, the trend was for young people to continue their education and enter professional fields rather than to work as laborers or service personnel. As a result, there is now a serious shortage of skilled workers in Moscow as well as in most other cities of the Soviet Union. At the same time, the city has a surplus of certain types of professional specialists.
5. There is a need to expand the passenger transportation network. The Metro lines are not long enough, and housing construction in the outlying districts has run ahead of transportation capabilities.
6. Much attention is being given to ecology and related environmental problems. "Dirty" industries are being moved out of the city, while new industries and industrial expansions are approved only when they have low requirements for labor, materials, and consumable material resources such as air and water.
7. The city is exhibiting continued growth, with large annual in-migrations. These cause a continued growth in demand for services. Attempts are being made to restrict this migration to those specialized workers who are in highest demand and to improve labor productivity as a means of reducing the shortage of workers.

The problems of the city are frequently intensified by the difficulty of reconciling immediate needs and long-range goals. Steps that appear promising for the immediate future have often led to problems in the more distant future.

The problems of the city are not local; they are universal, and extremely urgent. Their successful solution will create favorable conditions for the development of complex productive, creative, and cultural interchanges. It will speed up the scientific-technological revolution and the development of the productive forces of the society. This, in turn, will lead to further urbanization, and hence to further increases in the importance of cities.

2

BASIC FACTS ABOUT MOSCOW

HISTORY

The city of Moscow is mentioned for the first time in the chronicles of 1147 A.D., and after recovering from the raids of the Mongol-Tatars in 1237-38, it became the center of an independent principality. In the fourteenth century, it emerged as an important center of the Great Moscow Principality, which was one of several principalities founded in northeast Russia. During the last quarter of the fifteenth century, under Prince Ivan III Vasilievich, Moscow was proclaimed the capital of a centralized Russian government. In the sixteenth century, Moscow's size exceeded that of London, Prague, and other major European cities.

Despite removal of the capital to St. Petersburg by Peter the Great in 1717, Moscow retained its status as a large administrative, cultural, and political center. In March 1918, under the initiative of Lenin, Moscow became the capital of the Soviet Union.

PHYSICAL FEATURES

Moscow is located in the middle of the European part of the Soviet Union, between the rivers Oka and Volga. It is on the Moscow River at an average altitude of 120 meters above sea level. The highest points of elevation are to the southwest, at the Teplostanskaya Heights on the Moscow River (where the elevation is 200 meters), and to the

5

northwest, in the area of the Himkin reservoir, where the end of the south slope of the Moscow Heights is located. The eastern and southeastern parts of the city are located on the Meshcherskaya Plain. Many of the terrain features are a consequence of centuries of work by the population; the so-called cultivated layer, consisting of cultivated soil, remnants of old foundations, bridges, etc., approaches a depth of 10 to 20 meters in the central parts of the city.

The largest tributaries of the Moscow River within the city territory are the Yauza and Setun. There are also a number of small rivers, such as Neglinka, Presnia, and Hodinka, which are channeled primarily into underground pipes, and about 150 small streams. Within Moscow, there are also about 240 open reservoirs with a total area of 820 hectares, and there are other reservoirs outside the city.

CLIMATE

The climate of Moscow is moderate-continental. The average temperature during the coldest month (January) is - 10.2°C. The record winter temperature is - 42°C. The hottest month is July (18.1°C). The record high temperature is 36.8°C. The average annual rainfall is 582 millimeters, much of which falls in July.

POLITICAL GEOGRAPHY

Moscow is the capital of the Union of Soviet Social Republics and of the Russian Soviet Federated Socialist Republic (R.S.F.S.R.), 1 of 15 republics in the Soviet Union. It is the center of the Moscow province, or oblast, and the largest political, scientific, industrial, and cultural center in the country.

The area surrounding Moscow is divided into two basic urban zones: the inner zone, consisting of the suburbs that lie within 60 kilometers of the city boundaries, and the outer zone, which extends to a distance of 100 to 120 kilometers of the city limits. The two zones, together with Moscow itself, are referred to as the "Moscow city agglomeration."

The boundaries of the city are marked by the belt highway. This was established by decrees of the presidium of the R.S.F.S.R. Supreme Soviet (Council) in 1960 and 1961. Within these boundaries are several formerly independent cities of the Moscow oblast, Babushkin, Lyublino, Kuntsevo, Perovo, Tushino, and a number of other settlements and habitation points. The settlements outside the highway belt that are included under the jurisdiction of the Moscow City

Table 2.1. The Raions of Moscow

No.	Raion	Area Within City Limits (in square kilometers)
1	Babushkin	33.9
2	Bauman	6.3
3	Volgograd	29.7
4	Voroshilov	42.8
5	Gagarin	49.3
6	Dzerdjin	13.4
7	Zhdanov	14.2
8	Zheleznodorozhni	15.6
9	Kalinin	12.0
10	Kiev	18.9
11	Kirov	39.3
12	Krasnogvardeisky	68.8
13	Krasnopresnensky	13.5
14	Kuibishev	49.6
15	Kuntsevo	44.3
16	Leningrad	26.7
17	Lenin	13.8
18	Lyublino	55.1
19	Moskvoretsky	8.9
20	Oktiabr	17.6
21	Pervomaisky	34.1
22	Perovo	32.2
23	Proletarsky	22.3
24	Sverdlov	7.2
25	Sevastopol	31.3
26	Soviet	37.3
27	Sokolnitchesky	21.7
28	Timiriazevsky	35.3
29	Tushino	30.1
30	Frunzensky	15.5
31	Tcheremushkinsky	38.0
32	Zelenograd City	—
Total		878.7

Soviet of Workers' Deputies are Zelenograd, Vnukovo, Vostochnii, Meshcherskii, Nekrasovka, Rublevo, Severnii, and Zapadnii.

The city is divided into 31 administrative districts, or raions, plus the above-mentioned city of Zelenograd, which is part of the Moscow administrative system and is regarded as the thirty-second raion.

The division of the city follows the design of the Moscow General Plan. It preserves the radial distribution of the raions along the city arteries, forming two belts—an inner and an outer one. (Both of these are within the belt highway.) The 13 raions of the inner belt form the city center. The outer belt includes 18 raions created in part as a result of the construction of major residential blocks, and in part on the basis of the former cities of the Moscow oblast that are now included in Moscow.

The relative size of the 32 raions is shown in Table 2.1.

DEMOGRAPHY

The population of Moscow has been increasing rapidly, as shown in Table 2.2. The total population grew 12 percent in the eight years between 1970 and 1976, to 7.91 million people, and reached a population density of 9,002 people per square kilometer. The total population of Moscow and its surrounding areas in 1980 was approximately 13 million, and is expected to increase to 15 or 16 million by the year 2000.

The effect of two wars and of other processes that cause more male than female deaths and that cause the selective migration of men and women shows clearly in the dramatic reduction in the proportion of males in the population since 1912. (One can speculate about the

Table 2.2. Population Growth in Moscow (in thousands)

Year	Total	Percentage of Men
1912	1,618	54.3
1939	4,542	46.5
1959	6,044	42.6
1970	7,061	44.0
1975	7,632	45.0
1976	7,734	45.0
1978	7,910	NA

NA, not available.

reasons for the comparable preponderance of males before World War I.)

The rate of economic growth depends directly on the quality of the labor force, which in turn is closely related to its age structure. The population of Moscow by age and its change in composition are given in Table 2.3. The age structure is changing owing to three demographic processes: births, deaths, and migration.

Figure 2.1 shows the total, the natural, and the migrational population growth in Moscow for 1960-74. During this period, from 50 to 60 percent of the population growth was due to migration from the central economic region. This area includes Moscow and the ten oblasts (provinces) that surround it. It has a radius of approximately 240 kilometers, and has had long-standing production and labor ties with Moscow. Recently, the population growth rate has dropped to 47 percent, indicating an increase in migration from other, more dis-

Table 2.3. Distribution of Moscow's Inhabitants by Age

	Population in Thousands			Percentage of the Total		Population as Percentage of 1959 Population[a]	
	1959	1970	1977[b]	1959	1970	1970	1977[b]
Total	6,044.1	7,061.0	7,819.0	100	100	116.8	129.3
In age groups (in years)							
0- 9	797.3	799.0	—	13.2	11.3	100.2	—
10-15	456.3	538.4	—	7.5	7.6	118.2	—
16-19	369.9	418.5	—	6.1	5.9	113.1	—
20-24	598.5	631.9	—	9.9	9.0	105.6	—
25-29	553.3	443.4	—	9.2	6.3	80.0	—
30-34	622.5	684.4	—	10.3	9.7	109.9	—
35-39	407.7	531.2	—	6.8	7.5	130.3	—
40-44	390.0	643.8	—	6.5	9.1	165.1	—
45-49	493.8	455.6	—	8.1	6.5	92.3	—
50-54	416.2	349.2	—	6.9	5.0	83.9	—
55-59	331.4	489.2	—	5.5	6.9	147.6	—
60-69	395.9	699.8	—	6.5	9.9	176.9	—
70 and over	211.1	376.6	—	3.5	5.4	178.6	—

[a] 1959 = 100 percent.

[b] Age breakdown of population not available for 1977.

Figure 2.1.

Effect of Natural Growth and Migration on the Population of Moscow, 1960-74. (— – —), Net in-migration; (– – – –), natural growth; (————), total growth.

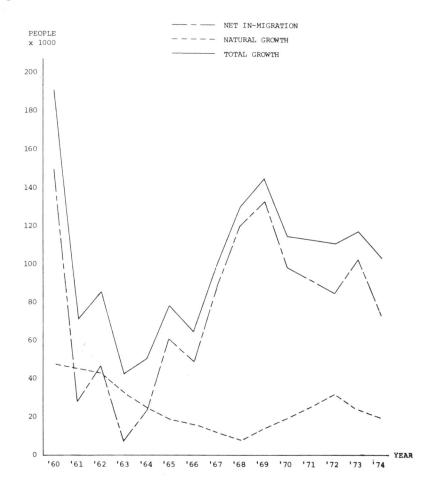

tant regions of the country. The most important role is still played, however, by the Moscow oblast; its population continues to increase owing to migration from other parts of the country and is a source of manpower for Moscow.

At the same time, Moscow supplies labor forces (in the form of exchanges) to other regions of the country, primarily in the urban areas of Siberia, the Far East, and Central Asia. There is a formal mechanism for outward migration. [Perhaps this is less ominous than it sounds.]

The demographic data indicate that since World War II, the relative size of the older age groups has increased, while that of the younger groups has decreased. This has resulted in a declining birth rate and a reduction in the available working population; in fact, there is a continuing shortage of labor, which currently amounts to over 500,000 people. [It is pretty clear that the problem is low productivity of the work force, rather than an absolute shortage.] If it were not for the net in-migration, the shortage would be even more severe. Yet, as is evident in Figure 2.1, net in-migration declined after 1969 and continues to decline. This reflects a policy of restricting in-migration and encouraging out-migration.

The bulk (72 percent) of the arrivals in Moscow come as a result of organized recruitment of workers by enterprises where manual labor is needed. There are large differences in migration rates for the different age groups. There is negligible migration in the groups under 15 and over 50 years of age. The population between 16 and 49 years of age has great mobility, particularly the group between 20 and 25 years of age. The young generation is attracted by the educational institutions of the capital, job opportunities, and other features of big-city life. A certain number also come to Moscow because of marriage. The migration contributes to the improvement of the age structure of the city, causing the slight increase in the natural growth rate that appears in Figure 2.1, and increasing the proportion of working-age population.

In contrast to the growth through net migration, the natural growth rate of the population is very low because of the low birth rate and the high death rate attributable to the relatively large number of older people.

It is worth noting that the work force is defined as healthy men and women between the ages of 16 and 55. Only 3.5 percent of the work force is not working. Students and pregnant women are considered to be working.

ECONOMY

Moscow's productive base consists of industrial enterprises and construction, design, and scientific organizations, which together employ the majority of the working population and occupy 20 percent of the city's territory.

The importance of the capital to the economy of the Soviet Union is illustrated by the fact that the economy of Moscow is responsible for 10 percent of the state budget revenues of the country. Industry in the capital includes about 1,400 enterprises in more than 20 industrial branches. The largest branches are machine construction and metal working, which account for 35 percent of the total production volume of Moscow, as measured in rubles. A substantial role in the industrial complex of the city is also played by the light manufacturing and food industries. Output highlights for 1973 and 1977 are listed in Table 2.4.

More than 400 enterprises that produce household goods are situated in Moscow, including more than 20 percent of the clock and watch output of the entire country, 15 percent of the television sets, 8 percent of the domestic refrigerators, and 4 percent of the washing machines.

The volume of construction work in the city can be estimated by the following figures: 1.2 million square meters of industrial and commercial area (excluding office space, schools, etc.) and 5.5 million square meters of residential area were constructed during 1974.

In 1977, 4.5 million square meters of living space, 19 schools, 130 retail stores with 34,300 square meters of sales space, 126 food

Table 2.4. Illustrative Measures of Production in Moscow, 1973-77

	Quantity	
Type of Output	1973	1977
Cotton and artificial fabrics (in millions of square meters)	470	386
Wool fabrics (in millions of square meters)	86.7	106
Silk fabrics (in millions of square meters)	311	267
Underwear (in millions of square meters)	40	34
Linen (in millions of square meters)	22.5	22
Leather shoes (in millions of pairs)	32	30
Furniture (in millions of rubles)	136	150
Meat (in thousands of tons)	166	142
Margarine and shortening (in thousands of tons)	NA	74
Canned food (in millions of units)	58	58
Pastry (in thousands of tons)	302	319

NA, not available.

establishments, 11,346 kilometers of communications lines, and 186 kilometers of mass transit lines were constructed. Overall construction in 1977 was 34 percent greater than in 1970.

Moscow has a well-developed structural materials industry. The production of complex structures and materials currently involves about 100 enterprises in five industries: (1) prefabricated housing construction and prefabricated concrete; (2) ceramics and adhesives; (3) nonferrous metals; (4) wood processing; (5) synthetic coating and insulation materials. The volume of output and the percentage of each field in the total volume for 1971 are listed in Table 2.5.

Moscow is the largest scientific and cultural center of the Soviet Union. More than 300,000 scholars work in scores of scientific research institutes. Approximately 900,000 students are studying in over 200 institutes of higher and specialized education. There are 25 theaters, 66 museums, 1,379 public libraries, over 300 clubs and "culture palaces," and 511 movie theaters.

TRANSPORTATION

Moscow is the largest railway center of the Soviet Union, with 11 railways linking the capital to all parts of the country. There is also direct connection with many foreign countries. At a distance of 5 to 120 kilometers from the city limits, the Great Circular Railway has been constructed for transit trips bypassing Moscow. Data on the railway activity in Moscow appear in Table 2.6.

Table 2.5. Outputs of Selected Industries in Moscow, 1971

Industrial Branch	Total Output in Millions of Rubles	Percentage of Total Structural Materials Output
Prefab housing and prefab reinforced concrete	229	34
Nonferrous metals	57	8.5
Ceramics and adhesives	87	13
Wood processing	116	17.3
Synthetic, coating, and insulation materials	152	22.7
Miscellaneous materials	29.7	4.5
Total	670.7	100

Table 2.6. Railway Activity in Moscow, 1972-77

	1972	1977
Outgoing freight (in millions of metric tons)	14.4	17.3
Incoming freight (in millions of metric tons)	52.6	54.8
Passenger trips originating in Greater Moscow (in millions)	550	650
Passenger trips originating and terminating in Greater Moscow (in millions)	530	626

Since completion of the Moscow Canal in 1937, the role of the city as a river port has grown considerably. The Volga-Baltic Waterway and the Volga-Don Canal opened the way from Moscow to the Caspian, Azov, Black, White, and Baltic Seas. There are three major river ports in the city—the western, northern, and southern. Water-borne cargo departing from and arriving in Moscow in 1977 amounted to 11.2 and 24.2 million tons, respectively.

Moscow is a major center for automotive traffic. Thirteen highways connect the city with the many republics and major cities of the country. The cargo transported by truck in 1977 amounted to 200 million tons.

Moscow has four airports—Vnukovo, Shermetyevo, Domodedovo, and Bykovo. The percentage of all freight transported by air is increasing.

During the period of socialist rule, intracity transport changed radically. The subway was constructed, and the trolleybus, bus, and taxi networks were created. In 1977, there were 5.4 billion intracity passengers. Further steps are being taken to improve passenger transport.

HOUSING AND UTILITIES

A great deal of housing construction has been underway, and the transition to high-rise buildings with improved apartment planning is quite advanced. New major residential blocks have been created to the southwest in Izmailov, Khoroshovo-Mnevnik, Fily-Mazilov, Novy Kuzminky, Perov, Medvedovka, Beskoudinovka, Tushino, and other districts. The reconstruction of the central districts of Moscow has been started.

At present, 97 percent of the housing area is in concrete buildings, 99 percent of the apartments have running water and sewer connections, 88 percent have gas, 11 percent have electric heating, and 82 percent have hot water.

Under the Soviet government, basic municipal services have been completely revamped. The capacity of the water supply stations has been increased, water purification plants have been constructed, and considerable work has been done in the field of gas and fuel supply. To improve the reliability of the water supply system, the Mojzaiskoe, Puzskoe, and Ozerinskoe Reservoirs were constructed. A new fresh water source is under construction, namely, the hydrotechnological facilities on the river Vazuza. Moscow is connected with the major sources of natural gas by the gas transmission pipelines Dashava-Moscow, Stavropol-Moscow, and Central Asia-Central Economic Region. Natural gas consumption in 1977 amounted to 15.3 million cubic meters. The gas network within the city consists of 2,730 kilometers of gas lines.

A system of power plants supplies the city with electricity and most of its heating needs. As a part of the Moscow energy system, the city is connected by a high-voltage network not only with the power plants of the central region, but also with major power plants on the Volga, such as the "V.I.Lenin" and the "XXII Congress."

The electric power consumed in Moscow is used primarily by industry (61 percent of total consumption). Second place is held by lighting needs (including personal consumption), 16.6 percent. Third place is occupied by the city transport system (trolleybuses, trams, subways), which uses 10.5 percent. Small motors, (e.g., elevators, winches, compressors) use about 8.6 percent of the energy, 2 percent is used by the electric railways of the Moscow railway network, and 1.3 percent by the water supply and sewage services.

In 1975, 94 percent of the heat for buildings was delivered from high-capacity power plants. Moscow's heating system is improving, and its pipeline network is growing; currently, it consists of about 5,000 kilometers. Centralized heating accounted for 66 percent of the total in 1970; the remainder was provided by individual building heating units.

Lighting the streets requires considerable amounts of work and money, increasing with the growth of the built-up areas and the extension of city streets. Lighting expenditures rose to 8.7 million rubles during the 1971-75 period. The total expenditures over the five years amounted to 40.4 million rubles.

EDUCATION

After the October Revolution of 1917, steps taken by the Soviet government allowed for the immediate construction of a new socialist system of public education based on genuine democratic principles.

In 1977-78, there existed 1,033 schools for general education of all types with 736,300 students. In addition, there were 177 professional-technical schools (with 95,500 students), including 104 giving degrees (57,900 students). There were 141 special middle institutes (221,800 students) and 75 institutes for higher education (with 644,900 students), including the Moscow Government University "M.V. Lomonosov," the Academy of Social Sciences of the Central Committee of the Communist Party of the Union of Soviet Socialist Republics, the Supreme Party Institute of the Central Committee, and certain military academies.

The public schools and the high schools for specialized training employed over 55,600 teachers in 1973. The universities employed approximately 38,000 faculty members. There are more than 300,000 scholars and scientists living and working in Moscow today, including 9,400 doctors and 67,600 candidates of science. Many of them successfully combine scientific research with teaching in the universities and the specialized high schools. Hundreds of academicians and associate members of the U.S.S.R. Academy of Science are simultaneously professors in Moscow universities.

Table 2.7. Educational Level of the Population of Moscow, 1970

	No. of People in Thousands			No. of People per 1,000 Citizens of Age 10 and Over
	Total	Men	Women	
University graduates	913	475	438	146
Some university education	230	119	111	37
High school specialized (technical schools and similar institutions)	624	249	375	100
General high school (complete)	1,060	437	623	169
Some high school	1,422	664	758	227
Total no. with at least some high school education	4,249	1,944	2,305	679

The educational level of the population is indicated in Table 2.7. In 1970, about 60 percent of Moscow's population had at least some high school education, and 16 percent had at least some college education.

ENVIRONMENTAL PROTECTION

The struggle against pollution of the environment is one of the most complex problems of modern cities. In order to preserve the environment of Moscow, it was necessary to totally redesign and reconstruct the production systems of many plants and factories. In addition, over 300 enterprises were moved beyond the city limits. Installations to prevent the emission of pollutants into the atmosphere have been constructed and are increasing in number in Moscow. The construction of water purification and sewer facilities has gained considerable momentum. Moscow has a metropolitan sewage treatment system that receives the waste of all enterprises and processes it. Thus far, only partial purification of sewage has been accomplished; some sewage flows into open reservoirs. The task of achieving 100 percent purified water still remains. In the near future, it is planned to attain a closed water cycle, in which the purified water will be returned for industrial use. This will require considerable capital investment.

In Moscow and its suburbs, a total of 4,000 hectares will be used for reservoirs by the year 1990. Another 1,500 hectares of reservoirs will be constructed in the forest belt. The water surface area per citizen of Moscow will rise from 6 to 15 square meters.

PARKS AND RECREATION

Ever since the formation of the Soviet government, great importance has been attached to the natural ally in the struggle for the purification of the air of large cities, namely, the forest.

The forest and park protective belt, covering 172,000 hectares, is required primarily to purify the Moscow air and as recreation for working people.

The area covered with plants and trees is increasing yearly. Between 1966 and 1970, an area of 226 hectares was converted to parks, 170 squares were created, and 200 streets were planted with trees and bushes. However, the work on the parks still lags behind the requirements of the city.

The areas set aside for the short-term recreation of the citizens of Moscow are located in the forest belt and the suburban zone within a 1.5- to 2-hour drive from the city. Furthermore, the general plan for the development of the city indicates the use for these purposes of more distant areas on the Oka River, the Moscow Sea, and the Ruzskoe and the Mojzaiskoe Reservoirs.

Currently, there are 70 recreation camps in the forest belt. Each of the Moscow raions has a recreation area of its own; they are located in the most picturesque areas. The executive committees of the raion councils have conducted operations aimed at clearing and cleaning up the territory and the reservoirs, constructing roads, and reclaiming flooded land. The General Plan for the development of Moscow calls for an increase in the number of people using the vacation resorts of the Moscow area up to a total of 5.7 million people annually.

Another recreation site is the Moscow River and the Moscow Canal. More than 800,000 people travel along them every summer.

Besides these areas of more active recreation, passive pursuits are also available. In the vicinity of Moscow, there are over 300 unique historical and cultural monuments, and special wardens are assigned the task of preserving them.

3

ORGANIZATION
OF THE CITY GOVERNMENT

LEGAL BASIS OF THE AUTHORITY OF THE
CITY SOVIETS

The Constitution of the Soviet Union, which is the basic legal document of the nation, states the following: "All power in the U.S.S.R. belongs to the people. . . . The people exercise governmental power through the Soviets [Councils] of People's Deputies which form the governmental foundation of the U.S.S.R. . . . All other bodies are under the control of, and are accountable to, the Soviet of People's Deputies. . . ." (Article 145).

In accordance with these statutes, the administration of Moscow is based on the R.S.F.S.R. law "On the City and Municipal Raion Soviets of People's Deputies of the R.S.F.S.R.," passed by the Supreme Soviet of the Union of Soviet Socialist Republics on November 28, 1978, and "On the Introduction of Amendments and Additions to the Decree of the U.S.S.R. Supreme Soviet entitled 'Basic Rights and Obligations of the City and the Municipal Raion Councils of Workers' Deputies'." These laws stipulate that the district and city soviets are the government organs in their territory, and, as such, they decide within the limits of their authority all local problems on behalf of the entire government and the working people of the city or the raion.

The raion and the city soviets are a crucial part of the government system. They implement on site the policy of the Party and the government. They must decide all problems dealing with the improvement of public services, the development of the raion and city economy, the coordination of enterprises and organizations of different administrative departments in the field of housing and municipal construction, the production of goods for the public, and service, social, and cultural projects.

According to law, the local (city and raion) soviets are responsible for those enterprises and organizations providing services intended primarily for the population of the city. Consequently, they are responsible for local industry, utilities, the municipal economy, trade, health care, and other organizations.

The authority of the soviet over industrial and sociocultural enterprises of higher subordination extends to territorial planning and coordination if these enterprises are within the soviet's geographic jurisdiction. [Note: The term "higher subordination," commonly used to describe government relations in the Soviet Union, indicates that an agency reports to or is under the authority of some other higher authority. In this case, an enterprise such as a steel mill is under the authority of a national-level Ministry of Ferrous Metallurgy, but the local city soviet has authority with respect to territorial planning. In fact, this is a source of continuing friction, for instance, if the ministry wants to expand the plant, but the city has other plans for that land or does not wish to provide housing, transportation, and utilities in that vicinity for the additional workers.] The local soviet has available an important tool for exercising its authority to coordinate: The approval of its executive committee is required for appointments and dismissals of the directors of certain enterprises that are subordinate to higher authority. Examples of such enterprises are trade concerns, public eating places, utilities, organs of housing and municipal construction, health institutions, and the social security and cultural organizations.

In order to ensure the active participation of these enterprises and organizations in the development of the raion and city economy, as well as to increase the concern of the local soviets for the resulting product of the enterprises and organizations on their territory, the raion and municipal budgets receive a portion of the profits of those organizations and companies that are under regional or republic—but not national (all union)—authority.

Successful execution of the functions of the soviets requires that they be given considerable authority. In particular, in certain cases, they are even authorized to countermand an order or a request issued by the head of an organization or enterprise of higher subordination. This applies to land use, construction in inhabited areas, environmental protection, housing, municipal, social, and cultural construction, public services, and the preservation of cultural monuments.

The local soviets are an organic part of the system of power. They are not just a part of the representative system, and one should not describe the socialist government as a conglomerate of independent territorial units without a directing center or with vague central power. Under socialism, government power is implemented by a system of organs that provide consistency between central and local units. The vitality of this power depends on the relations between the local and central units. These relations are based on the principle of democratic centralism. In this case, centralism implies that the local soviets are responsible to the superior organs of government power, and that they must abide by the legal acts of the Supreme Soviet as well as their own executive committees. The centralization of management of local soviets is motivated by economic, political, and organizational needs. Centralism provides a consistent national economic plan for the development of the local economy. The plan is approved by the Supreme Soviet. It stipulates the basic development policies of the local economy, and specifies the relations between higher government and the local management organs in the fields of housing construction, local industry, health care, and other areas of economic and sociocultural life. [In other words, every city government is a formal part of the national government—its local arm.]

What the local soviets have in common with other representative institutions is the order of their subordination, supervision, and control. Each of these institutions is responsible to and controlled by the electorate and the superior soviets. As for the executive and the regulating organs, they can act only as supervisors of the subordinate soviets. Thus, the decisions of any local soviet can be suspended by the executive and regulating organs of the superior soviet, but only the superior soviet itself can revoke these decisions.

The Moscow City Soviet is responsible to the presidium of the Supreme Soviet of the Soviet Union and the R.S.F.S.R., whereas its Executive Committee is responsible to the Moscow City Soviet and the Ministry Councils of the Soviet Union and the R.S.F.S.R. [Note: In some respects, Moscow is treated as a republic because of its unique importance, and therefore it may deal directly with the presidium of the Supreme Soviet of the Soviet Union.]

The Supreme Soviet exercises management of the Moscow Soviet through permanent committees of its members. In order to study the local state of affairs in the economic and cultural spheres, the committees receive reports from the organs of the Moscow Soviet.

At its sessions, the presidium of the Supreme Soviet of the Soviet Union examines the problems of the municipal soviet structure and the reports of organs of the local soviets. It makes decisions for improving the operations of these bodies.

All rights of Moscow in its relations with other cities, provinces, and republics on a government level are determined and regulated by the superior organizations.

There are economic, political, and cultural relationships and connections between Moscow and other cities, provinces, and republics. The economic relations involve primarily the industrial enterprises that are under the same ministries and departments. The political relationships are determined by the Central Committee and the Moscow City Committee of the Communist Party of the Soviet Union; these are based on friendship and cooperation with all cities, provinces, and republics of the country, for Moscow is the center of its entire political life. The same can be said of the cultural links as well; they are determined and implemented by the Ministry of Cultures of the Soviet Union and the R.S.F.S.R.

RIGHTS AND POWERS OF THE LOCAL SOVIETS

Being basic components of the system of representative power, the local soviets must act, primarily by the method of persuasion, to direct the public effort toward the implementation of the plans and directives developed by the Party and government organs, with the participation of the wide majority of people. At the same time, they are authorized to use, if necessary, government enforcement within the limits specified by the law.

As with all other organs of power, the city and raion soviets operate on the basis of law. This is indicated by the fact that they uphold the Constitution and the rest of the laws of the Soviet Union and the R.S.F.S.R., the decrees of the presidium of the Supreme Soviet, and the directives and orders of the government, and also by the fact that they issue acts in support of the government.

Local soviets are authorized to participate in debates and decisions on matters of state concern. However, they are authorized to make decisions only on the subjects of local concern included in their jurisdiction.

The Constitution of the Soviet Union states, "The Soviets of Workers' Deputies (zones, territories, provinces, raions, cities, settlements, villages) manage the cultural-political and economic development of their territory; they determine the local budget, supervise the activities of their subordinate management organs, uphold government law and order, contribute to the defense capability of the country, and protect the rights of citizens."

In order to perform the functions stipulated by the Constitution, the soviets as governmental organs have governmental authority. The Moscow municipal and raion soviets and their executive committees issue legal decisions and compulsory orders that apply in the territory where the soviet has jurisdiction. The basic organizational-legal form of activity of the soviet is the session.

The orders of the Executive Committee of the Moscow City Soviet are issued in accordance with the decisions of the Moscow Soviet as well as those of the Executive Committee. The decisions of the raion Executive Committees are made in accordance with the motions of the raion soviets and executive committees.

The Moscow Soviet Executive Committee (or the Raion Executive Committee) can issue orders on operative matters, which do not require group decisions, on the personal decision of the chairperson or deputies.

The most important feature of the soviets as governmental organs is that they have fiscal resources and authority. That is what ensures the implementation of their decisions. [Would that it were that simple!]

Another characteristic of the soviets as governmental power organs is their competence. "Competence" implies a set of governmental, economic, and cultural structures, completely or partially managed by the soviets, as well as the authority and responsibility of decision making in each of the above fields. There is no practical distinction between the jurisdictional competence of the soviets and that of their executive committees.

Based on an analysis of existing laws pertaining to local soviets and the work performed by them, the exclusive rights of the Moscow City Soviet and the raion soviets can be listed as follows:

1. Authority for the organization of the City Soviet:
    - to elect the chairman and the secretary of the soviet session;
    - to elect the Credentials Committee, approve its report, and confirm the authority of the deputies.
2. Authority for the formation of the organs of the Soviet, and the control of their activity and the work of the deputies:
    - to elect and change the Executive Committee of the soviet, including the chairman, deputies, secretary, and other members, and to review its reports;

- to determine the number and the names of the permanent committees, elect their members, determine their functions, and examine their reports;
- to approve the number and the structure of the deputy subcommittees and examine their reports;
- to decide upon relieving representatives from their obligations upon their request, owing to an inability to meet their obligations;
- during the period when the council is in session, to consent to the indictment of a deputy;
- to form the departments and administrations of the Executive Committee, and to approve their directors.

3. Authority in planning, auditing, and accounting:
   - to approve the balanced long-range and annual plans for the economic and sociocultural development of the city (raion); to organize and supervise their implementation; to approve the long-range and annual directives to the enterprises, companies, and organizations of municipal subordination, as well as the plans for the distribution, development, and specialization of these enterprises, companies, and organizations;
   - to study plans for the distribution, development, and specialization of the enterprises of local industry, public services, trade and public food services, cultural organizations and institutions, public education and health care, and the enterprises and facilities of higher subordination; if necessary, to submit proposals to the proper higher authorities;
   - to study proposed plans of enterprises, institutions, and organizations of higher subordination situated on the city's territory with respect to the development of housing and public services, highway construction, sociocultural and utility projects, the production of consumer goods and local construction materials, the environment, trade and public food services, public education, health care, cultural and other subjects related to public services; if necessary, to introduce proposals to the proper higher authorities, and approve balanced planning targets for the development of the city economy and the sociocultural development of the city;
   - to develop balanced plans for the allocation of labor and construction materials;
   - to prepare a budget that relates revenues and expenditures of the population [Note: The soviet is responsible for considering the disposable income available to the populace and the expenditures that the populace will have to make for various goods and services under control of the soviet; it prepares its budget plans accordingly.];
   - to develop the balanced plan needed for the development of the city economy;
   - to exercise control over the rational utilization of mineral, forest, water, energy, and other resources;
   - to exercise control over auditing and accounting in the enterprises, institutions, and organizations of city subordination.

4. Authority in the field of budget and finance:
   - to examine and approve the city budget, including total revenues with specific income sources and total expenditures;
   - to organize and control the implementation of the city budget;
   - to allocate any budget surplus;
   - to study proposals for changes in the city budget;
   - to study and approve the accounts used in implementing the city budget;
   - to audit the financial expenditures of the city.
5. Authority in the industrial field:
   - to direct the industrial enterprises of municipal subordination; to see that production-fiscal plans are implemented; to control the use of funds, the circulation of funds, and the quality of production; to approve the accounts of the fiscal economic activities and the proper distribution of profits;
   - to make decisions (with the consent of the superior organs of governmental management) concerning the organization, reorganization, and liquidation of industrial enterprises and the establishment of firms, associations, and trusts of city subordination;
   - to distribute the output of the city industry that is produced from local raw and waste materials.
6. Authority in construction, planning, urbanization, and land and water use:
   - to develop the general plan of the city and the design for the suburban zone; to examine these designs and to submit them, according to the existing practice, to the superior organs of governmental management;
   - to approve the proposals for detailed plans and designs for area development and for engineering designs and projects for environmental development;
   - to supervise construction on the city's territory;
   - to manage the construction and repair organizations of city subordination;
   - to approve proposals and lists of municipal construction sites within budget limits, as stipulated by law;
   - to control all land within the city limits; to exercise governmental supervision over its use;
   - to give permission for the development of mineral resources.
7. Authority in the field of housing, public services, and environment:
   - to manage housing, public services, and the environment;
   - to operate the engineering facilities that are under municipal subordination;
   - to manage the organs of housing and public services of higher subordination;
   - to supervise the records of workers and office employees in need of housing (control is exercised in the enterprises, institutions, and organizations, regardless of their subordination);
   - to distribute the housing stock owned by the soviet; to control the distribution of the housing facilities of organizations not subordinate to the city;
   - to make decisions pertaining to the organization of housing construction and other cooperatives in the city.

8. Authority in the field of transportation and communications:
   - to manage municipal transportation, the transport enterprises, and the organizations of municipal subordination;
   - to supervise transport enterprises and organizations of higher subordination with respect to their services to the public;
   - to supervise the communications enterprises and organizations for public services; to assist in the development of the telephone, mail, and radio-television networks, and in the repair and protection of communication lines.
9. Authority in the field of trade and public eating places:
   - to manage governmental and cooperative trade and public food services, and the enterprises and the organizations of trade and public food services on the city's territory and of municipal subordination;
   - to supervise the work of the enterprises and the organizations of trade and public food services of superior subordination;
   - to approve the plans for goods circulation in the trade and food service enterprises of higher subordination.
10. Authority in the field of everyday services:
    - to manage the everyday services to the population and the service enterprises and organizations under municipal authority; to implement the production-fiscal plans; to control the use of the basic and capital funds; to approve the formulas for fiscal and economic activities and the proper distribution of profits;
    - to supervise the everyday service enterprises and organizations of higher subordination.
11. Authority in the field of public education:
    - to manage public education and preschool and extracurricular child care; to provide compulsory education for all; to keep records of all school children;
    - to supervise the work of the homes for children and the preschool and extracurricular children's institutions.
12. Authority in the field of culture and general knowledge:
    - to conduct cultural-educational work; to manage the cultural-educational work of organizations and enterprises of municipal subordination and build up their financial bases; to control the activities of the other educational and cultural organizations regardless of their subordination;
    - to supervise the use of the cultural funds of enterprises, institutions, and organizations;
    - to manage motion picture distribution; to broaden the movie theater network;
    - to provide records and protect the historical, revolutionary, and memorial complexes and monuments.
13. Authority in the field of health care, physical culture, and sports:
    - to manage health care activities in the city, the city health institutions, the improvement of their material and technological fund, and the organization of public medical care;

- to inspect the work of the institutions of superior subordination; to report on unsatisfactory work to appropriate ministries;
- to enforce the sanitary requirements for the maintenance of residential and office buildings in the city; to conduct veterinarian supervision;
- to take measures to avoid, restrict, and eliminate noise in industrial, residential, and office buildings, as well as in the yards, streets, and squares of the city;
- to exercise governmental control over the enforcement of regulations for preserving the atmosphere, water resources, soil, and natural environment, including the sanitary requirements in this field;
- to conduct preventive work against the spread of infections and toward their elimination;
- to provide mother and child protection;
- to manage the department of physical culture and sports; to organize municipal sporting events.

14. Authority in the field of labor and employee training:
    - to keep records and regulate the distribution of labor resources throughout the city and work for their optimal allocation; to organize the employment of citizens;
    - to supervise the implementation of labor laws, work safety regulations, and safety programs of the enterprises, institutions, and organizations;
    - to plan the number of employees needed in public education, culture, health care, etc.

15. Authority in the field of social security:
    - to operate the social security system, providing prompt and adequate assignment and payment of the pensions specified by law;
    - to manage the institutions of social security of municipal subordination; to supervise the social institutions of higher subordination located in the city.

16. Authority in the field of public control, the implementation of socialist laws, and the protection of the government, the social order, and the rights of citizens:
    - to enforce the implementation of the laws of the Soviet Union and the R.S.F.S.R. as well as other official acts of superior organs of governmental authority and management; to protect governmental and social order, socialist property, the rights and legally protected interests of citizens, government institutions, enterprises, cooperatives, and other public organizations;
    - to establish a committee for public control and supervise its work;
    - to provide prompt and adequate consideration and decisions on all proposals, applications, and complaints of the working people;
    - to provide for the management of the subordinate organs of the Internal Affairs Ministry and the proper operation of the internal passport system;
    - to conduct the work of volunteer squads for the protection of social order and the community courts;

* to manage the activities of the City Fire Department;
* to uphold the laws pertaining to religious sects.
17. Authority in the field of security:
    * to implement the U.S.S.R. law for compulsory military service of all city employees and citizens as well as employees of enterprises, institutions, and organizations;
    * to conduct the civil defense of the city's territory.

STRUCTURE OF THE MUNICIPAL GOVERNMENT

The supreme legal and legislative institution of Moscow is the Moscow Soviet of the Workers' Deputies. It is elected every two years. It meets in full session twice a year. In 1975, the Moscow Soviet included 1,160 representatives, of which 543 were laborers, 517 women, 622 members and candidate-members of the Communist Party of the Soviet Union, and 538 non-Party members. Of the elected representatives, 327 were under 30 years of age, and 238 were members of the Komsomol (Young Communist League). Most of the current deputies are serving in the Moscow Soviet for the first time.

Between the sessions of the soviet, city management is in the hands of the Executive Committee of the Moscow City Soviet. [Like persons in the United States, the Soviets make extensive use of acronyms; hence the Moscow City Executive Committee is called MosGor-IspolCom, a word formed from the initial syllables of the name. The same form is used in every city, with only the first syllable changed to match the first syllable of the city's name.] The Executive Committee consists of a chairman, secretary, nine vice-chairmen, the chief architect of Moscow, the director of the City Finance Administration, and other deputies, for a total of 25 members. (A special twenty-sixth member was temporarily added with overall responsibility for the 1980 Olympic Games.)

The Executive Committee is elected at a session of the full soviet and meets every two weeks.

The presidium of the Moscow City Executive Committee meets weekly or more often as needed. It is also elected at a session of the full soviet. Its 15 members include the chairman of the Executive Committee, the secretary, the nine vice-chairmen, the chief architect of the city, the director of the City Finance Administration, the director of the Internal Affairs Administration [Police], and the first secretary of the City Communist Party.

In addition to the collective organs mentioned above, which are authorized to make actual decisions, there are some 21 permanent committees of deputies, which operate on a public basis. The committees can take actions that, in contrast to the decisions of the Executive Committee and the presidium, carry only the weight of recommendations. The organization chart of the city soviet is shown in Figure 3.1.

The Executive Committee

The chairman of the Executive Committee, the nine vice-chairmen, and the secretary, assisted by their secretaries, coordinate the work of the administrations and the services of the city economy. They also observe and keep accounts of the municipal organizations and the various organizations of administrative subordination that are closely related to the city economy.

The units under the Executive Committee are divided into three groups: (1) auxiliary agencies, assisting in the work of the Executive Committee itself, entirely subordinate to the Executive Committee and following its directions (General Department, Organization and Instructional Departments. Judiciary, etc.); (2) administrative agencies, immediately responsible for the operational management of economic or sociocultural activities; (3) functional agencies, responsible for coordination and regulation, as well as planning and inspection.

Among the functional agencies of the Executive Committee, a particularly important role is played by the City Planning Committee, which, with the help of its apparatus, analyzes the conditions of and develops projects for the development of the entire city economy and its individual administrations and monitors the implementation of plans. The structure of the City Planning Committee, whose acronym is Gorplan, is shown in Figure 3.2, within the dashed line.

The agencies that are subordinate to the Moscow City Soviet Executive Committee are organized in a system of 18 main administrations, 29 independent administrations, 9 departments, and a number of commissions, inspectorates, and other services. This system is shown in Figure 3.3.

Figure 3.1 (*overleaf*). Organizational Structure of the Moscow City Government.

Figure 3.2 (*overleaf*). Organizational Chart of the Moscow Soviet Executive Committee and the City Planning Commission (Gorplan).

Figure 3.3 (*overleaf*). The Distribution of Responsibilities on the Moscow Soviet Executive Committee. (For explanation of administrative offices, see Appendix.)

Fig. 3.2. Organizational Chart of the Moscow Soviet Executive Committee and the City Planning Commission (Gorplan).

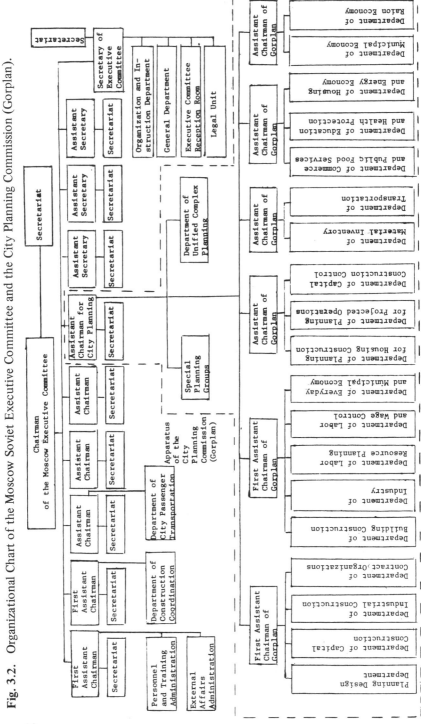

Fig. 3.3. The Distribution of Responsibilities on the Moscow Soviet Executive Committee.

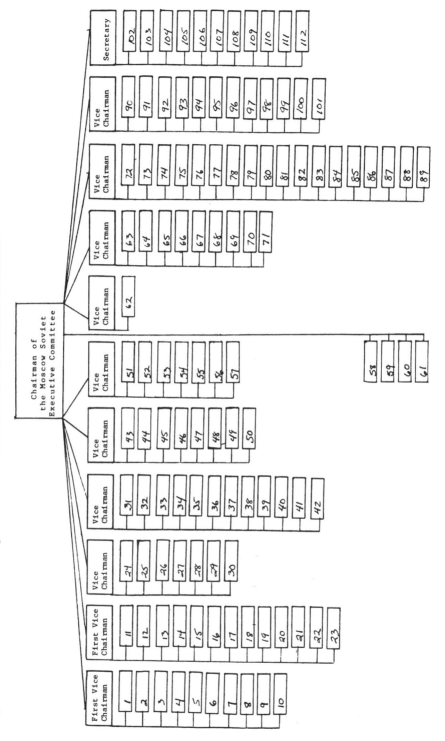

33

In order to perform its management functions, the Executive Committee has created a broad system of administrations and main administrations.

In 1975, the number of employees of the central organs of administration, plus the managers of the individual enterprises themselves, amounted to 40,629.

One of the basic features of the management structure of the city economy is that the majority of the economic branches have dual subordination, to the Executive Committee of the Moscow Soviet and to a particular republic or union ministry or agency. The structure of the branches and the services of the city economy under dual subordination is shown in Table 3.1.

STRUCTURE OF THE RAION (DISTRICT) GOVERNMENT

The supreme management organ of the raion is the Raion Soviet of Workers' Deputies, which is elected every two years. In 1975, the raion deputies in Moscow numbered 9,349. This included 4,404 laborers, 4,945 workers of other types, 4,242 women, 4,962 members and candidate-members of the Communist Party of the Soviet Union, 4,387 non-Party members, 2,590 deputies under 30 years of age, and 1,871 members of the Komsomol. Of the deputies, 4,594 were elected for the first time.

Sessions of a raion soviet are held not fewer than six times a year. Between the sessions, the management of the raion is carried on by the Executive Committee of the Raion Soviet.

The management structure of the Executive Committee includes four hierarchical levels: management of the Executive Committee of the Raion Soviet; administrations and departments of the Executive Committee; administrations and trusts of raion subordination; separate enterprises and institutions.

The broad range of problems handled by the Raion Executive Committee led to the creation of administrations and departments responsible for the specific management of the separate branches of the national economy and the sociocultural and administrative-political structure. The management structure is the same for all the executive committees of the raion soviets, and it includes the following: budget organs, planning commissions, and education, health, culture, social security, housing distribution, finance, trade, government statistics, and inspection departments; and economic organs, raion housing departments, repair-construction departments, departments of road and

Table 3.1. City Agencies Under Dual Subordination

Branch of the City Economy	Union or Republic Organ with Vertical Responsibility for the Economic Branch
Main Administration for Housing Economy	Ministry of Housing and Communal Economy of the R.S.F.S.R.
Administration for Fuel and Energy	
Administration for Water Supply and Sewage	
Administration for Municipal Services and Roads	
Administration for Everyday Services	Ministry of Everyday Services of the R.S.F.S.R.
Administration for Community Services	
Administration for Clothing Manufacture and Repair	
Main Trade Administration	Ministry of Trade of the R.S.F.S.R.
Main Administration of Food Services	
Administration for the Metal-Processing Industry	Ministry of Local Industry of the R.S.F.S.R.
Administration for Specialized Enterprises (for invalids)	
Administration for Applied Chemical and Rubber Products	
Bread Industry Administration	R.S.F.S.R. Ministry of Nutrition
Main Health Administration	R.S.F.S.R. Ministry of Health Care
Pharmacy Department	
Main Administration for Culture	R.S.F.S.R. Ministry of Culture
Main Administration for Internal Affairs (police and fire)	U.S.S.R. Ministry of Internal Affairs
Finance Administration	R.S.F.S.R. Ministry of Finance
City Department of Public Education	R.S.F.S.R. Ministry of Education
City Department of Social Security	R.S.F.S.R. Ministry of Social Security
Department of the Judiciary	R.S.F.S.R. Ministry of the Judiciary
City Registry Department	
Administration for Cinematography	R.S.F.S.R. Government Committee for Cinematography
Department of Publications, Printing, and Sales of Printed Matter	R.S.F.S.R. Government Committee for Publications, Printing, and Books
Committee for Physical Culture and Sports	Government Committee of the R.S.F.S.R. for Physical Culture and Sports

R.S.F.S.R., Russian Soviet Federated Socialist Republic.

bridge administration and development, raion food service organization, food service trust, department of public everyday services, and material and technology supply centers for the Executive Committee.

A typical structure for a Moscow raion soviet is shown in Figure 3.4.

FUNCTIONS OF THE CITY AND RAION SOVIETS

The soviets control and coordinate city or raion enterprises, housing and municipal construction, the construction of social and public service facilities, the production of consumer goods and local structural materials, and the development and implementation of measures for improving the environment, trade, public eating places, public education, health care, culture, and other areas related to public services.

In the process of performing the above functions, the soviets approve joint plans for the development of the city (or raion) economy, taking into account the corresponding plans of organizations of superior subordination. The soviets also develop formulas for the utilization of labor resources, local structural materials, and fuel, a formula for public income and expenditures, and other formulas necessary to plan the complex development of the city or raion economy.

The functions of the soviets also include the stimulation of socialist competition. This is a type of moral stimulation toward better and more productive work, which is organized by the local labor unions. A worker or a work brigade might set a certain target for itself involving extra work above the norm, or higher-quality work. For achieving this goal, the worker receives no extra pay, but rather the honor of being designated "best worker."

FUNCTIONS OF THE CITY (OR RAION) SOVIET EXECUTIVE COMMITTEE

Categories of Work

The City Raion Executive Committee is an executive and an administrative organ. Its functions include the following:

1. Internal organization of work:
   • preparation of the sessions of the soviet;

Figure 3.4 (*opposite*). Structure of a Raion (District) Soviet of Workers' Deputies. (For explanation of administrative offices, see Appendix.)

Fig. 3.4 Structure of a Raion (District) Soviet of Workers' Deputies.

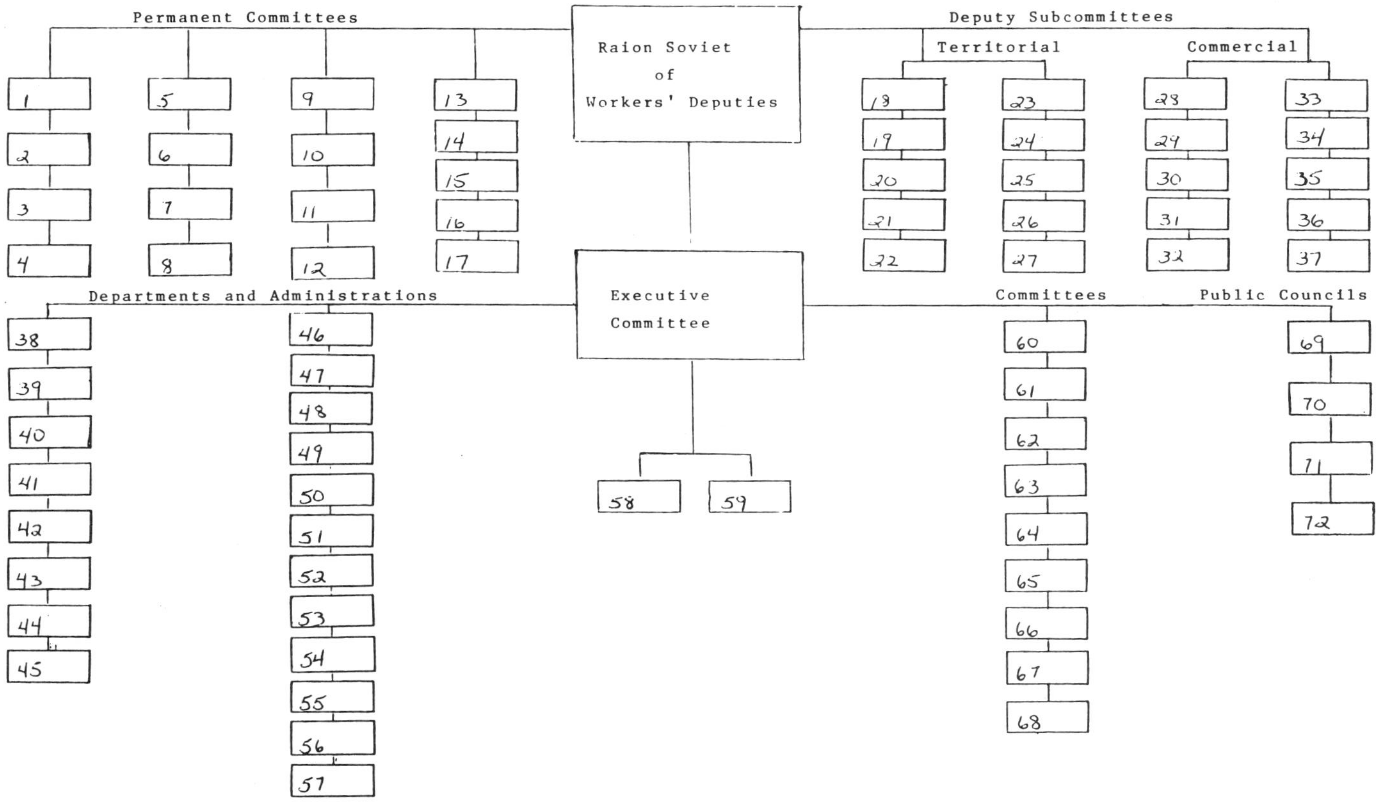

- development of the work plan of the Executive Committee;
- selection and appointment of employees of the executive apparatus;
- organization of soviet elections;
- assistance in the work of permanent committees.

2. Work related to the development of administrative-territorial units:
    - development and examination of the five-year plans for housing and municipal services, cultural and everyday services, and social services; and submission of the plans to the soviet for approval, together with the long-range and the current plans;
    - approval of the plans of enterprises and organizations of local subordination; control of their implementation;
    - organization and control of the implementation of decrees, decisions, and regulations of the soviet, the Executive Committee, and superior organs;
    - between sessions, ruling on matters concerning the social and economic development of the territory;
    - participation in the preparation of plans for social and economic development;
    - control over the preservation of social order and the defense of citizens' rights;
    - overseeing the enforcement of socialist obligations.

3. Work related to the satisfaction of the needs of the population:
    - receiving letters and petitions from the public; analyzing the reasons behind the complaints; developing measures pertaining to the petitions, letters, and complaints; issuing monthly reports on the number of communications, schedules for their processing, and an analysis of the correspondence;
    - generalizing the practical issues and proposals of the deputies and organizing their implementation;
    - control over the implementation of the decisions and the proposals of the electorate.

A Typical Raion Soviet

A large part of the management of the economy of a raion is handled by the raion soviet. Therefore, the functions of the basic sections of the Raion Executive Committee are described next.

1. Auxiliary bodies of the Executive Committee
    a. Organizational-Training Department:
        - controls and supervises the implementation of the petitions and proposals of the working people;
        - trains deputies and employees of the soviet and members of voluntary organizations;
        - organizes and involves the masses in the work of the soviet and the Executive Committee.

b. General Department:
  - keeps records;
  - reports, codes, reproduces, and distributes decisions and regulations issued by the soviet and the Executive Committee;
  - considers, appoints, and dismisses the aides of the Executive Committee;
  - administrates the services of the Executive Committee.

2. Functional bodies of the Executive Committee
  a. Planning Committee:
    - develops the joint annual and long-term plans for the development of the economy;
    - participates in the organization, control, and supervision of plan implementation;
    - analyzes the planning proposals of the Executive Committee agencies;
    - develops proposals and guidelines for the practical implementation of the planning requirements.
  b. Fiscal Department:
    - designs the raion budget;
    - provides financing for the economic branch agencies and for sociocultural undertakings;
    - controls and provides for the implementation of the budget;
    - supervises the maintenance of fiscal discipline and staff schedules;
    - supervises implementation of the fiscal plans of enterprises subordinate to the soviet, as well as the other organizations, enterprises, etc.;
    - organizes the assessment and collection of taxes for all levels of government.

3. Bodies for the economic branches

The bodies for the economic branches are under dual subordination, i.e., territorial and with respect to their particular branch of the economy. Such a combination enforces the implementation of the principle of democratic centralism, i.e., the centralization of management combined with local initiative.

The organs of the various economic branches develop, implement, and modify their plans. The soviet does not interfere in the professional work of the branches, but it supervises and demands constant and systematic reports on local needs and specifics. The soviet considers the plans and their adjustments and provides the necessary conditions for their implementation.

  a. Housing Administration:
    - maintains the housing inventory; issues the building logs for construction and repair; produces statistical reports on the housing stock;
    - develops the current and long-range plans for housing repair, the improvement of housing, and the technological level of operations;
    - conducts record keeping, reporting, and the training of employees for housing operation offices;
    - controls the physical condition and repair of the entire housing stock in the raion, regardless of subordination.

b. Capital Construction Department:
   - develops site lists for residential, cultural, and everyday service construction and the sites of raion subordination;
   - controls land use, the preparation of construction sites, and the structure and fiscal backing of the construction organizations;
   - controls construction, its quality, and the observance of budget limits.
c. Department of the Raion Architect:
   - supervises the legal aspects of construction and renovation in the raion;
   - develops designs for improving the raion's environment within the limits of general urban plans.
d. Department of Highway Development and the Environment:
   - develops the long-range and current plans for repair of local highways;
   - plans measures to improve the environment of the raion;
   - keeps an account of the condition of local highways.
e. Administration of Everyday Services:
   - develops plans for everyday services;
   - manages the activities of subordinate enterprises;
   - controls and analyzes economic activities.
f. Department of Trade:
   - organizes the study of population requirements for eating places and retail goods;
   - develops plans for the volume of trade in the raion;
   - plans for the long-range development of the trade network and the public eating establishments in the territory of the raion;
   - plans organizational and technological measures to improve trade services to the public;
   - organizes the selection and appointment of employees;
   - distributes goods among the trade enterprises;
   - keeps an account of sales;
   - supervises the minimum stock requirements for various goods in the trade network.
g. Department of Public Education:
   - develops measures related to the improvement of public education and preschool education;
   - develops long-range and annual plans and budgets for public education;
   - keeps accounts of the children of preschool age.
h. Department of Social Security:
   - handles pension allocations and the distribution of commodities to eligible persons;
   - organizes the payment of pensions and allowances;
   - keeps accounts of the people receiving pensions and allowances.
i. Department of Internal Affairs Administration:
   - organizes the prevention, interception, and complete exposure of crime;
   - organizes the correction and the reeducation of convicts on the basis of useful public work;

- organizes the personal passport system;
- organizes the training, distribution, and education of personnel protecting public order;
- organizes fire protection and automobile safety.

j. Department of Accounting and Distribution of Housing:
- maintains the waiting list of people eligible to receive housing;
- develops plans for the distribution of housing and for evictions and relocations from old and unsafe houses.

k. Office of Raion Technological Supplies:
- develops a balance list of required material resources;
- allocates available funds;
- provides centralized purchase and supply of material and technological resources to the enterprises, organizations, institutions, and establishments of the raion economy. [Note: This is equivalent to a Purchasing Department.]

l. Office for Citizen Registration:
- performs government registration and records births, deaths, marriages, and divorces.

Control and Inspection Functions of the Executive Committee

The Executive Committee supervises the implementation of the decrees and decisions of the management organs, i.e., the decisions and the orders of the Executive Committee, and the implementation of the approved suggestions, petitions, and complaints of the working people.

Immediate control over the former is the task of the employees of the secretariat, the leaders of the Executive Committee, and the ten-person Control Group of the chairman. The secretariat normally exercises control, with the Control Group addressing only the most important issues. The need for control and implementation schedules is determined by the heads of the Executive Committees at the time of the proposal's preparation as a decision or an order.

The Control Group monitors the implementation of decisions placed in its jurisdiction through questionnaires, memos, telephone communication, and site visits. Summary status reports are made to the chairman of the Executive Committee twice each month, with longer analyses when required. Provisions are made for extensions of deadlines, and there are procedures to modify controlled documents or remove them from the control list.

Since the staff of the Control Group is limited, it is not possible to reliably control the entire document output at present, and there has been an acute need for an improved system to control both decision documents and communications to the Executive Committee. One way to improve the control system is to implement an automated control system. In 1974, the Main Scientific Research Computing Center of the Moscow City Executive Committee developed and submitted for test runs the first stage of an automated system for operational management and information retrieval services. The first stage of the system is being applied to the decisions, orders, and regulations of the Executive Committee of the Moscow Council. The implementation of the complete system is expected to result in the following:

1. Improved quality of the issued documents;
2. Improved control of the schedules of decision documents;
3. Increased volume of documents being controlled;
4. Mechanization and automation of the collection, processing, and issuing of information pertaining to the controlled data;
5. Increased efficiency in the issuance of information by the Executive Committee of the Moscow Soviet and the reliability and readability of the control output;
6. Standard formats for the submission of control results to the leadership of the Executive Committee;
7. Organized availability of all data items to the Executive Committee.

To enforce the law and to protect the rights and interests of citizens, it is necessary to receive, consider, and resolve complaints brought by working people. The range of the subjects discussed by the citizens in their complaints to the executive committees is extremely wide. It includes all aspects of life and living standards of the local population. Consideration of complaints not only is important for the satisfaction of the personal interests of the citizens, the complaints are signals indicating shortcomings in the work of certain units of the government mechanism and violations of socialist laws. The chairmen of the executive committees carry personal responsibility for the arrangement of hearings and for action on the complaints of working people. They, their deputies, and members of the committees conduct interviews with visitors.

The procedure for filing complaints is specified in the official regulations issued by the organs of the government, such as the councils of ministers of the union republics and the executive committees of the soviets of the workers' deputies.

Regardless of the means by which a complaint has found its way to the management, it must pass through registration. Urgent letters are registered and reported to the supervisor immediately. Registration of the complaints is performed either in a log or on a card basis, in both alphabetical and chronological order. Entry of complaints and suggestions is also performed by means of books for complaints and suggestions. The regulations for the use of these books are stipulated by the official norms of the union republics and the executive committees of the local soviets.

The registry of the General Department fills out three cards for all controlled correspondence; the first card is stored in the reference file of the registrar, the second is sent to the Control Group of the General Department, the third is submitted to the appropriate department of the Executive Committee, together with the original document. The employees of the Control Group screen the file every day, select the cards of the documents whose expiration is within a few days, and remind the executors of the approaching deadline. Suggestions, petitions, and complaints of the citizens are removed from control by the management of the Executive Committee through either the directors or the senior employees of the secretariats. The employees of the Control Group indicate on the control cards the state of implementation of the letters removed from control. In order to provide prompt implementation of the citizens' letters and to complete analysis of the work on them, the Control Group issues monthly reports.

The General Department issues a report on the processing of the suggestions, petitions, and complaints of the citizens to the Executive Committee four times a year. This report is submitted to the management of the Executive Committee, the head of the General Department, the heads of the secretariats, and the senior aides of the chairman and secretary of the Executive Committee.

A decision on a complaint can be made only by officials or government organs who are authorized by law to do so. A decision must have a specified form. It can be written or verbal. The officials announcing a decision are under an obligation to specify reasons for satisfying or for turning down a complaint. Decisions must be motivated by and based on the law. Written decisions made by individual officials are usually in the form of a reply. Decisions of group organs must be issued in the form of legal acts, corresponding to the authority of the particular organ.

The plaintiff is sent the decision or an account of its contents. The following time limits are established for the consideration of complaints: up to 1 month for cases requiring additional research and checking; in other cases, not more than 15 days from the moment of filing with the decision-making authority; if the decision requires special checking and other measures, the deadline can be extended by the head or the deputy of the given organ for not more than 1 month. The author of the petition or the complaint must be notified of the time extension. [Note: It would be interesting to study the actual response times.]

STANDING COMMITTEES, DEPUTIES, DEPUTY GROUPS, AND PUBLIC ORGANIZATIONS

Standing Committees

Permanent or standing committees are created in order to involve the deputies and the broad masses of working people in the practical activities of the soviet. The members of the standing committees are recruited from the deputies of the soviet. The committees are organs of the soviet, responsible and subordinate to it. They are created to correspond to the basic branches of the industrial and sociocultural structure of the city government. The tasks of the standing committees include the following:

1. Organization of the inspection and supervision of the implementation of decisions of the soviet, Executive Committee, and electorate;
2. Development of proposals and preparation of their examination by a session of the council;
3. Preparation and the making of decisions;
4. Formulation of issues pertaining to the running of the soviet; participation in the preparation for a session;
5. Assisting in the implementation of decisions of the Soviet.

The work of the standing committees is coordinated by the Executive Committee. The latter offers practical assistance in organizing and seeing to the technical needs of the standing committees.

There are several specific standing committees of the raion soviets.

1. Planning and Budget Committee:
   • prepares and supervises the implementation of the plans and the budget of the local economy and culture;
   • coordinates the work of the various committees;
   • determines potential industrial productivity savings and the additional available local resources;
   • assists in determining the revenue of the soviet and the sources of additional revenues of the enterprises;
   • assists in implementing the quarterly and annual plans for the state and local tax revenues, rents, and government insurance;

• supervises fiscal budget discipline, prompt and adequate financing, and proper utilization of government resources.

2. Committee for Youth:
   • deals with the issues of upbringings, education, professional training, work, life-style, recreation, and health care of young people, and their participation in the economic and sociocultural structure.

3. Credentials Committee:
   • handles the issues of the authority of the deputies and their subsequent ability to exercise their representative's prerogatives.

4. Committee for Social Security:
   • works on the issues of the health care and social security of retired people, aged single people, and the disabled who require additional government aid.

5. Committee for Municipal Services and Highway Construction:
   deals with issues of public services and the highways, such as the following:
   • cleanliness and order in the territory;
   • mechanization of the refuse collection process;
   • cleanliness and order in housing areas;
   • clean air and water;
   • protection of architectural monuments;
   • supervision of green areas, public parks, and forests;
   • construction and repair of such amenities as sidewalks, ditches, drains, traffic signals, pavilions, and lighting;
   • supervision of the quality of construction and repair of highways and facilities;
   • assistance in the development of supporting industries and the mechanization of the highway construction;
   • supervision of local roads and underpasses and maintenance of the highways.

Deputies

The deputies are the elected representatives of the people in the soviets. The work of the deputies during the session is determined by the Deputy Status Law, which stipulates the rights of the deputies to introduce various proposals, motions, or amendments, to start inquiries, to issue information, to issue written statements and proposals, and to address questions to the Executive Committee and to the heads of departments, administrations, and organizations in the city and within the authority of the soviet. An important guarantee for taking into account the views of people's representatives, reflecting the interests of the working people, is the systematic handling of the proposals and notes of the deputies (both verbal and written) during the session. These notes and proposals are examined by the soviet or sent for consideration to the corresponding government or public organs and officials. The latter must examine the proposals within the specified time limits and notify the deputy and the Executive Committee of the results. According to the Deputy Status Law, a system of information is established in the raion and the city soviets. It informs the deputies of the activities of the soviet and its organs, the implementation of the plans and the instructions of the electorate, the measures taken in connection with the proposals and the notes of the deputies, and the latest amendments to the law. Providing the deputies with the necessary information enables them (1) to participate actively in the preparation and consideration of the issues, (2) to acquire the means for efficient solutions of emerging problems, and (3) to make competent decisions on the issues facing the soviet.

The law instructs the representatives to study public opinion thoroughly, to participate in its development by informative-explanatory and political-educational work among the electors, to carry on constant work in participation with law enforcement institutions, to assist in the implementation of decisions of the soviet, its organs, and the instructions of the electorate, and to help tighten their bonds with the leadership of public organizations, the organs of the public volunteer organizations, and the work collectives. The deputies are authorized to notify the soviet and its organs of the needs and the necessities of the population, to analyze—in the course of their work on petitions and complaints—the reasons for the complaints, and to introduce proposals into the soviet and other government organs and institutions.

The deputies work with the electorate, individually in the election districts and also in groups of deputies.

Deputy Groups

Deputy groups are established for sets of adjacent electoral districts for the coordination of activities and to avoid duplicate and overlapping work. They supervise the implementation of the plans of the enterprises and the organizations of the economy that are subordinate to the soviet, and they prepare material on the subjects debated by the soviet. They assist in the development of public activities, and organize the leadership of the neighborhoods, city blocks, and housing collectives. Their major task at present is to assist all deputies in the successful completion of their obligations to the electors, to help implement the instructions and decisions of the soviet, and to compile oral reports to the electors (which must be issued not less than twice a year, according to the Status Law).

Public Organizations

Public inspectorates and public councils are auxiliary elements in the system of the Executive Committee. They are created by the committee and act in an open and public manner.

The public inspectorates oversee the implementation of decisions of the soviet and superior organizations, and consider the letters and complaints of the working people.

Public councils direct their efforts toward the improvement of the work of a given branch of the economy that is subordinate to the soviet. The decisions of the public councils are implemented by orders of the directors of the corresponding branch sections of the Executive Committee.

ROLE OF THE COMMUNIST PARTY*

In any analysis of governmental operations in the Soviet Union, the pervasive influence of the Communist Party must be borne in mind. The key to the power of the Party is its organizational structure, which faithfully parallels the administrative structure from the lowliest work brigade in a factory to the presidium of the Supreme Soviet of the Soviet Union. Each element of the administrative organization throughout the Soviet Union has its counterpart unit within the Party apparatus. Each pair of governmental and political entities has many members in common, but one such member may hold quite different ranks in the two units.

The Moscow City Party Conference is the Party counterpart to the Moscow City Soviet, whereas the Moscow City Party Committee corresponds to the Executive Committee of the Moscow City Soviet. Furthermore, corresponding to the leadership of the Executive Committee (chairman, vice-chairman and secretary), the city Party is led by the first secretary. Members of the committee direct a departmental structure that mirrors the structure of main administrations, etc., of the municipal government.

The interlocking membership of these bodies is quite interesting. All members of the City Soviet Executive Committee are Party members. The more important of these are usually also members of the Party Committee. Conversely, the top members of the Party Committee are usually on the Executive Committee. It is not common, however, for the Executive Committee vice-chairman in charge of a particular function, housing construction, for example, also to direct the Party department for that area. Similarly, it is rare for the chairman of the Executive Committee (the mayor) also to the the first secretary of the Party Committee.

This may give a clue as to the actual role of the Party in the process of city government. It is one of supervision and coordination.

---

*This explanatory section was written by the U.S. authors.

Each element of the national Party organization reports to and receives its directives from its immediate superior in the national scheme, in a line leading directly to the Central Committee and the Politburo. The Communist Party of the Soviet Union is the policy-making body of the nation. The local units of the Party oversee the execution of this policy in terms of plan fulfillment and social attitudes. They act as gadflies to prod the administrators and workers and at the same time to lead them to greater achievements on behalf of the state and the people. They see it as their duty to criticize program failures and instances of corruption, incompetence, or inefficiency both through the forum of Party meetings and in the Party newspaper *Pravda*.

The City Party Committee has two more direct forms of control over the activities of the municipal government. The first stems from the fact that most senior officials of city agencies are Party members, and as such are bound to follow the directives of the Party units to which they belong. The second major factor is nomenklatura. This is a list of offices over which a Party unit exerts the right to nominate candidates and fire incumbents. Through nomenklatura, the City Party Committee controls the most important decision-making posts in the city government. It transforms top civil administrators into direct agents of Party policy regardless of their rank within the Party itself.

The second important role of the Party in addition to that of supervision is one of coordinating the activities of the various segments of the soviet social and economic system. On the municipal level conflicts continually arise between municipal agencies and those agencies that, although located within the city, are under the sole control of a republic or union ministry. These disputes may involve air pollution standards, the impact of expanding industrial capacity on municipal services, the allocation of housing, or any number of other issues. The Party is in a good position to mediate disputes of this type, given its pervasive presence, breadth of purpose, and directive power. Party deliberations are theoretically supposed to transcend petty and narrow-minded considerations, and to resolve issues according to the best interests of the society as a whole.

Throughout the remainder of this book, little will be said about the Party when describing the administrative activities of the city government. It should be kept in mind, however, that all these activities occur within the framework of Party supervision and coordination as described above. It may safely be assumed that few, if any, important decisions are made without the prior approval of some appropriate Party unit, and that the ultimate source of all power is the Party.

APPENDIX

Figure 3.3. Administrative Offices of the Moscow Soviet Executive Committee

1. Main Housing Administration
2. Question of the Capital and Current Repair of Houses
3. External Affairs Administration
4. Personnel and Training Administration[a]
5. Housing Accounting and Distribution Administration
6. Cooperative Housing Administration
7. Department of Nonresidential Buildings
8. Commission on Housing Questions
9. Main Scientific Research Computing Center (Glav NIVTS)
10. Coordinating Council[b]
11. function represented by Box 11 has been deleted
12. Main Moscow Construction Administration (Glavmosstroi)
13. Main Moscow Engineering Construction Administration (Glavmosinstroi)
14. Main Moscow Industrial Construction Administration
15. Main Moscow Industrial Construction Materials Administration
16. Main Moscow Architectural Planning Administration
17. Main Capital Construction Administration
18. Main Administration for Specialized Construction
19. Enterprise Construction[c]
20. Cooperative Construction
21. Study of the Removal from the City of Sanitarily Harmful or Fire-Hazardous Enterprises
22. Issues related to subway construction and State Planning Institute for Construction of Subways and Transportation Facilities
23. Department for Construction and Construction Materials
24. Everyday Services Administration
25. Communal Services Administration
26. Custom Sewing and Clothing Repair Administration
27. Water and Sewer System Administration
28. Metal-Processing Industry Administration
29. Household Chemical and Rubber Products Administration
30. Administration of Specialized Enterprises Which Use the Labor of Invalids
31. Main Health Protection Administration
32. Main Administration of Public Education
33. City Department of Social Maintenance
34. City Pharmaceutical Administration
35. City Veterinary Department
36. Commission on Youth Affairs
37. Commission on the Establishment of Personal Pensions of Local Important Significance
38. Commission on the Organization of Children's Recreation
39. Society of the Red Cross (supervision)
40. Main Administration for Professional-Technical Education Administration (supervision)

41. Moscow Society of Ornamental Dog Breeding (supervision)
42. Commission for Youth Employment
43. Main Trade Administration (Glavtorg)
44. Main Public Eating Administration (Glavobshpit)
45. Main Administration for Vegetable Production
46. Baking Industry Administration
47. Moscow Bakery Products Administration (supervision)
48. Main Administration for the Procurement, Processing, and Marketing of Secondary Ferrous and Nonferrous Metals
49. Main Administration for the Procurement and Processing of Secondary Raw Materials
50. Commission for the Struggle Against Drunkenness
51. Fuel and Power Administration
52. Apartment House and Hotel Administration
53. Natural Gas Inspectorate
54. Moscow Power Administration (supervision)
55. District Commission of State Municipal Technical Directorate (supervision)
56. Administration for the Operation of Administrative Buildings
57. Administration for the Operation of Large Apartment Buildings
58. General Leadership
59. Moscow Financial Administration
60. Civilian Defense Headquarters
61. Technology Administration[d]
62. Questions concerning the Olympic Games
63. City Planning Committee
64. Price Department[e]
65. Materials and Equipment Supply Administration
66. Administration for the Use of Labor Resources
67. Bureau of Technical Inventory
68. Commission for the Preparation of Propositions Concerning the Distribution of Space on the First Stories of Houses
69. City Statistical Administration
70. City Arbitration Administration[f]
71. City Commission for the Use of Labor Resources
72. Main Administration of Internal Affairs (Fire and Police Services)
73. Publication, Printing, and Book Sales Administration
74. City Designs and Advertising Administration
75. Justice Department
76. Moscow Bar
77. Registry Department
78. City Headquarters of the Volunteer Brigades, e.g., Auxiliary Police
79. Supervisory Commission[g]
80. Questions of the Council on Religious Affairs in Moscow
81. Issues related to the All-Union Voluntary Society for the Assistance to the Army, Air Force, and Navy of the Soviet Union
82. Moscow City Court (supervision)
83. Moscow Volunteer Fire Society (supervision)[h]
84. Moscow Society of Hunters and Fishermen (supervision)
85. City Military Commissariat (supervision)

86. Society for Furthering the Development of Water Transportation and for Safeguarding Human Lives on the Waterways of the Soviet Union
87. Moscow Society of Fishermen (supervision)
88. Commission for the Consideration of Registration Questions in Moscow
89. Commission for Civil Ceremonies
90. Main Motor Vehicle Transportation Administration (for freight)
91. Passenger Transportation Administration
92. Automobile Transportation Administration
93. Main Administration for Roads and Public Services
94. Forest and Park Administration
95. Department of City Passenger Transportation Coordination
96. Administrative Inspectorate
97. Issues related to the Moscow Telephone and Radio Transmitting Network
98. Issues related to the Bridge Trust and River Steamship Line
99. Issues related to the Moscow Rail Hub and Air Fields
100. Society for the Planting of Greenery and the Protection of Nature (supervision)
101. Scientific-Technical Council Concerning the Problems of Strengthening the Protection of the Environment and the Rational Use of the Natural Resources of Moscow and Its Greenbelt
102. Main Administration of Culture
103. Cinema Administration
104. Study to Organize Workers' Recreation
105. Organizational-Instructional Department[i]
106. Archive Administration
107. General Department
108. Supervision of the Reception Room of the Executive Committee
109. Legal Department (of the secretary)
110. Editorial staff of the Moscow Council Executive Committee Library
111. Agency for the Preparation of Materials for the Presentation of Government Awards
112. Commission for the Naming of Streets

Notes:

[a]Also runs technical schools.

[b]For implementation of management productivity measures.

[c]For example, this unit will supervise and inspect construction activities of an enterprise that might be building housing for its workers.

[d]To coordinate the planning and implementation of technological innovations in city agencies.

[e]Sets retail and wholesale prices, tariffs for commercial services, city transport fares, etc.

[f]Negotiates contracts between enterprises.

[g]This commission works with those who are not in a stable, fully employed mode of life. For example, when convicts are released from prison, this commission works to find them jobs, establish them in apartments, and in general, bring them back into the mainstream of Soviet society.

[h]There are many volunteer fire brigades organized at each enterprise and within each local housing administrative unit, or zhek.

[i]Serves as staff to the deputies and the permanent committees.

Figure 3.4. Administrative Offices of a Raion (District) Soviet of Workers' Deputies

1. Credentials
2. Planning and Budget
3. Construction
4. Housing
5. Industry, Transportation, and Communications
6. Everyday and Municipal Services
7. Public Education
8. Culture
9. Youth Affairs
10. City Improvement
11. Trade
12. Public Eating
13. Health Protection
14. Social Maintenance
15. Socialist Law and the Protection of Order
16. Physical Training and Sports
17. Department of Labor, Women, and Children
18-27. Mikroraion (Neighborhood) Housing Organization Office (Zhek)
28. Industrial Plant
29. Factory
30. Scientific Research Institute
31. Production Association
32. Combinat
33. Industrial Plant
34. Factory
35. Scientific Research Institute
36. Production Association
37. Trust
38. Planning Commission
39. Trade Department
40. Financial Department
41. Department of the Raion Architect
42. Department of Capital Construction
43. Department of Social Maintenance
44. Department of Housing Distribution
45. Department of Public Education
46. Housing Administration
47. Road Construction and City Improvement Administration
48. Everyday and Municipal Services Administration
49. Raion Food Trade, Industrial Trade, and Dining Trusts
50. Internal Affairs Administration
51. Repair and Construction Trust
52. Office of Raion Technical Supply
53. Bureau of Technical Inventory
54. Administrative Inspectorate

55. Inspector of City Statistics
56. Government Inspectorate for Fines
57. Registry Bureau
58. Organizational-Instructional Department
59. General Department
60. Commission on Housing Questions
61. Deputy Commission of the Installation of Telephones
62. Interdepartmental Commission
63. Administrative Commission
64. Supervisory Commission
65. Commission on Youth Affairs
66. Commission on the Struggle Against Drunkenness
67. Commission on Control over the Observance of Legislation Concerning Religious Cults
68. Commission on the Inculcation of New Civilian Ceremonies in Everyday Life
69. Public Inspectorate for Control over the Resolutions of the Raion Soviet Executive Committee
70. Public Council on the Work of House Committees
71. Public Council on the Work of Comradely Courts
72. Council on Assistance to Family and School

4

LONG-TERM PLANNING AND ECONOMIC DEVELOPMENT

BASIC PLANNING PROCEDURE

Planning, as a method of economic control, is carried out at every level of management, from the primary production units to the city economy as a whole. The supreme planning organ of Moscow is the City Planning Commission of the Executive Committee, the acronym of which is Gorplan.

Municipal plans are divided into long (10 to 25 years), medium (usually 5 years), and short (1 year) range. The General Plan for Municipal Development is designed for a span of 25 to 30 years by the Main Architectural Planning Administration of the Executive Committee. It is subject to approval by the state. This plan, together with other long-range plans dealing with municipal construction, determine over a long period of time the trends, pace, and magnitude of the development of the city's economy, the branches of industry, the raions, the trusts, and the individual enterprises. The work of the individual enterprises, trusts, and branches as well as the performance of the entire city economy are evaluated by the rate at which the perspective (long- and medium-range) and annual plans are implemented.

The basic social objective of the plans for the development of Moscow's economy is the further improvement of the living conditions of the population. These plans map the trends of scientific and technological progress, determine the volume of construction and renovation, and set the pace and the intensity of the utilization of industrial, material, labor, and fiscal resources.

54

The result of the planning process is the formulation of tasks for all the branches of the city economy. The completion of these tasks is aided by a system of economic incentives for the work of the labor collectives, based on the joint interests of the national economy, the separate branches, and the production units. The most important levers of economic incentive are prices, salaries, material incentive funds, income, credit, profitability, etc.

The development of the plan is a complex process of economic analysis and balanced planning computations. The balance method of plan development implies the coordinated development of the different branches of the city economy. For instance, the volume of construction and assembly work and the plan for capital investment are coordinated and consistent with the program of the construction and assembly organizations. This results in a motivated plan for construction and assembly work.

The impact of program growth with respect to labor requirements at enterprises and organizations is carefully calculated. The final coordination of enterprise and organizational growth must reconcile the development plans of the various raions of the city, the balanced development plans of all the economic branches for the city, and the development of several additional citywide plans such as water resources, the availability of important types of construction materials, overall labor resource availability, and so forth.

Planning in the City Planning Commission is divided into three stages: (1) establishing the basic features or policies of the plan; (2) development of proposals for the plan; (3) preparation of the plan itself.

During the first stage, the design organizations are bound by certain parameters (resources, time limits, etc.). The work is based on the assumption that after the available local resources are determined, the remaining necessary requirements will be satisfied from outside sources.

The second stage is developed after the preliminary work has been submitted to the superior organs (in the case of the City Planning Commission, these are the State Planning Agencies of the R.S.F.S.R. and the Soviet Union), which establish policies that act as the parameters of the second stage.

The second stage is the most important and time consuming in the entire planning process. Since the control figures issued by the superior organ are, as a rule, lower than the results of the first-stage evaluations, a proposed plan is developed after a series of iterative co-ordinating steps between subordinate and superior planning organs. The City Planning Commission, for instance, develops its plans on the basis of the planning proposals of the Main Administrations and Administrations of the Moscow Executive Committee.

After the approval and amendment of the planning proposals by the superior organs, the third and last stage, that of actual plan development, is entered. Following this, the plans in some cases have to go through a final approval process. The final plans must first be approved by the superior planning organs, and are then considered by the Executive Committee of the Moscow Soviet.

The schedules for the different stages of the plans are determined by the superior organs for their subordinates. They generally depend on the time span for which the plans are developed and the level of the planning organs. For instance, the deadlines for the development of the short-range (annual) plan by the City Planning Commission are as follows:

1. First stage (basic trends of the plan)—May of the preceding year;
2. Second stage (plan proposal)—October of the preceding year;
3. Consideration and approval by the session of the Executive Committee of the Moscow Soviet—December 1 of the preceding year.

Revisions of plans are made by the superior planning organ for the subordinate ones after a study of the suggested adjustments and the reasons for them. The deadline for revisions to the annual plan developed by the City Planning Commission is February 15 of the current year.

GENERAL PLAN FOR MUNICIPAL DEVELOPMENT

The social and economic impact of the post-war General Plan for the development of Moscow, which determined the long-range development of the city, can be seen in the continuous improvement of living and working conditions for high working productivity and highly organized everyday life and recreation for the population.

The program for the harmonious development of Moscow can be developed only after the rational distribution and intensification of the industrial production of Moscow and the Moscow area. Because of this, the government has issued an order stipulating that the current General Plan, approved in 1968 and forecasting the city development in the years 1980-2000, must be developed together with the structure of the raion plans and the plan of the Moscow region. This results in proportional development throughout the area and the geographic dispersion of economic activity; it also solves the problem of population distribution.

The intensive concentration of industrial power within a 50-kilometer radius around the city has resulted in an oversaturation of the area and threatens the protective forest belt with extinction. At the same time, the population of a number of peripheral districts is insufficient. Hence, one of the most important objectives in managing the development of the Moscow agglomerate is restricting the further concentration of industry and population in Moscow and the nearest suburbs and protecting its natural environment by stimulating the development of other nearby cities.

According to the 1968 General Plan, the territory of Moscow and the Moscow region is divided into two basic urban zones as follows: Moscow and the suburban zone within a radius of 50 to 60 kilometers from the city limits (this is the zone where further industrial growth is restricted), and the outer zone of the Moscow region within a radius of 100 to 120 kilometers from the city limits, which is the priority area for further industrial development.

The inner area, including the forest protective belt, is used for the regulated development of the farming economy, for resorts, for the settlement of the population that works in Moscow, for the basic facilities of the Moscow transportation network, and for the engineering facilities of the city. In the process, Moscow and the suburbs must have a sustained equilibrium between population size and available jobs.

The development of the forest protective belt of Moscow, as specified by the General Plan, must be directed so as to prevent the merging of the city with other settlements in the area. On the basis of the existing and newly developed forest areas, water reservoirs, and open farm zones, Moscow must be surrounded by a continuous green area, stretching from the suburbs to the parks around the city. The number of settlements in the forest belt must be limited through their consolidation. The environment and the architecture of these cities must improve.

According to the General Plan, the planning structure of the city is based on eight complex planning zones, forming an urban unit with the central city as the nucleus. The managed development of each of these zones is to provide an equilibrium between the working population and available employment.

The population of each zone should not exceed 1 million people. Each zone is to be divided into three to four planning districts (of

250,000 to 300,000 people each) with the necessary public administration and cultural-public service institutions as their centers. The planning districts must include residential districts (of 30,000 to 70,000 people each), with represents the basic units of the inhabited areas. The residential districts in turn must consist of housing groups of 3,000 to 5,000 people (with their centers for daily services) or microraions (where they are already established). The urban character of Moscow will be determined by the city center and its basic nucleus, surrounded by the park belt, as well as the newly created centers of the municipal planning zones, connected into a continuous system by traffic arteries and squares.

The General Plan stipulates the total eradication of old and inadequate housing facilities and the provision of individual family apartments with the number of rooms equal to the number of members in each family. In view of this, the average living space per citizen is planned to be increased to 13.0 to 13.5 square meters. [Note: In 1978, the average was 9.7 square meters, or 104 square feet, per person; see Chapter 7.] This implies an increase of the city housing stock to over 95 million square meters. The transition to housing constructed according to the standard norms has already begun. It will allow the construction of apartment buildings of differing heights and with varied space and volume characteristics, to satisfy the demands of each particular area.

The Moscow transport network will undergo regulated growth, based on development of the Metro, the highways, the railways, and the water and air transport of the city and surrounding areas. The planning objective is to provide the city population with a means of travel from home to work in less than 35 minutes.

Based on existing groups of industrial and productive enterprises, the creation of 65 production zones on the territory of Moscow is planned. The basic trends of the administration of industrial development of Moscow are the following: It is prohibited to expand or to build new industrial enterprises and workshops, science research and design institutes, experimental centers, construction offices, universities, or technical schools on the territory of the city or the forest protective belt. Such enterprises must be located in the suburban area of Moscow, lying primarily outside the belt. (This excludes enterprises and facilities needed for the immediate service of the population.) The industries whose growth within the city and its immediate suburbs will be permitted are those that do not use metals and energy, but that require high expertise (high-precision machining, tool industry, electrical appliances, etc.), as well as those that produce high-quality consumer goods.

At present, the city has no excess labor resources. Witness to this is the daily commuting to Moscow of the population of the surrounding area, as well as the positive balance of migration. Accordingly, industrial growth must come about by the reconstruction of enterprises and an increase in productivity through technological reorganization, wide application of advanced technology, and automation of the production processes, without increasing the number of employees or expanding the production area. The planned reorganization of industrial enterprises will not only increase output, but also will reduce the number of workers, allowing the employment of released labor resources in the field of public services. It is expected that approximately 350,000 people will be transferred from industry to the service field.

In the agglomerate outside the city limits, the reconstruction and expansion of existing enterprises are planned, in addition to the relocation of those being transferred from Moscow proper. A considerable amount of work is anticipated in the field of housing and municipal service construction. The ultimate goal of these measures is to halve the number of commuters, from 500,000 to about 250,000.

The organizations of Moscow have begun the design of the suburban area, determining the basic developmental trends of the Moscow agglomerate beyond the limits of the period covered by the General Plan.

In conclusion, it should be noted that the actual development of Moscow is accompanied by unavoidable deviations from the General Plan and the raion plans of Moscow and the vicinity. These include slippage in the deadlines for removing from Moscow and from the forest belt the enterprises and science research organizations that are polluting or environmentally unsatisfactory, pose fire hazards, or are inconsistent with the Moscow profile. There are also violations of the relocation guidelines by the enterprises and units of the city's industrial base. Prompt corrections are needed for deviations from the General Plan and the scheme of district planning for the Moscow area.

5

SHORT-TERM PLANNING AND BUDGETING

Article 97 of the Constitution of the Union of Soviet Socialist Republics stipulates the following: "The Soviets of Workers' Deputies supervise the work of the management authorities responsible to them, provide for the security of government order, for the implementation of law and for the observation of citizens' rights, manage the local economic and cultural structure, and formulate the local budget."

BUDGETING PROCEDURES

The budget of Moscow is a component—a substantial component—of the budget of the R.S.F.S.R. (The latter in turn is part of the budget of the Soviet Union.) It includes the city budget and the budgets of the 32 raions, including Zelenograd. The budget provides funds for financing the economic and sociocultural activities carried on by the Moscow Soviet of Workers' Deputies and its Executive Committee.

According to the regulations for planning the budget of the R.S.F.S.R., as set forth by the R.S.F.S.R. Council of Ministers, municipal authorities do the following:

1. Administrations and departments of the City Soviet Executive Committee formulate proposals for fiscal plans and estimates, based on the requirements established by the long-range Plan for Municipal Development, and submit these proposals to the City Finance Administration.
2. The raion finance departments formulate the raion budgets and submit them to the Moscow City Finance Administration; there is no overlap between these budgets and the proposals developed in (1) above;

60

3. The City Finance Administration formulates the combined city budget and submits it to the Executive Committee of the Moscow City Soviet for examination and approval;
4. On the basis of the plan for the development of the R.S.F.S.R. economy and that for the development of Moscow's economy, the Executive Committee considers the proposed city budget and submits it to the R.S.F.S.R. Council of Ministers for examination and inclusion in the proposed R.S.F.S.R. government budget. After discussion by the Council of Ministers, and prior to submission for approval by a session of the Moscow Soviet, the city budget is considered by the Budget Committee of the Executive Committee.

The Budget Committee of the Executive Committee does the following:

1. During the examination of the city budget, it reviews the reports of the administrations and departments on their fiscal plans and calculations, as well as the reports of the executive committees of the raion soviets on revenues and expenditures in the raion budgets. Also considered are proposals for adjustments to those figures;
2. It formulates a response regarding the overall budget of Moscow and submits it to a session of the Moscow Soviet of Workers' Deputies.

The session of the Moscow Soviet considers the city budget according to the report of the Executive Committee and the response of the Budget Committee. The following items are subsequently approved at this session:

1. The budget of Moscow in terms of total income, with specified major income sources, and total expenditures, with specified funds allocated to the local economy, social and cultural activities, and general management;
2. The amount to be deducted from state taxes and revenues that will be retained for the city budget;
3. The amount of capital funds available to the city.

The city budget specifies the raion budgets only in terms of total revenue and expenditures for each district, together with the amount of capital funds designated for these budgets. Raions report expenditures for broad budget categories—sports, health, etc. They have, however, considerable discretion within these areas, i.e., with respect to salaries, supplies, and even within the area of capital expenditures. In general, though, the only way a raion may effectively increase local revenues is to obtain funds from a higher level such as the city. It can decide to retain additional profits from enterprises under its subordination, but these are few, and funds from these sources amount to a small fraction of the total budget.

While approving the city budget, the session of the City Soviet can change the total revenue and expenditure figures anticipated for the city budget by the state budget of the R.S.F.S.R., provided it does not change the amount it retains from state taxes and revenues. For example, increased income could be made available from increased levies on industries of city subordination.

Any surplus, due to higher revenues or lower expenditures than anticipated, is allocated by the Executive Committee to financing the local economy and to social and cultural activities, including capital investments. This is true for raion budgets as well.

Budget deficits in raions are rare owing to very strict planning and expenditure discipline. The State Bank and the City Finance Administration exercise daily control by virtue of the fact that all funds and payments go through this bank.

The City Executive Committee implements the budget through the Finance Administration and other management organs of the committee. The session dealing with the report of the Executive Committee and the response of the Budget Committee examines and approves the report on the implementation of the city budget, and its decisions are published.

The central authority that carries out the fiscal planning of Moscow is the Moscow City Finance Administration (Gorfin), which performs the following functions:

1. Develops a proposal for the municipal budget based on studies of the proposals of the main administrations, the administrations, and the departments of the City Executive Committee, as well as the proposed raion budgets and the proposed budget for the city of Zelenograd;
2. Checks the consistency of the raion budgets (which are approved by the raion soviets) with the laws of the Soviet Union and the R.S.F.S.R. and the national economic plan for the city of Moscow;
3. Designs and implements the forms and methods of budget planning; establishes and maintains control over the work of the raion finance departments;
4. Works to improve the forms and methods of budget planning;
5. Develops proposals for resolutions and decisions of the Executive Committee concerning the composition and implementation of the Moscow city budget;
6. Keeps track of changes in income and expenditures introduced by the resolutions of the Council of Ministers of the Soviet Union and the R.S.F.S.R.; this is achieved through coordination of the R.S.F.S.R. budget with those of the city of Moscow and the raions.

Consolidated information regarding changes in the city and raion budgets, i.e., the modified revenue and expenditure plans of the city, is relayed periodically to the R.S.F.S.R. Ministry of Finance.

Control over the implementation of the budget with respect to revenue is exercised by comparing monthly reports on the implementation of the revenue plan with the city budget approved by the Moscow City Executive Committee. The results of the budget implementation are relayed periodically to the Executive Committee of the City Soviet.

Gorfin analyzes the fiscal-economic situation of the city economy. This analysis is examined annually by the R.S.F.S.R. Ministry of Finance.

Financing for raion organizations and enterprises is provided by raion finance departments within the fiscal limits approved by Gorfin. The Laws of the Raion Soviet and of the Budget Rights of Citizens place great power in the hands of the raion committees for development, examination, approval, and implementation of the budget, as well as for decisions on numerous financial problems.

While approving the raion budget, the raion soviets and their executive committees are authorized to increase or decrease the following revenues that stem from the raion economy or from other income sources: local taxes and rents (construction tax and land rent, tax on vehicle horsepower, entertainment tax, etc.); income from leases; profits of government properties; profits of specialized budgeted enterprises; fees for children in schools and boarding schools, etc.

The executive committees of the raion soviets are authorized to increase or decrease (according to the actual profits realized) expenditures for the following purposes:

1. Working capital for the economic enterprises of the raion soviet;
2. Raion operating expenses (cleaning of the raion, road maintenance, care of plantings, etc.);
3. Capital repair of roads and construction facilities;
4. Capital repair in budgeted enterprises;
5. Maintenance of schools, hospitals, clinics, and other budgeted enterprises, including the following functions: medical supply, equipment, and inventory, daily nutrition, educational expenditures (educational and writing supplies and materials for classes and lab courses in the general educational system, the schools for working youth, and the schools for children living in children's homes).

Total expenditures in the following budget categories are set by the Moscow City Executive Committee and may not be increased by the Raion Executive Committee without the approval of the Moscow City Soviet:

1. Wages of the budget unit as a whole; that is, they cannot raise the total salary budget of a unit. This serves as a check on inflation. The local group could,

for example, decide to increase expenditures for health care supplies, but could not hire additional personnel in this area.

2. Administrative-managerial expenditures (headquarters expenditures for elements of the Executive Committee structure and its sections).

The Raion Executive Committee may do the following:

1. Decide, with the approval of the enterprises, companies, and organizations (regardless of their departmental subordination), on the utilization of funds for housing and municipal, highway, cultural, and everyday service construction and on the construction of educational, public eating, trade, and health facilities;
2. Conduct renovation and expansion of schools, cultural and other clubs, and libraries using funds for capital repair and additional funds obtained during the implementation of the raion budget;
3. Increase the number of children in the preschool organizations and the number of beds in the boarding schools over and above the number specified in the plan with funds from their own budget, with notification to the Main Administration of Health and the City Education Department;
4. Solve problems dealing with the opening and closing of public schools, kindergartens, and nurseries, with the approval of the Main Administration of Health and the City Education Department;
5. Receive from the ministries and the departments new health centers, preschool child care centers, and schools for the use of the raion departments of health and education, with the approval of the Main Health Administration and the City Education Department;
6. Initiate, if necessary, new classes in the public schools during the academic year, financing them with funds from the raion budget;
7. Make decisions on subjects related to the improvement of living conditions using funds for the capital repair of housing facilities;
8. Depending upon economic feasibility and public demand, open, change the location, or change the specialization of trade enterprises, food establishments, and the everyday service centers managed by the district, with notification to city management.

The Raion Executive Committee can repair its administrative buildings and purchase necessary equipment using profits or surplus obtained during the implementation of the budget. Furthermore, it is authorized to spend surplus revenues due to extra profits or economy of expenditures. This does not apply to unutilized funds that were allocated to capital investments.

During 1974, such surpluses were used by raion executive committees to provide 17.2 million rubles for housing and municipal services, for capital repair, and for equipping public education and health enterprises. This represented approximately 2 percent of the total budget.

The budget committees of the soviets of workers' deputies, in cooperation with the entire community, are assigned the task of exercising financial control and also of checking on enterprises, companies, and organizations and systematically observing the implementation of the decisions of the executive committees and of the superior government authorities. The budget committees are also responsible for the supervision of the soviet organs dealing with executive and management functions. They perform considerable work on the preparation of reports on the implementation of the budget for the current period and the development of the budget proposal for the coming year.

The members of the permanent budget committees together with the public inspectors are authorized to supervise the work of the departments of the executive committees, the enterprises responsible to the executive committees, as well as the various other trusts, organizations, etc. They are entitled to all necessary reference materials and explanations, and they can examine all orders, resolutions, and other documents.

Systematic control over the work of the enterprises, companies, and organizations responsible to the soviets and their executive committees is one of the most important functions of the permanent budget committees. The committees assist the soviets in the timely solution of problems in the economic and cultural everyday service structure.

Active participation of budget committees in the development and implementation of local budgets contributes to the timely and complete acquisition of profits and tightens control over the expenditure of government funds.

REVENUE SOURCES

The city and the raions receive revenues through several mechanisms. These are described below.

Deductions from Profits and Other Enterprise Revenues

Deductions from profits and other enterprise revenues are paid by enterprises and economic organizations subordinate to the executive committee of the city or raion soviet. There are almost 23,000 enterprises and organizations associated with the raions and the city, of which 4,000 are the responsibility of the main administrations, administrations, and departments of the Moscow City Executive Committee. An enterprise pays a percentage of its annual profit to the governmental unit to which it is subordinate, and only to that unit. This unit may be a raion, a city, a republic, or the all-union (national) government. The actual percentage paid depends on the level of subordination and type of enterprise.

Income Tax

The income tax is paid by enterprises and organizations; this tax is constant with a basic industry, e.g., steel, oil, etc. Multipurpose industries may pay at various rates depending upon the variety of their products. An industry pays its income tax only to the governmental level to which it is subordinate: union, republic, city, or raion.

Local Taxes and Fees

Local taxes and fees include a tax on car ownership, which is paid to the raion in which the car is registered, and a land rent paid by the long-term occupants of individual (as distinguished from multi-family) dwellings. Land rents are also paid by enterprises according to their subordination. Apartment rents are paid to the local housing office, and are used directly by that office to maintain the housing complex.

State Funds and Other Income

State funds and other income are allocated to the budget of Moscow. They include the inheritance tax and other low-yield taxes that go to the city and raions.

Deductions from Various Taxes

As specified by the state budget of the R.S.F.S.R., deductions from various taxes are, in effect, planned grants from the republic and union governments, under which a jurisdiction retains a portion of the state taxes that it collects. A number of these taxes are described below.

Turnover Tax

The turnover tax is a wholesale tax (or value-added tax) that is levied at each point of sale (except retail), and represents a portion of the profit that is turned over to the state. Portions are retained by the raions and the city, with the remainder going to the state. In the Soviet Union, the turnover tax is one of the basic sources of income for the state budget and represents a powerful tool for the regulation of the activity of industrial production. This tax is imposed on highly profitable items not included among the primary necessities. It is not imposed on bread, meat, canned food, potatoes, vegetables, books, or children's goods. Since there is no sales tax, and since the turnover tax is not applied at the retail level, there is not tax on services.

In order to maintain low prices for children's goods, light industry and other enterprises sell clothing material at rates lower than cost. The discounts are: woollen fabrics, 25 to 35 percent; cotton fabrics, 20 to 50 percent; silk and synthetic fabrics, 25 to 32 percent. In order to cover the difference in the prices for the children's products, the state budget allocates 600 million rubles per annum from the turnover tax. This amount is allocated to Moscow, separate from the city budget.

The government of the Soviet Union has introduced a number of turnover tax deductions in order to stimulate the production of public-oriented items, to improve their quality, and to encourage the use of local raw and waste materials.

In order to make possible the planned activity of enterprises, production for 1975-76 was encouraged by fiscal authorities by reducing the turnover tax on over 1,012 items produced by national, republic, and local enterprises.

Personal Income Tax

Revenues from personal income tax are split between the raion and the union government, with up to 50 percent of the collected amount being retained by the raion. The exact portion is negotiated by the city on behalf of each raion and depends upon the characteristics of the raion, its needs, and its alternative sources of revenue. The tax rate is 8.2 percent of the first 150 rubles of monthly salary and 13 percent of the remainder.

"Bachelor" Tax

The bachelor tax amounts to 6 percent of salary and is levied on all those who do not have children. The revenue generated is split among the raion, city, and union governments.

CITY AND RAION REVENUES

Total city revenues in 1975 and the contribution of each source to the total are shown in Table 5.1. The total exceeded two billion rubles. (The planned budget showed a slight surplus: Revenues were expected to exceed expenditures by 3 million rubles.) Of the total,

Table 5.1. Sources of Actual Revenue, 1975

Income	Amount in Millions of Rubles	Percentage
Turnover tax	542.6	23.8
Payments from profits	1,202.6	52.7
Business income tax	11.2	0.5
Personal income tax	112.7	4.9
State taxes, local taxes	37.6	1.6
Nontax duties	31.7	1.5
Money and prize lotteries	8.4	0.4
Other income	333.4	14.6
Total income	2,280.2	100.0

the budgets of the raions and the city of Zelenograd were 867 million rubles. The remainder, 1.413 billion rubles, was directly in the budget of the city.

Another useful way of looking at revenues is in terms of fixed and other income. Fixed incomes are obtained from enterprises of local subordination. They include profit payments of enterprises and organizations of local subordination, local taxes and rents, state tax deductions, the tax on local entertainment, income from government properties, lease taxes, user fees for children in boarding schools, and overhead income from specialized sources. Other income consists of turnover taxes, personal income tax, bachelor tax, and various other smaller fees, duties, and taxes.

Table 5.2 indicates the importance of fixed income sources in the budget of Moscow. It can be seen that fixed income accounts for a much larger part of the city soviet budget (97 percent) than the raion budget (25 percent).

Because the major source of fixed income is the economic enterprises that come under the city and the raion executive committees, it is important to discuss these enterprises in some detail, particularly those in the fields of trade, public food service, and everyday services.

From 1966 through 1970, about 1,000 new stores with 13,700 employees, public eating enterprises [that is, restaurants and cafeterias] with 175,000 seats, and food-preserving centers with a capacity of 334,000 tons were built in Moscow. The turnover (sales) of the trade and the public eating enterprises for this period increased from 7.2 to 10.6 billion rubles. The large growth in sales made possible the

Table 5.2. Fixed and Other Income in City Revenues, 1975 (in millions of rubles)

Type of Income	Moscow Soviet		Raions		Total City Budget	
	Rubles	Percentage	Rubles	Percentage	Rubles	Percentage
Fixed	1,118.3	97.3	218.7	25.2	1,337	66.4
Other (turnover tax, personal income tax, etc.)	30.7	2.7	648.3	74.8	679	33.6
Total	1,149	100	867	100	2,016	100

Note: This table shows planned revenues for 1975 as adopted in December 1974.

successful attainment of the gross profit and expenditure targets of the enterprises and organizations.

The city's share of the profits from trade and public eating enterprises increased from 4.9 to 12 percent of profits, and amounted to 736.1 million rubles in 1975, or about one-third of the total budget. (The commodity distribution funds in trade and public food services amount to over 600 million rubles per annum.)

City revenues stemming from the trade of industrial goods are substantially higher than from the sale of food, in spite of the fact that trade taxes for industrial goods are lower. This is due to the different levels of distribution costs and expenses and the fact that there is considerably more waste in food sales.

The following were constructed during the ninth Five-Year Plan (1971-75): 1,000 new stores for 16,000 employees; 800 public eating centers with 155,000 seats; food-preserving centers with a capacity of 274,000 tons. The construction of trade and public eating enterprises was allocated 356,000 rubles, or 33 percent more than during the previous Five-Year Plan. The total gross volume of trade exceeded 13.6 billion rubles.

Everyday services are also quite important. They regulate money circulation in the country, since the bulk of the income of the population is spent in exchange for various services. Income from enterprises and organizations of the everyday service system is becoming an increasingly promising source of income for the city budget. Examples from several of these services are presented for illustrative purposes.

During 1971-75, the repair of common appliances and equipment increased by 30 percent. The profits of the repair factories increased from 3.4 to 4.4 million rubles, i.e., by 29.4 percent.

The amount of work by dry cleaning centers increased by 69 percent, while their profits increased from 1.9 to 5.2 million rubles, or by 174 percent. Repair and custom production of shoes increased in volume by 14 percent, while the profits increased from 2.6 to 3.5 million rubles, or by 35 percent. Photographic work increased by 39 percent, while profits increased from 1.5 to 2 million rubles, or by 33 percent.

During this period, the profit of the enterprises of everyday service and personal custom tailoring increased from 37.2 to 62.4 million rubles, i.e., by 68 percent. However, payments into the budget for this period remained almost the same; they increased from 26.8 to 27.2 million rubles, i.e., by just 1.5 percent. This is a result of granting greater authority to the everyday service enterprises to utilize and reinvest their profits for expanding existing facilities and constructing new ones. There has been a substantial increase in the portion of the profit reinvested in growth and a relative decrease in deductions for the budget. Thus, whereas in 1967 the payments into the budget by the everyday service enterprises represented 72 percent of their profits, owing to an increased investment for growth, this figure was reduced to 44 percent by 1970.

As a whole, the budget payments of the local enterprises and organizations during 1975 represented 59 percent of the budget, i.e., 89.5 percent of the budget of Moscow and 19.4 percent of the raion budgets. Other forms of fixed income, primarily from the same enterprises and organizations, contribute another 6 percent, for a total of 25 percent of the raion budgets.

In accordance with Party and government decisions to increase the authority of local soviets in the area of economic and cultural development, a number of necessary steps were taken to enlarge and stabilize the income base of the local soviets. Since 1969, for example, raions have been receiving income from the distribution of lottery tickets. Since 1970, they have received 50 percent of the income of the 3 percent government loan bond sale. This is a lottery bond, with the bond principal being used by the state.

Local fixed income sources represent a smaller part of the district budget. For 75 percent of their revenues, they are dependent upon other income, namely, deductions from government taxes and revenues. Thus, the turnover tax deductions, the income tax, and the tax on bachelors and undersized families become the basic source of income for local raion budgets.

An especially important part is played by the turnover tax. It contributes up to 90 percent of the budget in some raions, although there are districts where it amounts to less than 3 percent. In 1975, the raions were scheduled to receive 508 million rubles in turnover tax, while the union (national) budget was to receive 5 billion rubles in turnover tax from enterprises and organizations in Moscow.

In addition to the turnover tax, the raion budgets retain 10 percent of the bachelor tax, that is, the tax on singles and childless couples. These deductions are differentiated according to raions and contribute anywhere from 1 to 60 percent of the raion budget. In Moscow as a whole, this deduction represents 5 percent of the budget, or approximately 100 million rubles.

The raion budgets receive certain local taxes and rents in their entirety: the tax on private [i.e., leased] structures, land rent, and the tax on private vehicles.

The executive committees of the city and the raion soviets are authorized to lower tax rates and to introduce additional deductions on local taxes and rents for specific taxpayers or groups of taxpayers. They can also stop collecting the tax on private vehicles altogether.

BUDGET EXPENDITURES

Between 1955 and 1975, the Moscow budget tripled in size while the raion budget grew even faster, quadrupling in size. Table 5.3 shows the distribution of expenditures in the overall city budget for 1975. The planned expenditure budget for 1975 amounted to 2.013 billion rubles, 43 percent of which is accounted for by raion expenditures.

A major part of the raion budget is allocated to sociocultural enterprises and undertakings, housing construction, development of the raion economy, and enhancement of the environment.

Capital expenditures represent 48 percent of the total budget shown in Table 5.3. They are divided as follows: housing construction, including capital repair, 27 percent; municipal construction (highways, bridges, water-pumping stations, equipment for passenger and freight transportation, etc.), 12 percent.

Over 50 percent of all the budget funds of Moscow is allocated to the sphere of the national economy. Each year these expenditures increase. Capital investments account for almost three-fourths of this.

Table 5.3. Actual Budget Expenditures, 1975

Type of Expenditure	Amount in Millions of Rubles	Percentage
On social welfare	1,218.6	56.4
Housing construction	646.1	29.9
Communal and public services	412.8	19.1
Other expenditures	159.7	7.4
Sociocultural measures	822.5	38.0
Education	323.6	15.0
Health care	469.6	21.6
Social security	29.3	1.4
Other	121.5	5.6
Total	2,162.6	100.0

[*Note*: Expenditures by and for "profit-making" enterprises do not appear in this budget.]

Table 5.4 indicates the source of these funds. They are allocated to housing construction, the construction of everyday service and trade centers, and the acquisition of equipment and vehicles for the public transportation system.

Approximately 10 percent of the total expenditure for the national economy is used to cover operating deficits, including the subsidy allocated to the public transportation system. It is expected that, in view of the continued growth of all branches of the city economy, these expenditures will continue to increase.

Housing stock construction and maintenance consume 60 percent of the total budget amount allocated to the national economy.

Table 5.4. Expenditures for Capital Investments, 1975 (by source of funds)

Source of Funds	Amount in Millions of Rubles	Percentage
Capital investments from budgetary means	1,008	79
Capital investments from turnover measures	267	21
Total	1,275	100
Including amount spent for capital repairs and public services	246	19.2

Owing to the improved quality of housing construction, budget expenditures for construction were to increase by 10 to 15 percent in the period 1971-75. Budget expenditures for the maintenance of the housing stock increase every year. The bulk of these expenditures (75 to 85 percent) goes toward the capital repair of old buildings. During 1971-75, 485 million rubles was allocated to capital repair. This represented over 80 percent of all funds set aside for capital repairs and equipment.

The cost of heating apartment buildings and of supplying hot water is a major part of the housing maintenance budget. Over 50 percent of these expenses is covered by government contributions from the union budget. Owing to the growth of the housing stock, this contribution will increase, even if the existing rates are kept constant. Housing expenditures are also rising because of improved building maintenance and operation.

The budget expenditures of Moscow for health care during 1971-75 increased 1.5 times over the previous five-year period. The General Plan for the Development of Moscow sets a goal of 17.5 hospital beds per 1,000 persons and 15 to 20 visits annually per capita for health care. This would result in a 40 to 50 percent increase in the budget for medical care.

The major part of the health budget is allocated to hospitals, clinics, and dispensaries. From 1966 to 1970, health care expenditures increased by 25 percent. As a whole, the expenditure per hospital bed per annum increased by 11 percent during that period.

During the ninth Five-Year Plan (1971-75), capital investments for health care amounted to 171 million rubles, or 45 percent more than in the previous five-year period.

On January 1, 1970, new higher expenditure norms were introduced for the maintenance of hospital beds in the various medical centers. Food norms in the maternity and children's hospitals were increased by 19.6 percent. Expenditures for medical supplies increased as follows: for maternity and children's hospital beds, by 14 percent; for tuberculosis wards, by 30 percent; for surgical clinics, by 12.5 percent. The bed supply inventory norms have increased by 105.5 percent for the new beds and by 63.3 percent for the existing ones. As a result, by 1970, these expenditures reached 5.3 million rubles.

During 1966-70, expenditures for medical equipment more than doubled. Wage costs increased by 15.6 percent as a result of an increase in personnel and higher saleries.

The network of centers protecting the health of mothers and children (mother and child consultation centers, maternity hospitals, day-care centers, etc.) is expanding continuously, and so it their budget. During this 1971-75 period, day-care center expenditures increased by 13.5 percent and expenditures for children's sanitariums by 25.6 percent.

The drugstore network of the city consisted of 900 stores in 1975. A substantial expansion of this network and an improvement of its hardware and equipment are being planned; drugstore construction is being allocated 6 million rubles.

Considerable importance is attached to improving the social security of the population. This is expressed primarily in the increased construction of homes for the aged and disabled and the better quality of their services. During 1966-70, the number of beds in homes for the aged and disabled increased by 2,420, while expenditures for their maintenance increased by 71.4 percent. The average annual expenditure for the maintenance of a bed increased from 697 to 852 rubles, i.e., by 22.2 percent, including the following: food, by 35 rubles; salaries, by 78 rubles; miscellaneous expenditures, by 42 rubles.

Pensions for science workers and for those disabled since birth are paid from state insurance, whereas pensions and other aid for war veterans were shifted to the budget of the republic. This resulted in a decrease of the Moscow budget by 1.6 million rubles.

At the same time, in order to improve the social security of the population, expenditures out of the city budget for this purpose increased by 83.3 million rubles, or 20.4 percent, from 1966 to 1970. In the future, the share of these expenditures in the city budget will increase, owing to more retired citizens and increased payments per person.

The most vivid indicator of the consistent improvement in the material and cultural standard of living is in the area of sociocultural development. In view of the tasks of Communist construction, the Twenty-fourth Congress of the Communist Party of the Union of Soviet Socialist Republics acknowledged the necessity "to ensure the further development of public service funds as an important source for the improvement of the material and cultural standard of living of the Soviet people. During the five-year term (1971 to 1975) free material items and services are to be increased, together with monetary payments to the population from surplus funds, by 40%."

Expenditures for sociocultural undertakings represented 35 to 38 percent of the budget of Moscow in 1975, and they too are increasing annually. For the years of the eighth five-year term alone, they amounted to 2.836 billion rubles.

During the five-year period 1966-70, 1.2355 billion rubles was spent on the overall education of the citizens of Moscow. This includes preschool institutions, museums, libraries, theaters, and other cultural institutions as well as the traditional public school system. Of the total amount, 921.5 million rubles was spent to support the primary, secondary, and vocational schools of Moscow. Expenditures for the maintenance of a class increased by 10 percent, while expenditures for the salaries of teachers and assisting personnel increased by 8.3 percent and those for other needs by 24.1 percent. Even if expenditures for running one class had remained the same, total expenditures during 1971-75 for the financing of the public schools would have increased by approximately 30 percent owing to an increase in the number of teachers and administrative personnel. The growth of expenditures for education is also caused by the introduction of new subjects into the school curriculum.

The transition of regular schools to an extended-day schedule resulted in an average increase in expenditures of 75 percent.

Extracurricular institutions—Pioneer palaces, children's sports centers, clubs of young naturalists, centers for travel and tourism, and the rest—are becoming increasingly important in the education of the young, and increasing expenditures are being allotted for such purposes.

Children's music schools have also been expanding. Their number increased from 45 in 1966 to 65 in 1970, while budget expenditures grew from 1.5 to 1.7 million rubles.

During the ninth five-year period (1971-75), 25 million rubles was allocated for the construction of extracurricular educational centers.

Preschool institutions in Moscow have been constructed, but with recognition of the declining number of children. Owing to the transfer of some of the population from the central areas to new sections of the city during the ninth Five-Year Plan period (1971-75), preschool centers for 62,000 children will be constructed, at a cost of approximately 80 million rubles.

The average expenditure from the budget for one child in the preschool centers amounts to 390 rubles per annum. In 1970, the budget of Moscow allocated 77.5 million rubles for the maintenance of kindergartens and nurseries. The estimated increase in expenditures for the preschool institutions amounted to 30 percent for the years 1971-75.

It should be noted that parents pay a user charge for these institutions; in nurseries, it is 9 rubles per year.

Passenger transport is one of the most important problems in any modern city. Its solution is related to the expansion of the network of surface routes, the construction of underground tunnels, and more and better vehicles. This naturally leads to a growth in expenditures for the development, maintenance, and operation of the city's transport system, which carried 4,867 billion passengers in 1975, or 730 trips per capita.

Until recently, deductions from the income of surface urban passenger transport were a profit source for the budget, though this decreased every year. For instance, while the budget received 28.7 million rubles from this source in 1966, in 1969 the amount was only 4.9 million. At present, surface passenger transport in Moscow is operating at a loss. In 1972, the budget contribution to cover operating losses of surface passenger transport amounted to 22.8 million rubles.

The cost of new vehicles is considerably higher than that of the old ones. For instance, the new bus LIAZ-677 costs more than twice as much as the old ZIL-158. The cost of the trolleybus ZIU-5 is 31 percent higher than the cost of the old MTB. The cost of the tram Tatra is 64 percent higher than the average cost of the old tram KM.

Owing to increased fuel usage, higher fuel quality requirements, higher salaries for drivers, and amortization, the operating costs of the new vehicles have also increased.

Expenditures for the replacement of obsolete vehicles, expansion of the vehicle fleet, and construction of new parking areas and repair plants amounted to 300 million rubles for the period 1971-75.

The underground passenger transport system (Metro) has a special role. With its development, Moscow acquired not only comfortable transportation, but a substantial source of income for the city budget as well. The Metro is a profitable enterprise whose payments and donations to the budget are consistently increasing. For instance, from 1959 to 1969, the contribution of all Metro enterprises to the budget increased from 19 to 25.1 million rubles.

Even this profitable mode of transportation, however, is changing in its relationship to the budget. The Metro lines not only require capital investments for construction, but they are incurring higher operational expenditures. At a constant uniform cost per ride of 5 kopecks, the operational expenditures are increasing at a considerably higher rate than the profits. During 1966-71, operating expenses increased by 27.6 percent, reaching 55 million rubles per annum. For the same period, profits from passenger rides increased by 16 percent, to 76.4 million rubles per annum.

The growth of operating expenditures is related to higher salaries for personnel, the increased cost of supplies and equipment, and increased amortization deductions. In 1970, these deductions increased from 31.1 to 32.5 percent. During 1971-75, 38 kilometers of new lines was constructed for the Metro, at a cost of 302 million rubles.

In 1976, the total length of the Metro was 176 kilometers, it carried 1.8 billion passengers, and its income from passenger transportation was about 90 million rubles. The operating costs exceeded 80 million rubles and the profits were cut in half compared with the annual contributions during the 1966-70 period.

Cleaning and lighting the city requires considerable expenditures in terms of labor and money, which increase with the expansion of the city territory and the growth of the street network. During 1966-70, annual expenditures for lighting increased from 6.4 to 8.7 million rubles, i.e., by 35.9 percent. The total expenditures for the five years amounted to 40.4 million rubles. Expenditures for garbage collection increased from 12.6 to 19.3 million rubles per annum, and amounted to a total of 71.6 million for the five-year period.

At present, the mechanized collection of garbage using compacting trucks is being widely implemented. During 1966-70, the annaul cost of cleaning per square meter dropped from 48.4 to 41 kopecks, or by 17 percent. (This is an average figure, which includes refuse collection, street and sidewalk cleaning, street washing, snow removal, yard sweeping, etc. The total cost of cleaning and collection is divided by the land surface that has no structures yet built upon it.)

During 1971-75, 50 percent of the solid waste was processed for the recovery of secondary materials. This has a considerable economic effect. For instance, 200,000 tons of waste paper yields an income of 4 million rubles.

The development of parks in Moscow is also accelerating. During 1966-70, annual expenditures for planting in the city increased from 5 to 7.5 million rubles, i.e., by 50 percent, and amounted to a total of 33.4 million rubles over the five years. During 1971-75, 35 million rubles was allocated to the city parks and natural environment, including 20 million rubles for the construction of greenhouses, 12 million for planting, and 3 million for the building of water towers and roads in park zones and rest areas.

The figures quoted indicate that one of the most expensive undertakings of park development is plant growing. Plant growing, however, provides a certain annual income, and thus it covers planting expenditures to some extent.

Bridge and highway construction is the most important component of urban development. During 1966-70 alone, approximately 5 million square meters of roads was built and reconstructed, together with 7 traffic intersections, 8 highway tunnels, 56 pedestrian passageways, and 2 bridges. This work, which helps develop the industrial base, required 256 million rubles.

During 1971-75, highway construction was to be increased by 6.2 million square meters; in addition, 4 traffic intersections, 5 bridges, 9 road tunnels, and 37 underground passages for pedestrians were to be built. The sum allocated to these plans amounted to 378 million rubles.

The construction and maintenance of cultural centers have also played an important role in the development plan of Moscow. The budget expenditures for cultural institutions amounted to 53.1 million rubles during the eighth Five-Year Plan (1966-70). From 8 to 10 movie houses and 10 to 15 libraries are to be built in the city every year. Furthermore, 11 cultural centers, previously supported out of the budget of the republic, have been transferred to the budget of Moscow. As a consequence, annual budget expenditures for theaters during 1966-70 doubled, from 0.639 to 1.304 million rubles; expenditures climbed from 0.438 to 1.145 million rubles for the maintenance of museums and exhibitions.

The plans for 1971-75 specified a considerable growth in the construction of cultural institutions, with 69 million rubles allocated for this purpose. Movie theater construction alone consumed 57.6 million rubles. The movie theater network was to grow during this period by 20 theaters with a total of 24,000 seats. The plan for 1976 was to have 23.5 seats per 1,000 citizens.

The library network of the city is being expanded and modernized. Expenditures for the maintenance of libraries increased from 4.3 million rubles in 1966 to 5.5 million in 1970, while the average expenditure for the maintenance of one library increased by 1,426 rubles per annum.

The development of recreation areas on the territory of the city and park areas of the suburbs of Moscow requires not only the participation of the budget of Moscow, but also the provincial budget, trade union funds, and resources of the ministries and enterprises whose employees use these areas. During 1971-75, 11.2 million rubles was allocated for this purpose.

Financing major sports facilities (stadiums, swimming pools, sports centers, race tracks) involves the funds of sports societies and the enterprises that manage social and cultural development. The capital investment allocated to the construction of such facilities for 1971-75 amounted to 24 million rubles.

Water supply and sewage treatment operations form a complex system of engineering and technological equipment, playing an important part in the life of every city. Water supply development in Moscow was allocated 68.4 million rubles during 1966-70. Developments planned for 1971-75 required 204.6 million rubles, i.e., three times more than for the previous five-year period.

Thanks to the commencement of operation of the industrial water supply and recirculation systems of a number of Moscow enterprises, the need for capital investments for water supply has dropped to 50 million rubles. Meanwhile, savings in operational costs of industrial enterprises due to these new systems amounted to over 14 million rubles.

The construction of sewer plants and equipment will gain new impetus but will require considerable expenditures. Such projects received 97.7 million rubles during 1966-70. During 1971-75, the efforts to increase the capacity of the sewer plants and the length of the sewage pipe network received 187.5 million rubles, or about double the previous amount.

MODERN MANAGEMENT EFFORTS*

The rising cost of materials and labor combined, with a generally low birth rate, has contributed to the recent emergence in the Soviet Union of a labor shortage and a drive for greater productivity and efficiency. In particular, the use of management science techniques and electronic computers is expanding into every aspect of the national economy.

At the municipal level, the shortage of workers is even more severe, owing to the relatively low level of salaries paid for many city jobs and the low social status that is identified with them. There is a great desire, therefore, to utilize labor-saving methods and computers in the operation of local government. One problem has been the slow rate at which computers have been made available to municipalities. In 1973, for instance, there were only 13 operational computers serving the Moscow municipal government, and all of these were first- or second-generation equipment, in constrast to third- and fourth-generation computing hardware used in New York and other major U.S. cities.

---

*This section was written by the U.S. authors.

In 1971, by decree of the Twenty-Fourth Congress of the Communist Party of the Soviet Union, local governments and their subsidiary organizations were charged with improving the efficiency of their operations through the adoption of modern management techniques and tools, including the use of automatic (computerized) systems of management, referred to as ASU. ASU is a catch-all term, covering any computer application that contributes to the administration of an organization, somewhat analagous in usage to the U. S. term "management information system." Soon after the decree, ASUs began to sprout, at least in the design stage, in agencies throughout the local governmental structure of most medium- and large-sized cities. In 1973, the first soviet complex of upward-compatible, third-generation computers, complete with peripherals and fully developed software, was unveiled in Moscow. Developed jointly by the Soviet Union, Bulgaria, Hungary, East Germany, Poland, and Czechoslovakia, the RYAD computers (ES-1010, ES-1020, ES-1021, ES-1030, ES-1040, ES-1050, ES-1060) and subsequent modified versions were close equivalents to the small- and moderate-sized members of the IBM 360 series of machines and were said to be program compatible with them.

The increasing availability of these machines began to make possible the realization of the ASU designs stemming from the 1971 Party Congress decree. During the late 1970s, most large agencies in Moscow were in the midst of converting their procedures from manual to automated modes and, at the same time, providing for the integration of their operational and control data into more comprehensive systems covering the management of whole sectors of the local economy. All of these sectional or branch management systems are in turn to contribute to an enormous integrated ASU governing the entire municipal administration of the city.

The key organization in the expansion of computer usage in Moscow is the Main Scientific-Research Computing Center, which is subordinate directly to the Executive Committee of the Moscow City Soviet. The center has some 500 employees at three locations in the city. Its role is threefold: (1) It coordinates and plans the work of all computing centers of departments and enterprises directly subordinate to the Moscow City Soviet; (2) It acts as a service bureau for those agencies that do not themselves have computer capability; (3) It undertakes original and self-initiated research including the development of ASUs for individual organizations and branches of the municipal economy, and of the overall integrated city management system, "Moskva," which is discussed below.

As an indication of the powerful role played by this center, in addition to handling approximately 60 percent of the computing requirements of the city government, all requests for new and replacement computers from those agencies having their own computer capability must be screened and evaluated by the center before being passed on to the State Committee for Science and Technology and the State Planning Commission for funding.

The activities of the center appear to be primarily routine data-processing tasks, including the support of a job-matching or employment system for municipal agencies, the automated billing of utility charges, fees, and rents for the apartments controlled by the city, and a form of purchasing system.

By far the most interesting activity of the center is its role in the design and development of Moskva and its component subsystems. The goal of this complex system is to ensure the optimal orderly development of the city through a general improvement in the quantity and quality of relevant information supporting and influencing municipal management decision making. The designers feel that in a centrally planned entity such as Moscow, it is scientifically possible to quantify the interrelationships and dynamics of the city organism so that, given certain annual quotas of materials, labor, and financial resources, decisions can be made that will optimize the desired output. This output is defined as the improvement of conditions under which residents and visitors live, conduct business, and obtain services in Moscow. [The U.S. authors consider this ambitious scheme to be without scientific merit and utterly hopeless.]

In order to realize this ambitious goal, four levels of automation have been incorporated into the overall design. At the most basic level, local ASUs are being implemented that address management problems of individual enterprises within the municipal service economy, primarily systems of an informational, accounting, and routine data-processing nature. City officials feel that the number of such ASUs may eventually reach several tens of thousands. The second-level ASUs are called "branch" automated managment systems. Such systems are concerned with the problems and tasks of all enterprises linked either organizationally within the structural framework of the city or geographically within the 30-district scheme utilized for the administration of service delivery. With some 55 to 60 service agencies and 30 districts currently in Moscow, it is contemplated that the number of branch ASUs will eventually approach 100.

The third level of automation, the "interbranch complex" ASUs, must handle the key problem of the optimal development and functional coordination of complexes of closely interrelated branches. An example of such a group, characteristically unified by a common goal, is the interbranch complex ASU Glavmosstroi (Main Administration of Construction). It encompasses all or part of eight branches, including the Main Administrations for Architecture, Housing Construction, Industrial Construction, Engineering Construction, Construction Materials, Housing Management, the Administration for Production Enterprises, and the Construction Transportation Division of the Main Administration for Auto Transport. Some 11 such interbranch complex ASUs are planned.

Finally, there is the all-city ASU Moskva. Feeding upon information passed up from the subordinate ASUs, Moskva attempts to solve problems involving development goals for municipal services, possible local compositional variants in these development goals, and the need for balance among the development plans of the interbranch complexes. Among the subsystems of Moskva are those dealing with city service planning, operational control and management, various resource needs and availabilities (financial, material, technical, population, labor), social programs, and management science progress.

Having produced a model for this system, a plan was developed for the introduction of computers and the development of component ASUs through 1990. Within this framework, a total of 36 ASUs at all four levels has been developed to date and implemented to some degree. These systems are supported at approximately 24 computing centers employing 3,500 people. By 1990, the introduction of 87 ASUs is planned, serving 115 client organizations at various levels. A total of 135 computers (primarily those of the RYAD type) will be utilized at that time, with a general productivity of 15 million operations per second. The planners in Moscow estimate that their 1990 data-processing volume will be 167 billion bytes per year.

Some examples of ASUs already developed and at least partly operational in Moscow are listed below.

1. "Gorplan"—a system developed for the City Planning Commission, which is centered around a complex of planning algorithms intended for the development of the 20-year, 5-year, and annual plans for municipal services, for interbranch complexes, and for districts of the city.
2. "Finances"—developed for the Finance Administration to monitor and control the execution of the municipal budget.
3. "Material Technical Supply"—developed for the administration of the same name to manage the supply and purchasing functions that are the responsibility of the Moscow City Soviet Executive Committee.

4. "Population and Labor Resources"–the job-matching system mentioned above.

5. "Kurs"–developed to automate the distribution and management of all housing that is subordinate to the City Soviet.

6. "Signal"–an interesting system developed to monitor and control the execution of all orders from administrative agencies as well as decisions of the Executive Committee itself. It is somewhat analogous to project management systems in the United States. The authors of the system claim that its implementation has resulted in: higher-quality directive documentation (owing to informational requirements of the system); better-quality control of execution deadlines; increased effectiveness of information output for the Executive Committee; and increased reliability and clarity of control results.

7. "Mossoviet"–the goal of which is the improvement of the operational administration of municipal services by the Moscow City Soviet through the use of econometric and management science techniques.

The above seven ASUs were developed by and are run at the Main Scientific-Research Computing Center of the Moscow City Soviet Executive Committee. They are run on the Center's Minsk 32 (second generation) and ES-1020 computers, and were developed at a stated cost of 11.2 million rubles, or 15.7 million dollars at the somewhat arbitrary but nonetheless official exchange rate.

Among the Branch and Interbranch ASUs are the following:

8. "Glavmosstroi"–for the automated development of five-year and annual programs of municipal construction, and for the coordination of the member organizations of the interbranch construction complex. Developed at a cost of 8.8 million rubles, it utilizes six second-generation computers, four of the URAL type and two MINSK 32s. The system supports a complex of branches that constructs more than 5 million square meters of general housing in Moscow each year, in addition to schools, hospitals, theaters, commercial buildings, etc. Typical tasks of the system are: development of hourly assembly and transport schedules for such items as mortar, concrete, asphalt, and other materials and equipment; monitoring the actual execution of hourly and daily assembly schedules; calculating yearly plans for resource requirements and work programs for construction trucks; and preparing management summaries and reports for top administrators of the various construction agencies. Each day this system processes 30,000 characters of information, much of it gathered by means of 140 radio transmitters and 200 teletypes in direct communication with construction organizations and sites. As was mentioned above, it is the heart of an enormous operation involving eight of the largest agencies in the Moscow city government.

9. "Glavmosavtotrans"–for the centralized management of urban freight flow, including the optimization of truck routes, inventory control, and maintenance operations. The system utilizes one ES-1030 and two URAL 14 computers, and was developed at a cost of 6.13 million rubles.

10. "Start"—an automatic traffic control system developed at a cost of 2.5 million rubles, and utilizing an M-6000 minicomputer.

Additional ASUs exist for such services and organizations as the food and retail trade network, municipal taxi system, Metro operation, emergency ambulance service, epidemic forecasting and control service, police department, bread-baking and distribution industry, tailoring industry, municipal laundry and hotel operation, water supply and sewage system, and the management of social welfare services.

These systems are in various stages of implementation and are constantly being expanded. Together with certain urban models currently under development, they represent the city's central effort to meet the economic and labor requirements of the coming decade and beyond.

6

PERSONNEL

Because of the extremely wide scope of municipal services and responsibilities compared with those of most Western cities, the size of the Moscow civil work force dwarfs that of New York City. Some 1.4 million of a total of 5.1 million workers in the city are employed by organs of the Moscow City Soviet. [Note: This can be compared with only 300,000 in New York City, whose population is only slightly smaller.]

This manpower is spread throughout the massive bureaucracy of over 50 main administrations, departments, bureaus, and inspectorates of the government, together with their subsidiary enterprises, trusts, and factories. [Note: Exact employment figures are very difficult to acquire from the Soviet Union for a variety of reasons, not the least of which is the secrecy surrounding such agencies as the police and fire services. Nevertheless, Table 6.1 presents rough estimates for most large agencies, gathered from personal interviews with agency officials and from a variety of other sources.]

Note: The material contained in this chapter is derived primarily from the original Soviet report for this project and from personal interviews by the U.S. authors with municipal officials of Moscow. Additional material was derived from "Gotovim Rabochie Kadri (Skilled Workers Are Being Trained)," *Gorodskoe Khozaistvo Moskvy*, pp. 9-12, Moscow, August 1977.

Table 6.1. Estimated Number of Moscow City Employees (by agency)

Agency	No. of Employees	Year
Main Administration for Construction—Glavmosstroi	250,000	1969
Main Administration for Trade—Glavtorg	200,000	1975
Administration for Consumer and Everyday Services	103,000	1976
Main Administration for Catering and Food Services	100,000	1975
Public Education Department—Mosgorno	100,000	1976
Main Administration for Auto Transport—Glavmosavtotrans	96,000	1976
Main Administration for Engineering Construction—Glavmosingstroi	30,000	1976
Administration for Municipal Services	20,000	1975
Administration for Water Supply and Sewage Disposal	16,000	1977
Main Administration for Planning and Architecture—GlavApu	10,000	1969
Administration for Forests and Parks	5,000	1975
Main Administration for Housing	3,600	1977
Subtotal	933,600	
Main Administration for Public Health[a]	102,000	
Administration for Taxis and Light Autos[b]	64,000	
Administration for Passenger Transport[c]	50,000	
Other[d]	250,400	
Total	1,400,000	

[a]In 1975, there were 67,700 doctors in Moscow, of which 53.8 percent, or 36,401, were employed by this administration. At the same time, there were 121,900 secondary medical personnel in the city. By conservatively assuming that this category includes all other employees of medical organizations, and that the same percentage of these work for the city as is the case with doctors, it is calculated that some 102,000 employees work for the Main Administration of Public Health, 36,401 doctors and approximately 65,600 other personnel.

[b]There are over 16,000 taxis in Moscow plus an undetermined number of passenger cars maintained, driven, and made available by this administration. The 64,000 employee figure was obtained by assuming the fleet of nontaxi autos to be small, and estimated a four-to-one ratio of employees to vehicles (see below).

[c]There are over 10,000 buses, tramcars, and trolleybuses in service in Moscow. Several bus depots exhibited a surprisingly consistent ratio of four employees to one vehicle. Assuming this ratio holds also for surface electric transport, and adding in administrative personnel, we estimate an employee total of 50,000.

[d]The major agencies in this category, and for which no detailed figures are yet available, include the following: Main Administration for Industrial Construction, Main Administration for Construction Materials, Main Administration for Capital Construction, Main Administration for Culture and related agencies, Main Administration for Internal Affairs (police and fire), local industrial administrations (metal processing, chemical and rubber products, etc.), and municipal staff agencies (finance, cadre or personnel, civil registry, etc.).

In spite of these large figures, the city is [or claims to be] in need of additional employees. Figures quoted by municipal officials place the shortage at anywhere from 110,000 to 130,000 workers. These needs are concentrated, in general, in what are perceived to be less desirable fields of employment and the trades. The prestige that has been associated with engineering, economics, and science has turned young people away from vocational courses and led to the present situation. A Moscow deputy mayor stated that there was a great need for bakers, barbers, waiters, and nurses. The need for the last is so great that when nurses reach retirement age, they are placed on full pension but are encouraged to continue working at their regular salary. In general, although understaffing is a problem experienced by virtually every city agency, it is most serious in the service sector, which has a need for 80,000 more workers.

ADMINISTRATION FOR PERSONNEL AND TRAINING

The Administration for Personnel and Training is responsible for the recruitment and some of the training of city employees. It is also responsible for handling promotions and recommending people for high positions. As mentioned earlier, the Party will usually play a role in influencing the placement of key people. This is an ever-present background factor that affects the routine operations of the Personnel Administration.

Some 65,000 new municipal workers are trained on the job every year and some 13,000 in trade schools. There are 29 operational training centers in the city governmental system, in addition to a large number of smaller training shops located within various enterprises. These number over 640.

In such a tight labor situation, recruitment is a particularly competitive procedure. Such perquisites as new apartments and favorable placement on waiting lists for new cars are used to bolster the financial package of salary and bonuses to attract qualified workers. Nonetheless, there are times when an agency wishes to dismiss an employee. It is easiest to fire a worker when he consistently violates the labor law through lateness, absenteeism, or avoidance of his duties. When he is simply a poor worker, a series of conferences involving the manager, the worker, and the labor organizations take place, culminating in the administration of an examination by a special qualification commission whose decisions are usually final. Since every citizen has a right to work in the Soviet Union, if the manager is successful in firing an employee, he becomes at the same time responsible for finding the worker a new job. [Note: The consequence of this is that it is too difficult to fire someone and it is not worth the bother, from a manager's point of view. The situation in U.S. civil service systems is not much different.]

Personnel Placement

The main objective in choosing the most rational form of division and cooperation of labor in enterprises is the correct placement of production personnel. The placement of personnel has to guarantee the optimal division of functions among executives, the maximal clarification of those functions, and the cooperation and coordination of workers responsible for various aspects of production and service.

The way to solve these problems is to prepare professional-technical job descriptions and qualification manuals indicating all a worker should know and be able to do, and to compose instructional charts that explain the most rational ways to perform a given type of work. In order to clarify the duties of executives and to establish close cooperation among them, specific charts have been made of the organization of labor, which show the most rational delineation of executive functions as well as other useful information.

It is possible to judge the degree of cooperation between basic and supporting workers by means of the coefficient of labor cooperation, which is calculated by the formula:

$$CLC = 1 - \frac{Ts}{T},$$

where *CLC* is the coefficient of labor cooperation, *Ts* is the time spent unproductively during a given period as a result of poor service at the place of work, and *T* is the total work time for the same period at the same place of work. This coefficient can be calculated for groups of workers and for separate places of work.

The correct placement of personnel indicates that workers are placed according to their ability and practical skills so that the use of skilled labor does not depend on the completion of unskilled work. Also, the difficulty of the work should not exceed the skill levels of the workers themselves.

An integral part of personnel placement is professional selection, defined in the rules as "the process of choosing from a group of candidates for a given position those people from whom one can expect with most certainty successful completion of the given work." The problems of professional selection for production work consists of determining a person's ability, inclinations, and suitability for one or another type of work. It is, of course, not meant that the administration, solely by its own judgment, should decide what a worker should be, a lathe operator or a mill operator; the aim is simply to avoid giving workers work for which they do not have the necessary qualifications.

Professional selection is done first by establishing any medical restrictions for work in a given area, second by establishing psychological restrictions, and third by using various tests that establish a subject's reaction time, attention span, ability to calculate, and so on, depending on the most important job requirements.

Associated with the problem of placement is the problem of orientation. Whereas placement is usually determined at the enterprise, when a new worker is hired or transferred to a different post, the problem of orientation should be dealt with considerably earlier. While still in high school, a young person should receive at least minimal information on the existing branches of the economy, the various types of technological processes and equipment, and the development of different spheres of human endeavor. Such information, which the polytechnical instructor in school ought to provide, will allow persons taking up independent life to choose a future occupation carefully and to decide at which enterprise they will work or which institute they will enter. Of course, the problem of orientation should be dealt with at the enterprise also. The administration is expected not only to make decisions about hiring, but also to bring about the most appropriate choice of work for each applicant.

The career personnel in an organization will also take part in orientation, help decrease turnover in the work force, and help ensure the most rational placement of workers.

Further refinements in the placement of personnel in factories should depend on modern methods of organizing labor. These include careful analysis of the degree of progressiveness in existing placement techniques, a search for the most rational form of combining professional and labor functions, perfection of methods for operating several machines simultaneously, definition of the most effective way to organize labor brigades, and professional selection and orientation. The placement of labor in factories, which is a direct expression of the division and coordination of labor, creates a complex organism—the socialist production collective.

EVALUATION OF SPECIALISTS AND
TECHNICAL MANAGERS

The first criterion for evaluating specialists and technical managers is ideological-political quality. The optimal composition of this quality obviously can be determined by means of generalization and analysis. The factors most often encountered that characterize the ideological-political qualities of workers are: political maturity; ideological conviction; thorough understanding of the basic aims and goals of the society and an active attempt to further the speedy resolution and implementation of those aims; the ability to subordinate personal and narrow-minded interests to social interests, and active participation in community activity; a broad political outlook and the continuous attempt to expand it.

The second criterion of evaluation is professional competence. The most widely used factors are: degree of specialized education; amount of work experience in one's field; amount of experience in the given or in a similar position; expansion of general and specialized knowledge within the educational system.

The third criterion, psychological compatability within the labor collective, is for the most part expressed by the degree to which the worker is able to work without causing conflicts.

The fourth criterion is creative ability. Depending on personal abilities and traits, creative initiative is made evident in several ways, each of which may serve as a corresponding factor of evaluation. The first is inventiveness and conceptual ability expressed in the development and introduction of new applications and proposals, including proposals for various competitions, and conceptualization of one's own work. The second is scientific and methodological work, as shown by the introduction and development of scientific and research topics, standards, and methodological materials. The third is the introduction of recent developments from outside. Fourth is the publication of books, monographs, brochures, articles in journals and newspapers (both circulated and wall posters [!]), translated articles, and patents. All of this, of course, must be related directly to the worker's basic activity. Fifth are giving lectures on his or her experiences at technical classes in the organization, and also appearances to give information, talks, and announcements in both the organization and elsewhere.

The fifth criterion of evaluation, discipline, is defined by the extent to which work time is utilized and the intensity of work.

The sixth criterion, completeness of work, is manifested in the completion of work on time and in the quality of work performed.

The seventh criterion of evaluation, the community activity of workers, deals with four factors: whether the worker takes part in community work; the significance of that work; the amount of time spent on it; and finally the social discipline or degree of willingness and conscious effort put into the community work.

7

MUNICIPAL SERVICES

In this chapter, the objectives, planning procedures, departmental structure, and other characteristics are described for a number of important public services: housing, health and education, preschool children's institutions, transportation, public works, water and waste water, parks, public safety, trade and public food services, and everyday and communal services.

HOUSING

[Note: Housing appears to be the most pressing concern of the city government, for the housing shortage is severe. In 1973, the first deputy mayor of Moscow remarked that the biggest social problem in the Soviet Union was two women sharing the same kitchen. Indeed, about a quarter of the families did not have their own apartments but had to share with one or more other families. Consequently, housing construction has high priority. More money is spent on this area and more employees work in it than any other. In large Soviet cities, a typical promotion path is from head of the housing activity to mayor (chairman of the executive committee), an indication that the magnitude of the task and the executive responsibility are second only to those of the mayor.]

Basic statistics about the housing stock of Moscow are presented in Table 7.1. The extent of the housing shortage can be seen

Table 7.1. Moscow Housing Statistics (1976 data unless otherwise indicated)

No. of apartment buildings	52,000
Municipal	24,000
Other	28,000
No. of apartments, 1973	2.044 million
Usable housing area, 1973 (in square meters)[a]	
Total	107.5 million
Per capita	14.5
Living space, 1973 (in square meters)[a]	
Total	72.2 million
Per capita	9.7
Living space in municipal apartments (in square meters)	47 million
Living space in other state-owned apartments (in square meters)	17.5 million
Living space in cooperative buildings (in square meters)	6.5 million

[a]"Usable housing area" includes all space within an apartment; "living space" excludes kitchens, bathrooms, hallways, and closets.

in the per capita living space, which is only 9.7 square meters, or about 104 square feet. The planning norm, or target, is 12 square meters per capita, as shown in Table 7.2.

The emphasis on housing construction is evidenced in the pattern of municipal expenditures for housing, which is shown in Table 7.3, and by the fact that slightly more than half (51.2 percent) of the housing stock available in 1971 had been constructed during the preceding decade. An average of 500 apartments per day was being completed during that period, and 4.9 million people moved into better housing. The growth of the housing stock since 1913 appears in Table 7.4.

Table 7.2. Planning Norms for Housing

Living space per person	12 square meters (to be raised soon to 15 square meters)
Kitchen	7-9 square meters
Vestibule	Greater than 1.4 meters wide
Living room	17-20 square meters
Single bedroom	8-9 square meters
Double bedroom	12-13 square meters

Note: There are 10.76 square feet per square meter.

Table 7.3. Expenditure for Housing (in millions of rubles)

For municipal housing construction, 1971-75	3,500
For all housing construction (including cooperatives, industrially sponsored housing, etc.), 1971-75	4,000
Budget expenditure for capital repairs of municipal housing, 1971-75	485
Budget expenditure for maintenance of municipal housing, 1971-75[a]	approx. 140
Maintenance budget for municipal housing, 1975	303
Capital repair budget for municipal housing, 1975	140
Routine repair budget for municipal housing, 1975	73.4

[a]The budget for housing maintenance includes the cost of thermal energy (heat), but over half of this expenditure is defrayed by an allocation from the national budget.

Construction

Most of the housing in the city (61 percent) was constructed and is owned by the municipal government. Ministries, their subordinate enterprises, and other nonmunicipal authorities own approximately 23 percent. Construction cooperatives, consisting of groups of individuals who collectively own their apartment buildings, account for some 8 percent. Some small, privately owned dwellings continue to exist in rural areas of the city. [Although technically owned by the state, in effect they are leased for an indefinite term and can be passed on by inheritance.]

Before 1968, over 200 different construction organizations were building residential structures in Moscow. Because of the resultant lack of coordination and inefficient planning, the city found that it was not able to make significant headway in overcoming the severe housing shortage it was experiencing. A solution to this problem was sought through the consolidation of most of these organizations into one municipal agency, the Main Administration for (Housing) Construction, Glavmosstroi, thereby combining the planning, construction, and management of the bulk of Moscow's housing under the direct control of the City Soviet Executive Committee.

A number of agencies are nevertheless involved in housing construction: the Main Administration for Architecture and Planning (Glavapu), the Main Administration for Capital Construction (Glavuks), the Main Administration for (Housing) Construction (Glavmosstroi), the Main Administration for the Construction of Engineering Projects

Table 7.4. Growth of Housing Stock in Moscow

| | 1913 | 1940 | 1961 | 1970 | 1973 | 1976 | Projected | |
							1981	1990
General housing area (in millions of square meters)	16.9	28.2	59.7	93.8	107.5	117.1	139.9	141-146
Living space (in millions of square meters)	11.9	18.5	40.0	64.0	72.2	77.1	90.8	95.0
No. of apartments (in thousands)	190	325	880	1,781	2,044	–	–	–
Average per capita general area (in square meters)	10.44	6.21	9.88	13.25	14.51	15.14	–	–
Average per capita living space (in square meters)	7.35	4.07	6.62	9.04	9.74	9.97	–	–

Source: Moskva B Tsifrakh, 1971-1975, Statistika Moscow, 1976.

(Glavmosingstroi), the Main Administration for Construction Materials (Glavmospromstroimaterialu), and the Main Housing Administration (Glavmoszhilupravlenie). Figure 7.1 illustrates the interrelationships among the city's various housing agencies.

The basic function of Glavapu, the Main Administration for Architecture and Planning, is the implementation of a consistent, scientifically based urban policy in the construction of housing and park areas. The head of Glavapu is also the city's chief architect. Glavapu includes the Scientific Research and Design Institute of General Planning, Mosproect-1 and Mosproect-2 (two design institutes), "Mosinproect" (an institute for the design of engineering structures and communication facilities), the Scientific Research Institute for Standard and Experimental Design, and the Expert-Technological Administration.

Glavapu is financed from funds of client organizations that have requested the design work, as well as from budget funds for long-range planning, scientific research, and experimentation.

The Main Administration for Construction Materials, Glavmospromstroimaterialu, includes industrial enterprises that produce concrete- and steel-fabricated building elements, bricks, wood products, and plastics.

The Main Engineering Construction Administration, Glavmossingstroi, handles the development of major highways, underground communications and transportation facilities, and other major engineering projects. Its activities are planned entirely by the City Planning Commission, Gorplan.

Glavuks, the Main Administration for Capital Construction, combines the functions of expediter and monitor of wholesome, planned, optimal urban construction. It inspects completed construction and authorizes payment for it.

The Main Housing Administration, Glavmoszhilupravlenie, develops proposed annual and long-range plans for housing management and capital repair for the city as a whole, and separately for each raion. This agency is responsible for the operation and maintenance of the housing stock after it is built and allocated.

Glavmosstroi, the Main Administration of Construction, is the principal organization in Moscow for the construction of apartment

---

Figure 7.1 (*opposite*). Administrative Bodies for the Design, Construction, Allocation, and Operation of Housing in Moscow.

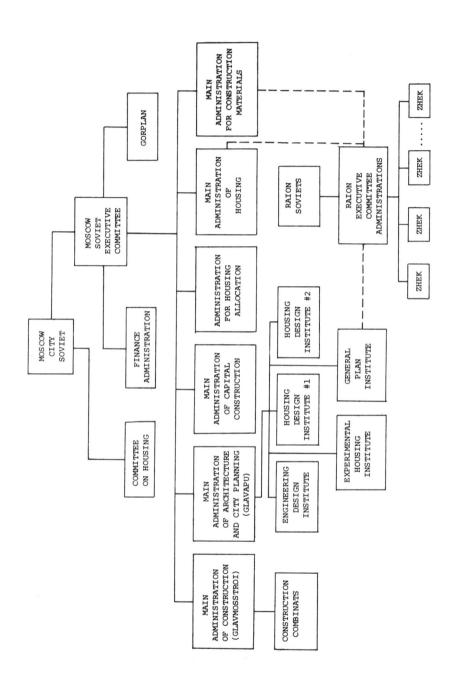

97

houses, buildings for municipal or service use, and certain industrial facilities. Its activities represent 70 percent of the total construction work in Moscow, and its employees number in excess of 250,000. The construction and labor plans of Glavmosstroi are subject to the approval of Gosplan, the State Planning Committee.

Most of the construction is handled by Residential Construction Combinats (RCCs) that are subordinate to Glavmosstroi. These RCCs are enterprises that prepare an entire line of elements for the prefabricated buildings, arrange transportation of construction materials to the construction site, assemble the buildings, perform subsequent finishing work, and finally turn over the completed building to the Main Administration of Housing for operation.

There are several types of construction combinats. In order to fulfill their functions, they each have a plan and a corresponding budget. Each RCC has factories for panels, partitions, and other elements. The RCC has an annual plan for the industrial output of these factories. Most is used by the RCC itself, but some may be sold elsewhere, even to other combinats. Most RCCs are "single-profit centers" using a single balance sheet and budget. Some, however, have their industrial and construction activities as separate profit centers, for example, RCC no. 1 of Glavmosstroi.

RCC no. 1 completed 1.2 million square meters of living space in 1974. It employs 8,000 workers, 3,000 at the various construction sites and 5,000 distributed among four principal factories that specialize in bathroom modules, walls and balconies, roofs, and external walls. Typically, it specializes in standard 9- and 16-story buildings, although experimental structures of over 20 stories have been erected.

Coordination between the many factories and construction sites, as well as with the transport combinats of the Main Administration of Auto Transport (Glavmosavtotrans), which move the completed units to the assembly site, is maintained by Glavmosstroi through the operation of their main computer center. The center communicates directly with the various units in the system via teletype, radio, and telephone so as to maintain and adjust the annual, monthly, weekly, daily, and even hourly work plans. The directors claim that this information system is at the heart of the agency's ability to construct over 5 million square meters of living space per year.

Administration

Upon completion of a building's construction, it is turned over to the Moscow Administration for the Accounting and Allocation of Housing and the Raion Soviet Executive Committees.

The Moscow Administration for the Accounting and Allocation of Housing plans housing distribution over the entire city. It assigns housing to citizens whose homes are to be torn down as old or inadequate or because of city reconstruction and environmental improvement. It also assigns new apartments to overcrowded and new families. Furthermore, the administration manages the accounting and distribution sections of the raion executive committees.

The raion executive committees play a major role in the development of the housing industry. The entire existing municipal housing fund of the city and about 25 percent of the capacity of the construction organizations of the Moscow Executive Committee are administered by the raion executive committees.

Assignment of Housing

All housing facilities owned by the government, public organizations, and house-building combinats are distributed under public control according to the general instructions of the Moscow City Soviet as directed to the raion executive committees.

The raion executive committees each form a Housing Committee, including members of the soviet as well as representatives of the trade unions and of business organizations. The enterprises (companies, organizations) have similar committees.

The Housing Committee of the Raion Soviet considers and makes recommendations on the following matters: certification of citizens as eligible for improved housing; provision of housing facilities to citizens on the waiting list; allocation of housing enterprises and organizations; admission to residential construction coops; prompt occupancy of new buildings.

The certification of a citizen as eligible for housing is handled by the Raion Executive Committee of the citizen's current raion of residence, or by the Housing Committee of the place of employment if the citizen works for an enterprise or organization carrying on construction work or receiving housing facilities according to certain quotas. Retired citizens are provided with housing by their former employers on the same basis as current employees.

Gaining eligibility status for housing requires an application that describes present housing conditions and is certified by the appropriate authority of the building in which the applicant currently resides. Families eligible for housing are registered in official books certified by the seal of the Raion Executive Committee (or the enterprise). The books are maintained in accordance with established requirements for strictly accounted documents in the accounting and allocation departments for housing facilities in the raion soviets, enterprises, and organizations. Each year from January 1 to April 1, these departments update their lists of eligible citizens.

The lists of the people who are to move into a new building are approved by the Executive Committee of the Raion Soviet one to two months prior to the delivery of the building to the tenants.

The apartments of the buildings erected at the expense of certain enterprises are given to tenants according to lists approved by the administration of the enterprise as well as by the local factory trade union, with subsequent notification to the Executive Committee.

The authorization to occupy is issued by the Allocation Department on the basis of and in agreement with the decision of the Executive Committee of the Raion Soviet. The order is sent to the zhek (described below), regardless of departmental hierarchy, and is stored as a strictly accountable document.

The directors of each zhek, regardless of the hierarchical structure, notify the Raion Executive Committee Allocation Department of all vacated living area within three days of its vacation by the tenants. The departments keep a definitive account of the final data on housing distribution for each city section, and these are submitted to the Moscow City Accounting and Allocation Administration. The data on vacant housing are submitted on a monthly basis.

An automated management system (ASU) for the distribution of housing facilities (ASU "Kurs") went into operation in the mid-1970s. This system is designed to improve the efficiency of the distribution procedures for housing accommodations, thus contributing to the harmonious development of the city economy.

Housing Management

The organization of actual day-to-day housing management in Moscow exhibits the usual dual subordination system characteristic of most of Soviet society. Figure 7.2 illustrates this. The municipal Main Administration of Housing is jointly subordinate to the Moscow Soviet Executive Committee and to the R.S.F.S.R. Ministry of Housing and Communal Services. Whereas the general administration of the city's housing is decentralized to the individual raions, the city agency maintains a network of enterprises and factories that perform services and design work determined to be too complex or specialized to be handled at the raion level. Depending upon the extent of a raion's housing service and maintenance network, a problem may be handled at either the raion or the city level.

Figure 7.2. Organization of Housing Management in Moscow.

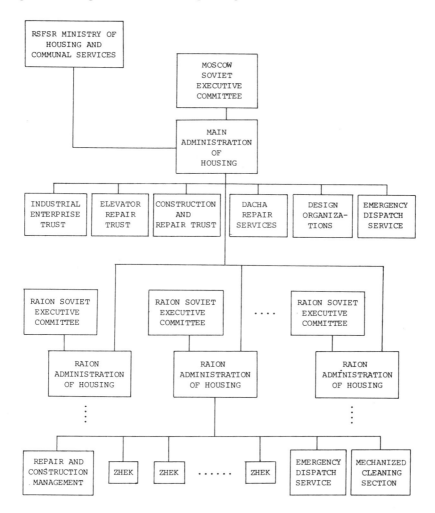

Figure 7.3 illustrates the organization of housing services in a typical raion. Here again, there are various service organizations at the raion level that are available to serve the needs of the zheks in the raion. Depending upon the size and development of a given zhek, the assistance of the raion may or may not be required to handle a given problem. Note that the Raion Administration of Housing Services is dually subordinate to the Raion Soviet Executive Committee and the City Main Administration of Housing Services.

Day-to-day housing management is decentralized to individual Housing Operation Offices (Zhilishehno-Ekspluatsionnie Kontori, or

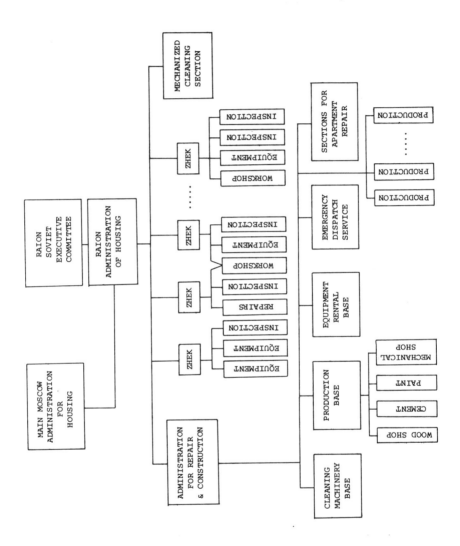

zheks). In 1975, there were 620 zheks organized under the (then) 30 raions in Moscow and their raion housing management administrations. In addition, there were some 40 zheks organized to manage housing belonging to organizations and authorities other than the city government. Figure 7.4 illustrates the organization of a typical zhek.

A zhek operates on a self-supporting basis, and is organized to carry out the technical operation and repair of the housing within its area. It has a number of major responsibilities and functions: (1) maintenance and operation of the housing stock, including the maintenance of yards and space between buildings, cleaning, the removal of refuse, and the separation of scrap materials for recycling; (2) the sanitary condition of the housing and its territory; (3) capital and current repairs of the housing stock; (4) grass and trees inside the zhek area; (5) the condition and cleanliness of its internal streets, paths, and passageways; (6) the supply of heat and hot water to local institutions; (7) maintenance and cleaning of raion playgrounds. If a playground is operated by an organization or enterprise in the zhek area, the organization itself may care for the playground. The zhek is not responsible for traffic signs, lights, etc.; these are the responsibility of the Government Automobile Inspectorate (traffic militia).

Much of the work of the zhek is performed under contract with other organizations. For example, for the mechanical cleaning of internal streets within the zhek, the zhek contracts with the raion for necessary service. The price paid is the same fixed price per square meter that applies to all of Moscow. Note that street cleaning applies to both summer and winter and therefore includes snow plowing and snow removal as well. In similar fashion, the zhek contracts with the same Raion Administration of Municipal Services for refuse collection, as described below. Indeed, the zhek earns money through the ultimate sale of edible garbage to an agricultural entity for feeding hogs. It also contracts with Moslift (the city elevator trust) for maintenance and repairs of elevators and with Mosingremont (the Moscow Trust for the Repair of Engineering Structures) for repairs to the heating plant, etc. The zhek does not have a choice of contracting organizations, and it does not negotiate prices. These are established citywide. However, it should be noted that the zhek can fine one of these agencies if it fails to perform according to the contract, and the amount of the fine is specified in the contract itself.

Figure 7.3. Typical Organizational Structure of a Raion Administration of Housing in Moscow.

Figure 7.4. Typical Organizational Structure of a Housing Operations Office (Zhek) in Moscow.

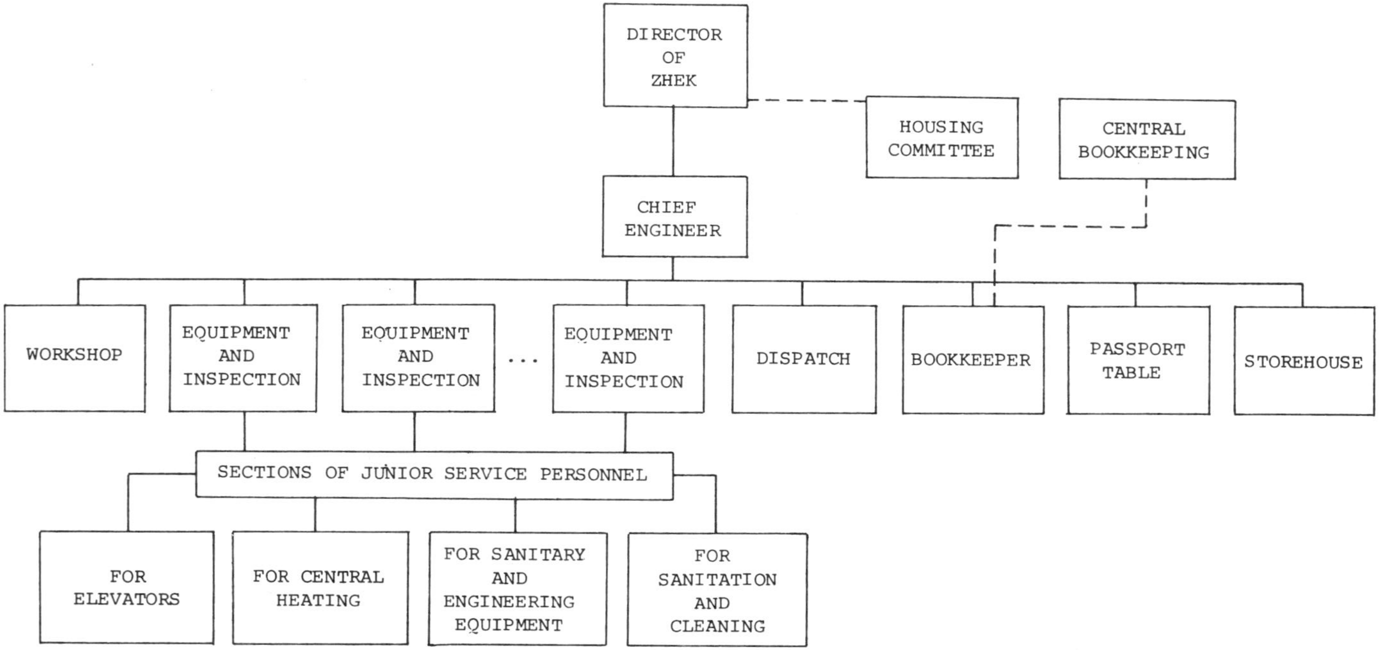

A description of one particular zhek may help to clarify how zheks in general are organized and operate. Zhek no. 2 is 1 of 25 in the Leningrad Raion in the northwestern part of Moscow. The zhek has a population of about 7,500, and has 83,000 square meters of living space in 18 recently constructed apartment buildings. They contain a total of 2,014 apartments. There are also 19,000 square meters of enterprises, shops, nurseries, etc.

A zhek receives revenues from these sources: (1) rents from residents; (2) leases from canteens and shops; and (3) direct subsidies or grants from higher levels of government.

The expenditures of the zheks usually exceed their rental and lease income, so that much of their funding comes from the raion budget. Since this particular zhek is new and has significant lease revenue, its budget is roughly in balance at 115,000 rubles per year.

As mentioned above, many services are provided to a zhek under contract with higher-level agencies. Zhek no. 2 has a contract with an enterprise of the Leningrad Raion Administration for Roads and Public Services for street cleaning, for example. The contract mentions the total area to be swept and identifies the streets to be swept, the conditions and frequency of cleaning, and the fine if it is not all cleaned. The price for cleaning one square meter of streets twice a day is 7.8 kopecks. This must be multiplied by 365 days to calculate the annual total. The zhek is divided into six sectors, and there are inspectors working for the zhek who examine the area to make sure that it has been properly cleaned. The zhek has substantial monitoring responsibilities, enforces standards of cleanliness on citizens, and can force shops and enterprises to maintain their areas properly.

In addition to the work done under contract, the zhek has its own maintenance staff capable of performing certain work. This particular zhek has approximately 90 people. There are norms for the number of employees per zhek, which are related to its area. The 90 employees include cleaning personnel, operators of the building incinerators, building workers of various kinds, dispatchers (see below), technicians of various types, a chief engineer, an economist, a bookkeeper, clerks, gardener, and one teacher-organizer for children. Table 7.5 gives the staffing norms for the administrative and management personnel in a typical zhek.

The zhek is responsible for organizing children's sports and clubs of various types: photography, radio, skating, knitting, musical ensembles, and so forth. There is an effort to have many activities for children to prevent their becoming delinquent and engaging in various

Table 7.5. Staffing Norms for Administrative and Management Personnel in a Zhek

Position	Staff Categories, Depending on the Amount of Living and Equivalent Nonliving Area, in Thousands of Square Meters					
	Over 70	50-70	35-50	20-35	10-20	5-10
Director	1	1	1	1	1	1
Chief engineer	1	1	0-1	—	—	—
Senior engineer	1	0-1	—	—	—	—
Engineer	—	—	1	1	0-1	—
Technician	1 per 15,000 square meters	4	2-3	1-2	1	0-1
Senior accountant (with chief authority)	1	1	1	1	1	1
Accountant	1	1	—	—	—	—
Account for the portfolio	2	2	2	1-2	1	0
Economist	1	1	—	—	—	—
Senior statistician	0	—	0-1	—	—	—
Agent-dispatcher (and storekeeper)	1	1	1	1	0-1	—
Cashier (and bookkeeper)	1	1	1	0-1	—	—
Secretary-typist	1	0-1	—	—	—	—
Total	16+	12-15	9-12	6-9	4-6	2-3

antisocial acts. Crime prevention is primarily a responsibility of the zhek. It may also have contacts with the police and with school officials about delinquent children. For minor destructive behavior, the culprit is called to the zhek office for a talk with the officials. The zhek used to organize the auxiliary police, but it no longer has that responsibility. Enterprises now do this and encourage their workers to volunteer for such activities.

Efforts to strengthen the zheks have been undertaken recently. Transferring them to a self-supporting basis (with subsidies as necessary) and the attempt to create zheks with a minimum of 65,000 to 70,000 square meters of living space are examples of these moves. Central accounting offices have been created in each raion housing agency serving all the zheks in the raion. Payment on a piece-work basis was instituted for custodians as a work incentive, and a central supply warehouse was created in each raion, reducing the number of such structures by 94 percent.

Within the zheks there also have been innovations. One is the Central Dispatch System. The Dispatch Center typically consists of a large room containing a communications console that faces a large wall schematic of the zhek area. The wall map shows the streets and buildings of the zhek, and contains a set of lights within the outline of each building. When a resident telephones the Dispatch Center, a light indicates the building from which the call is made, as well as whether it is made from the elevator or a corridor phone in that building. The center is called whenever various repair or janitorial services are required and in case of emergency. The dispatcher takes appropriate action to notify repair crews, mechanics, or raion agencies.

Lights on the wall map and signals and switches on the console permit the automatic monitoring of gas leaks, hot water pressure and temperature, water leaks, and elevator operations. Two-way intercom communication is possible with all elevators, lobbies, and entranceways in the zhek. Locked doors to buildings can be unlocked automatically upon receipt of a signal from the dispatcher. Finally, there are several television monitors in the center that are connected to cameras located throughout the grounds of the zhek.

The first dispatch centers started operating in 1974. The creation of these centers, which now exist in over 200 zheks, has significantly improved response time and efficiency in the internal service systems of the housing network.

It should be noted that the dispatch centers receive extra attention owing to recent developments in the implementation of ASUs in the city housing agencies. Within the ASUs the dispatch centers will act as coordination centers for the operational management of the housing of the microraions and as a source of primary data.

Daily summaries from the center will be transferred to raion dispatch centers (the second level of management), where they will be immediately sorted. The necessary data will be sent to the agency computer center. After data processing, the raion housing administrations and the Main Moscow Housing Administration will issue an account of the emergencies and the unforeseen work in the housing system.

The Central Dispatch Office of each raion housing administration is connected with all dispatch centers by intercom. The office receives periodic data on service requests and their disposition.

The third level of the housing operations management system is the Central Dispatch Center of the Main Moscow Housing Administration. The functions of this center include the coordination of and operational control over the raion dispatchers and emergency services and the accumulation and processing of data from the raions on unforeseen repairs. Computers are widely used in this system.

As a result of these and other improvements, gross income from housing rose from 2.94 to 3.41 rubles per square meter of area operated during the period 1971-75. In 1971, 85 percent of the expenditures for routine repairs went toward wages, with only 15 percent for materials, whereas in 1975, the figures were 60 and 40 percent, respectively. The number of raion workers was reduced from 19,300 to 12,500, and the indexes for timely repair work completed were improved. All this suggests more efficient housing operations.

There is one additional factor in the management of the housing system. In zheks containing over 20,000 square meters of living area, building committees may be elected in major residential units to advise the zhek management, organize socialist competition and sports activities, and perform inspections. These are strictly voluntary groups without any managerial role or authority.

Maintenance

Income and Expenditures

The maintenance and operation of the housing stock require substantial expenditures. The housing sector meets all operational expenditures other than capital and current repair by means of its own income. The gross income in 1972 from the operation of the housing stock amounted to 123.1 million rubles, whereas the monthly income per square meter of housing area was 23.3 kopeks.

The following figures illustrate the structure of the total income: apartment rents, 54 percent; leases on space other than living space, for stores, etc., 18 percent; charges, e.g., for parking, 13 percent; miscellaneous, 15 percent. In spite of the large percentage represented by rents, the rent for a tenant family is not more than 5 percent of family income.

The fee for electricity is 4 kopeks per kilowatt-hour and for gas it is 16 kopeks per person per month regardless of actual gas usage. A charge of 45 kopeks per person per month for water supply and sewage disposal are also included in the rent bill.

The uninhabitable building spaces can be leased to enterprises and organizations. In order to improve the financing of housing maintenance, since 1968, 80 percent of the rent on such leases remains in the possession of the zheks and is used for the maintenance and repair of the building. In 1975, this income amounted to 28.2 million rubles compared with 9.5 million rubles in 1967.

Expenditures for the technical maintenance of the water supply, sewage, and electricity networks and the equipment of the buildings are covered by the income from their operation that is received by the zheks. In 1971, this amounted to approximately 12 million rubles.

Preventive maintenance of gas equipment is done at the expense of the gas distribution companies. The latter spend more than 2.5 million rubles per year for this type of service.

Norms for Current Repairs

Current repairs consist of systematic work performed to prevent buildings and equipment from prematurely depreciating, and to repair minor defects occurring during operation. In financial terms, the volume of the work for current repairs is expressed as 0.75 to 1 percent of the reconstruction cost of the building. Some 73 million rubles has been spent annually for this work in recent years.

Current repairs of the buildings are performed every three years. During the intervening period, only emergency repairs are handled.

Current repairs are performed by permanent employees of the zhek. The number of workers needed to perform current repairs and routine maintenance is determined on the basis of the work expenditure norms listed in Table 7.6. These take into account the work required for the water, sewage, and heating systems, electric networks, and other equipment in the building.

The building maintenance workers are staff employees of the zhek. As mentioned above, they are also responsible for the sanitary conditions of the building, equipment, and the general order and quiet on the building territory.

The Moscow Soviet Executive Committee established the following average annual norms for the cleaning of the housing area by superintendents. Each indicates an area of a particular type for which the employment of one superintendent is required.

- improved surface (asphalt, etc.)   960 square meters of streets
      1,500 square meters of yards
- other surfaces (gravel, cobblestone)   1,600 square meters of streets
      2,700 square meters of yards
- unimproved surfaces   2,500 square meters of streets
      4,200 square meters of yards
- gardens and greenery   5,200 square meters

Table 7.6. Work Expenditure Norms for Current Repairs

Construction Elements, Equipment, and Type of Work	Profession of the Worker	Unit of Measure	Quantity
		Norm per Worker	
Roof surface	Roof	Square meter	8,800
Steel	repairer		
Soft surfaces (rubber, etc.)			11,000
Miscellaneous (tiles, asbestos-cement, roof slates, cast iron slabs, wood, etc.)			12,000
Wood structures in stone houses with useful lives as follows	Carpenter	Square meter of living area	
Up to 10 years			18,000
Over 10 years			11,000
Wood buildings			8,000
Buildings with miscellaneous partitions			10,000
Masonry, plastering, partitioning in stone buildings with useful lives as follows	Mason, plasterer	Square meter of living area	
Up to 10 years			20,000
Over 10 years			13,500
Wood buildings			16,300
Buildings with miscellaneous partitions			14,000
Water supply, sewage, central heating, hot water as follows	Mechanic-sanitary technician	No. of apartments	
Water and sewage without bathtubs and hot water			180
Water and sewage plus bathtubs and no hot water			160
Water and sewage with bathtubs and hot water			150
Central heating of the building (separate or group)		Square meter of living area	9,000
Central heating from a city plant or a local station			13,000
Water towers		No.	15
Electrical network and equipment	Electrician	No. of apartments	
With surface cables			700
With wall cables			1,200
Electric motors			40

In buildings with garbage chutes, cleaning norms are increased by 15 percent.

Calculating the Number of Workers Required for a Housing Area

This example illustrates the method used in the Ukraine to determine the number of porters needed for a building. It is similar to that used in most large Soviet cities.

The number of porters needed is determined by three factors:

1. The area of streets, sidewalks, and yards to be cleaned by the workers of a given building;
2. The cleaning norms for one porter, which are established by the City Executive Committee;
3. An adjustment for the kind of road surface, the intensity of traffic, and the time of year.

The cleaning norms call for one porter for each 2,500 to 3,000 square meters in oblast (provincial) centers and one for each 4,000 square meters in other towns. Because the norms are stated in terms of area cleaned, all other activities that a porter does must be converted into an equivalent area. Table 7.7 shows the conversion rates. If, for example, a building were associated with 16,120 square meters of streets and sidewalks, 7,350 square meters of courtyards, 5,880 square meters of lawns, 215 trees, and 47 sewer shafts, then the following conversion could be made:

Table 7.7. Rates for Converting Other Activities into an Equivalent Area Cleaned

Activity	Unit of Measure	Equivalent Area in Square Meters
Cleaned area of street	100 square meters	100
Cleaned area of yard	100 square meters	60
Cleaned area of attic or basement	100 square meters	50
Cleaned area of lawn	100 square meters	60
Caring for greenery	1 tree	10
Carrying garbage container up to 50 meters	1 container	30
Inspection and cleaning of sewer shafts	1 shaft	40
Cleaning of outhouse	1 outhouse	40
Cleaning and clearing of garbage chute	1 chute	50

Area of streets and sidewalks	(16,120/100) × 100 = 16,120
Area of courtyards	(7,350/100) × 60 = 4,410
Area of lawns	(5,880/100) × 50 = 2,940
Greenery	215 × 10 = 2,150
Sewer shafts	47 × 40 = 1,880
Total equivalent area	27,500

If the norm is 3,000 square meters per porter, then nine porters are needed.

Once this calculation has been made, allowance must be made for the number of days off these nine porters will take each year. If each porter takes 1 day off each week and takes 12 days of vacation during the year, then the nine workers will have a total of 576 person-days off during the year. Two additional porters will have to be hired to make up for these losses, so that a total of 11 will be needed for the building.

Norms for Capital Repairs

Capital repairs are divided into complex and optional. Complex repairs imply repair of the entire building, whereas optional repairs deal with separate structural elements of the building or of its engineering equipment.

Table 7.8. Selected Norms for Complex Capital Repairs (duration of repairs in months)

| | Complex Buildings | | |
Work Volume in Thousands of Rubles	Using Light Cranes, Elevators, and Hoists	Using Tower Cranes for Large Prefabricated Structures	Combined and Wooden Buildings
Up to 5	3	–	3
6-10	4	–	4
11-20	4.5	4	5
50-60	8	5	9
91-100	10	7	a
121-150	a	8	a
171-250	a	10	a
More than 250	a	a	a

a Specified in the design.

The norms for the duration of complex capital repairs are established in two versions, depending on the degree of mechanization of the work. A brief summary of norms for the length of time it takes to complete repairs of a building is listed in Tables 7.8 through 7.11. The norms for all the repair work include work related to the improvement of the environment (stove installation, drilling holes in walls and partitions, finishing work, etc.). [Note: This illustration is included in order to demonstrate the high degree to which work standards have been developed. However, the U.S. authors are not aware of the extent to which these norms are utilized in practice and achieved. They seem useful only for gross planning purposes and not for the supervision and evaluation of a particular repair job.]

General supervision over the quality and schedule of repairs and the expenditure of materials is performed by the principal engineers of the zhek.

A substantial reserve of funds for the improvement of the housing environment is earned in the process of making optional repairs at the expense of the tenant, where one can employ the best, most

Table 7.9. Selected Norms for Optional Capital Repairs (duration of repairs, in months)

Type of Structural Elements and Type of Repair Work	Work Volume in Thousands of Rubles					
	Up to 1	1.1-2.5	2.6-5	5.1-10	10.1-15	Over 15
New waterproofing of basements						
Sheet type	1.0	1.5	2.5	3.5	–	–
Cast	1.5	2	3	4	–	–
Facade repair						
In stone buildings	1	2	2	3	4	4
In wood buildings	0.5	1	–	–	–	–
Roof repair (regardless of materials)						
Up to 100 square meters	0.5	1	1.5	–	–	–
From 100 to 300 square meters	1	1.5	2.0	–	–	–
From 300 to 700 square meters	1.5	2	2.5	3	–	–
Over 700 square meters	2	2.5	3	3.5	–	–

Table 7.10. Selected Norms for the Improvement of Facilities (duration of repairs, in months)

Type of Work	Work Volume in Thousands of Rubles			
	Up to 1	1.1-2.5	2.5-5	Over 5
Assembly and repair of central heating	1	2	2.5	3
Assembly and repair of the water and sewage systems	1	2.5	3	3.5
Assembly and repair of the house gas systems (including the transfer to gas stoves)	1.5	2.5	3.5	4
Yard repair	0.5	1	1.5	2
Installation and repair of the electric lighting systems	1	1.5	2	2.5

durable, and costliest materials if the client requests them. The Moscow Housing Repair Trust has performed the following amounts of repairs at the expense of the tenants: 1.65 million rubles in 1968; 4.2 million rubles in 1970; 6.32 million rubles in 1972; 8.14 million rubles in 1973; and over 11 million rubles in 1974.

In summary, the housing stock of Moscow is undergoing major qualitative improvements, and it has changed from primarily wooden buildings fewer than six stories high to concrete high-rise buildings. Construction is continuing at a rapid rate and accounts for a large portion of the city budget, and the result is gradually improving housing conditions.

Table 7.11. Selected Material Expenditure Norms for Repairs (per construction volume of 1 million rubles)

Type of Material	Unit of Measure	Quantity
Rolled ferrous metals	Ton	13.5
Construction nails	Ton	20
Lumber	Cubic meter	750
Cement	Ton	40
Window glass	Square meter	900
Soft roof-surfacing material	Thousands of square meters	5.4
Gas pipes	Ton	2.1
Paint	Ton	1.0
Electric cable	Kilometer	2.5

HEALTH CARE

Health care is a separate branch of the city economy. This branch provides medical-preventive and sanitary antiepidemic services, health centers, and drugstores for the public. The objective of the health care system is to attain optimal correspondence between the needs of the public for medical care and their satisfaction.

The health care system includes a number of municipal and nonmunicipal agencies and facilities. These include the Main Health Administration and the Pharmacy Administration of the Moscow Soviet Executive Committee, the Emergency Ambulance System of the R.S.F.S.R. Ministry of Public Health, and numerous other clinics, hospitals, and institutes under the jurisdiction of the various republic ministries. Figure 7.5 shows the general organization of the city's public health system. Tables 7.12 and 7.13 present basic data about the city's health system.

The Department of Education and Health Protection of the City Planning Commission (Gorplan) is responsible for the long-range coordination of this system. By means of multiyear plans, Gorplan

Table 7.12. Statistics of the Moscow Public Health System (unless otherwise indicated, January 1, 1978, data)

	No.
Medical research institutes and laboratories, 1973	70+
Medical universities, 1973	3
Medical schools, 1973	27
Medical doctors	70,800
Citizens per doctor	110
Other medical personnel	135,000
Hospitals	246
Hospital beds	109,100
Hospital beds per 1,000 citizens	14
Ambulance stations, 1973	24
Sanatoriums and rest homes, 1973	39
Patients in sanatoriums and rest homes, 1973	4,600
Drug stores	415
Medical establishments, i.e., polyclinics and first-aid stations (such as found in factories), which treat only outpatients	923
Construction costs per hospital bed, 1970	7,540 rubles
Capital investment for hospitals and medical centers for the period 1971-75	171 million rubles

Figure 7.5. Organization of the System of Public Health in Moscow.

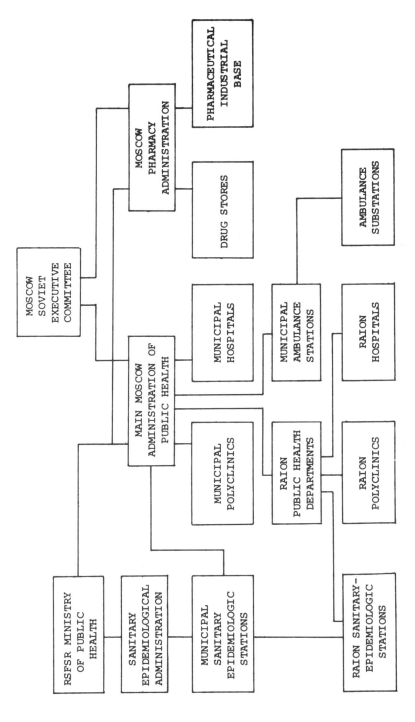

116

Table 7.13. Hospital Centers in Moscow, 1970 (facilities with at least some inpatients)

Raion	No. of Medical Centers
Babushkin	8
Bauman	10
Volgograd	2
Voroshilov	6
Gagarin	4
Dzerdjin	6
Zhdanov	6
Zheleznodorozhni	2
Kalinin	10
Kiev	7
Kirov	9
Krasnogvardeisky	6
Krasnopresnensky	10
Kuibishev	8
Kuntsevo	8
Leningrad	7
Lenin	9
Lyublino	9
Moskvoretsky	12
Oktyabr	15
Pervomaisky	13
Perovo	6
Proletarsky	8
Sverdlov	10
Sevastopol	3
Soviet	3
Sokolnitchesky	12
Timiriazevsky	5
Tushino	7
Frunzensky	10
Tcheriomushinsky	4
Zelenograd City	1
Total	236[a]

[a] This figure includes all hospital centers in Moscow, including those not subordinate to the Moscow Soviet (which numbered 218 in 1970).

establishes the number of clinics, hospitals, and pharmacies and the distribution and level of capital investment. In general, it sets the system's goals and provides plans for their achievement.

The planning sections of the Main Health Administration and other operational agencies are responsible for concrete and current planning. This might involve, for example, the location and construction of specific hospitals, clinics, and so forth.

The organizational structure of the administration can be represented in the following way: The polyclinics, the hospitals, and the sanitary-epidemiological stations are managed by the raion health departments, which in turn are managed by the Main Public Health Administration of the Moscow Soviet Executive Committee. The drugstores and the industrial bases for their products are managed by the City Pharmacy Administration. (See Figures 7.6 and 7.7.)

The Main Public Health Administration includes the following departments: medical treatment and preventive care for children and mothers; personnel and medical training institutions; medical centers; planning and finance; economic-technological, e.g., medical engineering experts who develop advanced X-ray and other equipment; and management, engineering, and operational departments. There also exists a department that produces medical supplies and a specialized department of self-supporting medical activities.

The basic objectives of the Main Public Health Administration of the City Executive Committee (Glavgorzdrav) are the following: the organization of city health care on a prophylactic basis, providing easily accessible and qualified medical care for the public; management of the sanitary work; alerting the public to disease possibilities and necessary remedies.

The municipal health facilities (hospitals, polyclinics, etc.) are under the direct supervision of either the raion soviet executive committees or that of the city, depending upon the size, purpose, and client population of the facility. Thus, a large, general-purpose hospital with specialized treatment facilities is likely to be under central municipal jurisdiction, whereas a small hospital that serves primarily the routine needs of the local population will be administered by the raion public health agency. The central Main Health Administration nonetheless guides the work of the raion health establishments.

Current health efforts emphasize increasing the number of hospital beds and improving the quality of the medical equipment in the existing hospitals and in those under construction.

A great deal of attention is also given to the construction of polyclinics. Planning of the polyclinic network is conducted by micro-

Figure 7.6. Organizational Structure of the Main Moscow Administration for Public Health.

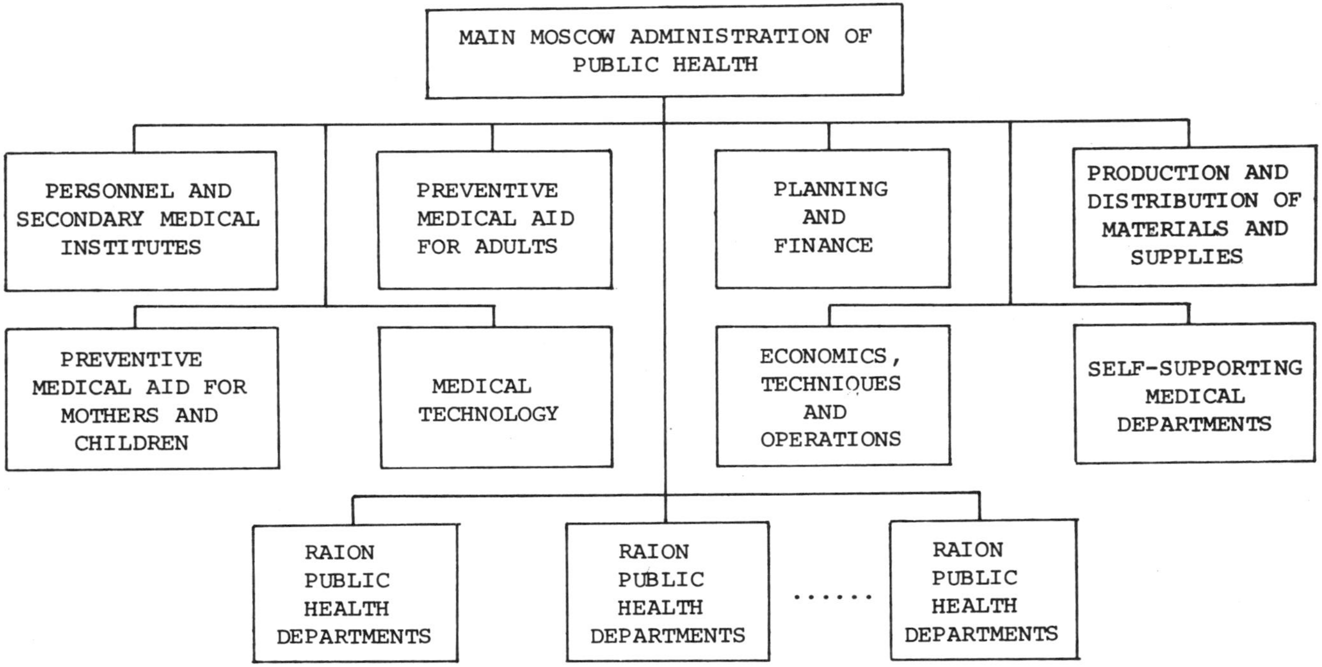

```
                    MAIN MOSCOW ADMINISTRATION OF
                          PUBLIC HEALTH

  PERSONNEL AND      PREVENTIVE        PLANNING          PRODUCTION AND
  SECONDARY MEDICAL  MEDICAL AID       AND               DISTRIBUTION OF
  INSTITUTES         FOR ADULTS        FINANCE           MATERIALS AND
                                                         SUPPLIES

  PREVENTIVE         MEDICAL           ECONOMICS,        SELF-SUPPORTING
  MEDICAL AID FOR    TECHNOLOGY        TECHNIQUES        MEDICAL
  MOTHERS AND                          AND               DEPARTMENTS
  CHILDREN                             OPERATIONS

  RAION              RAION       . . . RAION
  PUBLIC             PUBLIC            PUBLIC
  HEALTH             HEALTH            HEALTH
  DEPARTMENTS        DEPARTMENTS       DEPARTMENTS
```

Figure 7.7. Organizational Structure of a Sanitary-Epidemiologic Station.

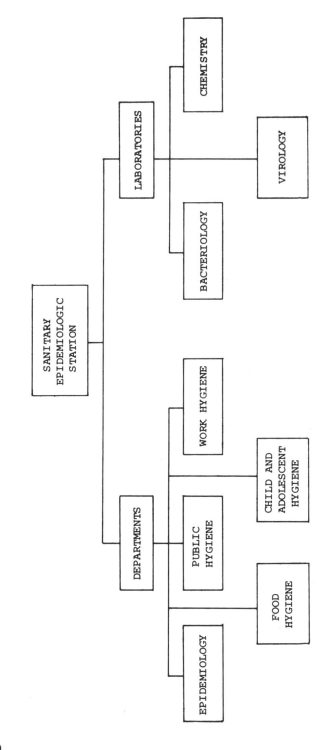

raions and involves considerable complications as to optimal distribution, owing to difficulties in forecasting their population size as well as sex and age structure.

In the Moscow hospital network, a considerable portion of the budget for beds (primarily in specialized medical centers) comes from the Health Ministries of the Soviet Union and the R.S.F.S.R. and their departments. This may be in recognition of the fact that the system is used by a large number of patients from other cities.

The administration also guides the work of City and Raion Sanitary and Epidemiological Stations. These stations conduct inspections and measure air, water, and noise pollution in the city. They also perform occupational health and safety inspections through a separate unit within their network. In addition, personnel of this unit also instruct employers on how to maintain a healthy and safe working environment.

The life expectancy in Moscow is now 73 years. This has led to an increased demand for hospitals and rest homes. There are some 1.4 million pensioners in the city, with men eligible to retire at age 60 and women at age 65.

From 1966 to 1970, there was an increase of 2,420 places for the aged and for invalids in rest homes. Maintenance expenditures by the city increased by 71.4 percent during this period.

The average annual expenditure per bed went up by 22.2 percent, from 697 to 852 rubles. This 155-ruble increase was due to food (35 rubles), salaries (78 rubles), and administrative costs (42 rubles). The total city allocation for the construction of rest homes for the period 1971-75 amounted to 11.2 million rubles. Table 7.14 shows the growth of health services in Moscow since 1940.

EDUCATION

The Main Administration of Public Education is one of the principal components of the city's education system. It provides public schools and boarding schools for the population, including general ten-year schools and special (usually vocational) schools with eight grades. Other components include preschool institutions and activities.

The organizational structure of public education can be represented in the following way: The Main Administration of Public Education of Moscow (Mosgorno) manages the work of the schools. It includes special sections for its various activities. Each city raion has a Raion Department of Public Education. Mosgorno guides and inspects the work of the raions and exercises financial control through

Table 7.14. Growth of Health Services in Moscow (as of December 31 of the indicated year)

	1940	1960	1965	1966	1967	1968	1969	1970	1972
Hospitals	190	290	285	280	273	273	271	270	260
Beds	36,000	67,800	79,800	81,800	83,600	86,200	87,300	89,400	99,400
Beds per 1,000 population	84	107.2	120.3	122.1	123.1	124.6	123.7	124.7	134[a]
Outpatient clinics	—	1,120	950	1,056	1,046	1,049	1,083	974	988[b]
Maternity/child clinics	—	333	298	316	314	303	297	282	—
No. of spaces for maternity	—	4,840	4,608	4,708	4,833	4,596	4,597	4,612	—
No. of pharmacies	—	—	297	301	342	354	356	372	390

[a]In 1975, there were 157 beds per 10,000 population; the planned figure for 1990 is 175.
[b]The 1975 norm for clinical visits was 35 visits per shift per 1,000 population. The planned 1990 norm is 15 to 20 visits per year per inhabitant.

audits. The general management of the development of this field is conducted, as is the case with any field, by the City Committee of the Communist Party of the Soviet Union and the Moscow Executive Committee on the basis of the long-range and current plans that are developed by the City Planning Commission (Gorplan). The curriculum is developed by the Ministry of Education, although certain limited revisions may be made by the City Soviet Executive Committee, for example, to promote English-language schools.

Mosgorno has the structure shown in Figure 7.8. The schools themselves are under the raion education departments, known as RONOs.

Planning for the growth and location of educational institutions cannot be based solely on census data, since variations in the number of children in the microraions change the city plans substantially. For a more accurate estimate of the number of students in the general schools, the raion planning committees together with the RONOs develop plans for the admission and graduation of the students, considering migration among microraions. The calculations are adjusted to take into account the living area included or removed from the territory of a given school. On the basis of the plan for the distribution of students among classes, the fiscal authorities calculate the staff quota of teachers, service personnel, salaries, and other factors relevant to the operational and maintenance budgets.

The demand for schools is expressed by the session coefficient, which is different for the different raions. It is defined as the total number of pupils divided by the number attending school in the first shift. (The normal school day is five to six hours.) The goal for 1975 was to have 90 percent of all students attend single-shift schools, i.e., a session coefficient of 1.11, and during 1976-80 it was to reach the point where no school had more than one shift per day.

The growth of the adult working population influences the number of students that are on an extended daily schedule, a program that has also grown considerably in recent years. A child on an extended daily schedule attends a school from breakfast until approximately 6 p.m. Facilities for after-school recreation, study, and rest are provided at the school for these children of working parents. At the same time, the number of students in schools for working young people has dropped sharply. This is explained by the growing number of students in the ninth and tenth grades of the general schools and the increasing network of specialized vocational schools.

The vocational school network illustrates an interesting case of municipal planning. Beginning in the early 1960s, it became fashionable

Figure 7.8. Organizational Structure of the Moscow Main Administration of Public Education.

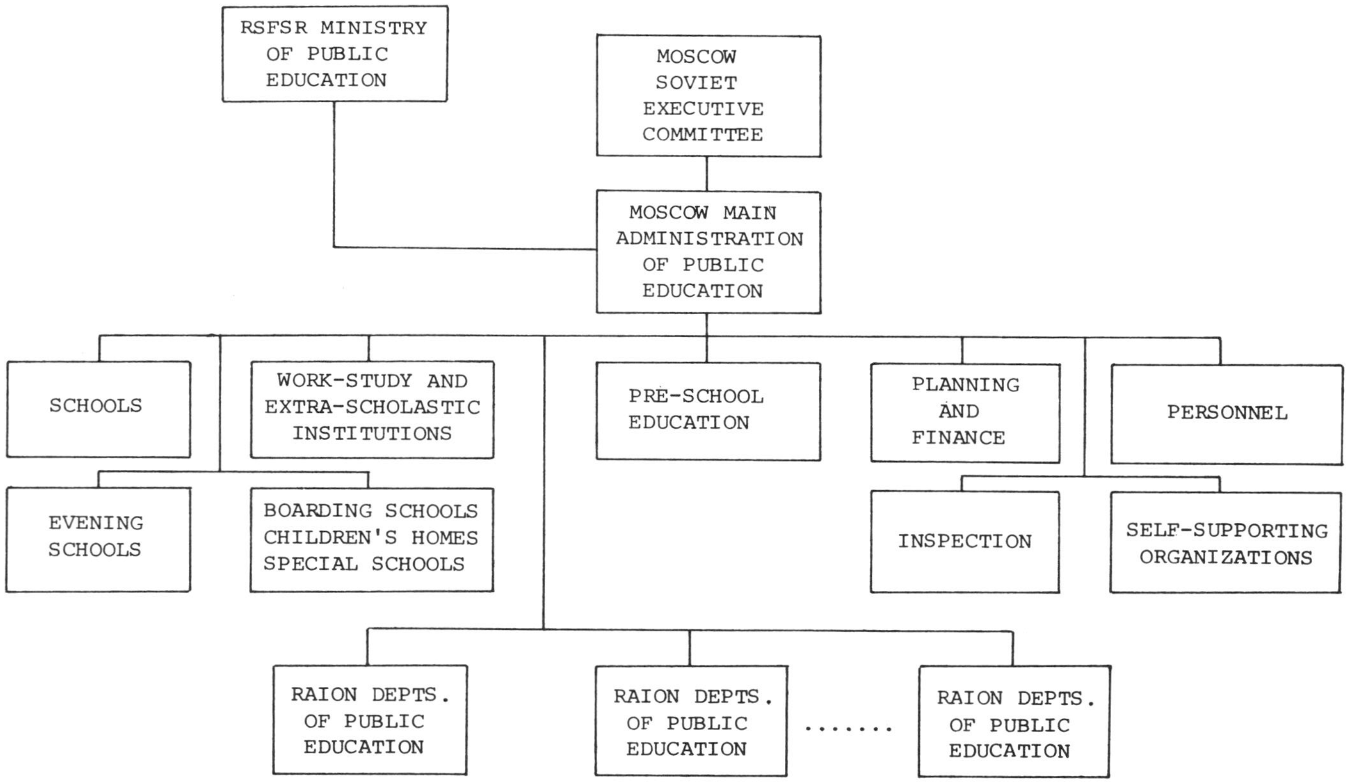

for more and more children to continue their education in universities and institutes rather than become laborers. This resulted in a serious shortage of skilled laborers and a surplus of professionals in certain fields.

In 1964 or thereabouts, the Moscow City Soviet decided to correct this imbalance by establishing more vocational schools. These schools offered free tuition, an additional stipend to students, a highly qualified teaching staff, and a number of privileges to graduates. Students learned several technical trades and had practical experience in each by the time they graduated. As a result of the effective "selling" of this program, these schools became quite popular.

The number of day students in the general schools and their distribution by grade level are shown in Table 7.15.

In 1977, there were 1,033 schools; 5 were primary (grades one to four), 83 were eight-year, and 877 were secondary (ten year). The distribution of the schools among the districts of Moscow appears in Table 7.16.

In the general and specialized schools in 1977, there were 4.0 teachers per 1,000 citizens. In that same year, there were 44 teachers per 1,000 students. The public schools and high schools for specialized training employed over 55,600 teachers. The number of city and raion education employees, both administrative and teaching staff, was approximately 100,000, including approximately 140 in the central office of Mosgorno.

Capital investments for the construction of schools for general education during 1971-75 amounted to 111.8 million rubles. The capital cost for one student for an average school was 740 rubles, and for

Table 7.15. Education Statistics, 1970

	Grades One to Four	Grades Five to Eight	Grades Nine and Ten	Total
No. of schools	–	–	–	1,025
No. of classes	9,530	9,636	2,915	22,081
No. of students	356,210	350,813	97,767	804,790
Average class size	37.4	36.4	33.5	36.4
No. of seats	–	–	–	619,070
Session coefficient	–	–	–	1.30

Note: By 1977, statistics were collected in a slightly different manner, and the relevant enrollment figures were: grades one to three, 234,400; grades four to eight, 380,800; grades nine and ten, 105,900; total, 721,100.

Table 7.16. Number of Schools by Raion, 1970

Raion	No. of Schools
Babushkin	37
Bauman	21
Volgograd	50
Voroshilov	34
Gagarin	35
Dzerdjin	30
Zhdanov	34
Zheloznodorozhni	26
Kalinin	25
Kiev	31
Korov	44
Krasnogvardeisky	46
Krasnopresnensky	33
Kuibishev	49
Kuntsevo	49
Leningrad	45
Lenin	30
Lyublino	30
Moskovoretsky	22
Oktyabr	48
Pervomaisky	54
Perovo	53
Proletarsky	41
Sverdlov	29
Sevastopol	45
Soviet	47
Sokolnitchesky	26
Timiryazevsky	41
Tushino	32
Frunzensky	26
Tcheriomushinsky	36
Zelenograd City	19
Total	1,168

schools with an extended daily schedule, 1,457 rubles. The latter schools include additional sports, recreational, and study facilities, as well as beds and expanded food services. Children of working parents stay at school until approximately 6 p.m., at which time their parents are able to take them home.

PRESCHOOL CHILDREN'S INSTITUTIONS

Preschool children's institutions (nurseries and kindergartens) are also considered to be in the education system. The work of these institutions is directed by the Main Administration of Public Education and the raion departments of public education (RONOs).

There are two kinds of preschool institutions, nurseries and kindergartens. Nurseries are for very young children, aged three months through three years. The demand for these facilities is declining owing to a shift in attitudes of young mothers in Moscow. Increasingly, mothers prefer not to work, but to raise their young children instead, at least up to the age of two or three years. Kindergartens serve children aged three to six years old. At age seven, children enter the first grade of general school.

Although the goal of the city is to provide a place for all who wish to enroll, this has not yet been met, and in some of the new residential raions, there is a waiting list of applicants for admission to the kindergartens. Preference for admission is given to: families in which the father is deceased; families in which a parent is ill; low-income families; and families in which a parent is vital to certain industries that intervene on their behalf (they may also subsidize the fee payments).

The children may attend six days per week, and are given breakfast, a midday meal, and an afternoon snack. The kindergartens have large playrooms with toys, gymnasiums, beds, and separate playgrounds for each age group. Music teachers, teachers for preparatory schoolwork, and nurses are in attendance.

The institutions are operated within three different organizational settings, by public education authorities, by public health authorities, and by enterprises. In 1978, the number and enrollments under each was as follows:

1. In the system of public education, 1,070 institutions with a total of 201,700 children—these are the most popular institutions and they are usually nearest to the home.
2. In the system of public health, 390 institutions with a total of 45,800 children—these are primarily for handicapped children.
3. In other departments, 1,137 institutions for 148,500 children—these are operated by enterprises for the children of their employees, and are generally very well equipped, with music teachers, etc. (The stake of enterprises in preschool institutions is clear; they are suffering from a labor shortage and wish to attract women into their work force.)

The total child population in 1970 amounted to 543,786. The percentage enrolled in preschool institutions was 62.3 percent. As

Table 7.17. Recent Preschool Enrollment

No.	1960	1965	1966	1967	1968	1969	1970	1972	1975
Nurseries	636	697	683	624	593	546	509	479	480
Children (in thousands)	65.8	73.3	69.8	61.6	56.0	52.6	49.6	47.0	53.2
Kindergartens	1,698	2,311	2,359	2,285	2,257	2,176	2,106	1,939	1,987
Children (in thousands)	171.1	289.0	302.4	294.4	290.7	283.9	277.8	290.5	NA

NA, not available.

Table 7.17 shows, the numbers of nurseries and kindergartens declined from their peaks in the mid-1960s, as did their enrollments, although a modest upturn was evident again by 1975. The distribution of institutions throughout the city is shown in Table 7.18.

Capital investment for the construction of children's preschool institutions for 1971-75 was 72.3 million rubles; the capital cost of

Table 7.18. Distribution of Preschool Children's Institutions Among the Raions of Moscow, 1977

Raion	No. of Institutions
Babushkin	94
Bauman	52
Volgograd	85
Voroshilov	80
Gagarin	77
Dzerdjin	66
Zhdanov	45
Zheleznodorozhni	47
Kalinin	49
Kiev	68
Kirov	90
Krasnogvardeisky	73
Krasnopresnensky	76
Kuibishev	97
Kuntsevo	119
Leningrad	102
Lenin	58
Lyublino	72
Moskvoretsky	61
Oktyabr	114
Pervomaisky	149
Perovo	129
Proletarsky	92
Sverdlov	66
Sevastopol	78
Soviet	111
Sokolnichesky	48
Timiryazevsky	83
Tushino	68
Frunzensky	77
Tcheriomushinsky	77
Zelenograd City	33
Total	2,536

the facilities per one child was 1,200 rubles. In general, 80 percent of the expenditures of the preschool institutions are met by the state, and 20 percent are paid by the parents. Fees differ according to the salary of the parents, ranging from 2.50 to 12.50 rubles per month. They also are dependent upon the age of the child, with higher fees for older children. Children of invalids are enrolled free of charge.

TRANSPORTATION

Planning and Organization

In the Soviet Union, there are basic principles used in planning intracity passenger transportation. The primary mode used in cities of less than 0.5 million population is express bus. In cities between 0.5 and 1 million population, rapid tram is the primary mode, and in cities over 1 million it is the Metro (subway).

There are also planning norms for commuting time. In cities with less than 250,000 population, 80 to 90 percent of the workers should experience door-to-door travel times no greater than 30 minutes. For larger cities, the target is relaxed to 40 minutes. (However, actual travel times are admitted to be 20 to 30 percent greater than this norm.) Another norm calls for mass transit stops to be located no more than 500 meters from any residence.

Moscow's transportation system is administered by a number of distinct agencies with separate responsibilities for subway, surface mass transit, taxis, traffic control, and freight transport.

The Metro Administration

The Metro Administration, which manages the city's extensive subway system, was an agency of the Moscow City Executive Committee until 1976. At that time, control was transferred to a department within the All-Union Ministry of Transport in a move designed to ensure uniformity and efficiency in the development of all the rapid transit systems in various cities throughout the country. Under the new arrangement, a close working and coordinating relationship continues to exist with municipal authorities, although policies and operational directives now emanate from a union ministry in much the same fashion as do those of the fire and police services.

Passenger Transport Administration

The Passenger Transport Administration manages passenger transportation on the three basic modes of surface mass transit: buses,

Figure 7.9. Organizational Structure of the Passenger Transport Administration.

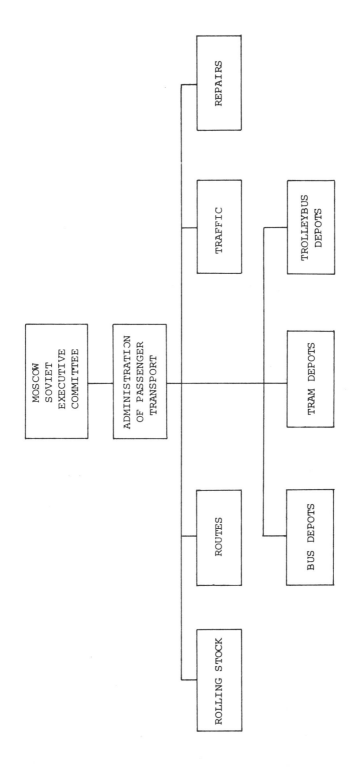

trams, and trolleybuses. For each of these modes, the Executive Committee maintains the following plan indexes: the number of passengers transported, the number of passenger-kilometers, the capacity utilization coefficient, income, expenditures, and profit. Figure 7.9 shows the divisional structure of the administration.

Administration of Taxi and Automobile Transport

The Administration of Taxi and Automobile Transport manages the taxi and fleet auto services. Its departmental structure is shown in Figure 7.10.

More than 20 taxi parks and several parks for rental and pool cars serving various Moscow organizations are attached to this administration. These and other fleets are stocked as a rule with "Volga" GAZ-24 cars.

Department of Municipal Passenger Transportation

The Department of Municipal Passenger Transportation, which is distinct from the Passenger Transport Administration, is responsible for coordinating the city's mass transportation services. It periodically (once every two or three years) studies passenger flows on all three modes of transportation. The study is carried out by personnel of the various transportation organizations, with the assistance of students, pensioners, and school children. It is financed by the Moscow City Executive Committee. The basic goal of these studies is to acquire analytical data for: extending passenger transportation to new microraions; increasing the capacity on overloaded routes; improving routes in order to improve transportation services for the population (to lessen the length of rides, to bring transportation closer to points of origin of passenger flows, to lessen the number of transfers); establishing express routes; and choosing sites for transportation factories and facilities.

Main Moscow Administration of Auto Transport (Glavmosavtotrans)

Glavmosavtotrans specializes in the centralized transportation of various local cargoes and in containerized shipping. In 1968, it handled 70 percent of the volume of local truck haulage in Moscow. Figure 7.11 indicates the constituent departments of the agency.

Traffic Control

Traffic control is the responsibility of the Government Automobile Inspectorate, or militia, which is directly subordinate to the Ministry of Internal Affairs.

Figure 7.10. Organizational Structure of the Administration of Taxi and Automobile Transport.

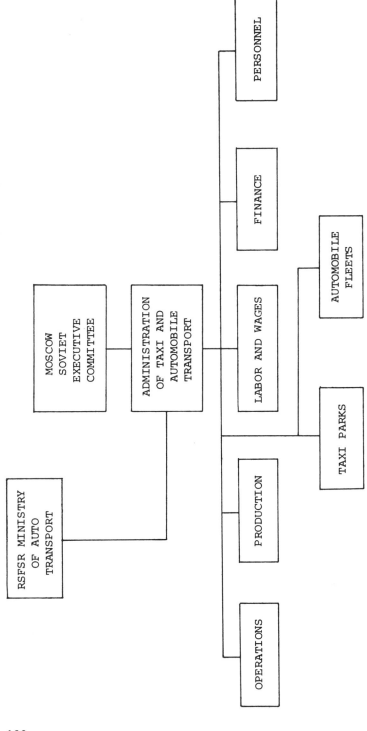

Figure 7.11. Organizational Structure of the Main Moscow Administration of Auto Transport (Glavmosavtotrans).

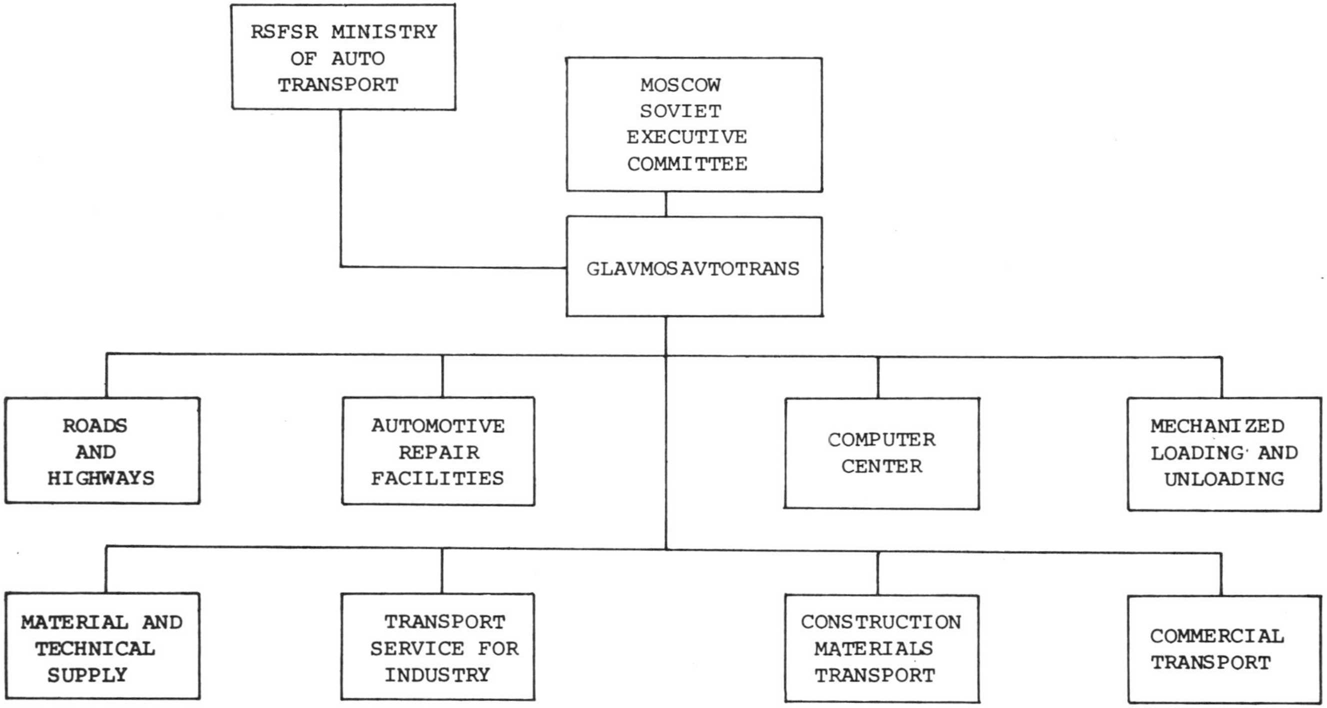

Operations

Table 7.19 illustrates the growth of the transport system. [Note: Not only is the system expanding in the manner indicated, but the usage of the system by the population also is increasing. In 1965, there were 588 trips per capita on public transit facilities; this figure rose to 610 by 1970 and to over 700 in 1975. This is a possible indication of better and more convenient service. However, a less favorable interpretation is also possible: Per capita usage is increasing because more

Table 7.19. Growth of the Moscow Public Transport System

	1940	1960	1965	1970	1975
Metro					
One-way trackage (in kilometers)	77	208	306	400	475
Stations	22	56	75	89	103
Rolling stock units	NA	1,017	1,406	1,832	2,269
Passenger trips (in millions)	377	1,038	1,329	1,628	1,966
Trolleybus					
Length of individual lines (in kilometers)	199	540	712	844	962
Rolling stock units	NA	1,360	1,785	2,101	2,249
Passenger trips (in millions)	201	793	801	785	910
Tram					
Length of one-way trackage (in kilometers)	541	485	446	472	462
Rolling stock units	NA	1,779	1,621	1,517	1,334
Passenger trips (in millions)	1,842	838	701	630	637
Bus					
Length of routes (in kilometers)	985	1,902	2,538	2,753	3,412
Passenger-kilometers (in millions)	NA	NA	4,961	7,985	9,600
Passenger trips (in millions)	220	990	1,254	1,519	1,781
Taxi					
No. of taxis	NA	4,684	10,118	14,234	16,149
Total annual mileage (in millions of kilometers)	NA	364	842	1,347	1,573
Total annual fare producing mileage (in millions of kilometers)	NA	268	648	1,147	1,338

Source: Moskva B Tsifrakh 1971-1975, *Statistika*, Moscow, 1976.
NA, not available.
Note: A tram is a street car; it runs on fixed rails in the street. A trolleybus looks like a bus but is powered from an overhead electric cable and, like an ordinary bus, does not run on rails.

transfers are required to travel to and from the newly developed residential areas in the outer reaches of the city. This interpretation is supported by the discussion on surface transit below.] Table 7.20 shows the changing pattern of usage by transport mode.

Metro

The Metro continues to be the centerpiece of the public transit system in Moscow. Begun in the early 1930s, the length of the routes had reached 151 kilometers by 1975, and construction was still continuing. Six lines are arranged along five chords that cross one another in the center of the old city and radiate in ten directions toward the city perimeter. The seventh line forms a continuous circle around the city core, connecting the other six lines as well as all the major rail terminals and other major municipal facilities. Present construction is extending the lines further into the new residential raions on the periphery. A map of the system appears in Figure 7.12.

Table 7.21 provides data on the operations of the Metro network.

The Moscow Metro continues to show an operational profit, though this is steadily diminishing. Table 7.22 illustrates this trend. The main reason for this decline is the constant expansion of the network. As service improves and the length and number of routes grow, fare revenue increases but at a slower rate than expenses. The 1976 goal was 176 kilometers of operational routes. The General Plan calls for 320 kilometers by 1990, and an eventual network of 450 kilometers. This expansion is planned at a construction cost of approximately 16 million rubles per kilometer.

Table 7.20. Changing Patterns of Public Transport Usage (percentage of passengers carried by each mode)

	1912	1935	1940	1950	1960	1965	1970	1975
Metro	—	2	14	26	28	32	36	37
Trolleybus	—	1	8	17	22	20	17	17
Bus	—	5	8	12	27	31	33	34
Tram	100	92	70	45	23	17	14	12

Sources: Y. A. Limonov, *Metropolitan*, Izdatelstvo "Transport," 1971, p. 347; *Moskva B Tsifrakh 1966-1970*, Izdatelstvo "Statistika," 1972, p. 45; *Moskva B Tsifrakh 1971-1975*, Izdatelstvo "Statistika," 1976, p. 63.

137

Figure 7.12. System Map of the Moscow Metro. The numbers refer to stations, as listed in the Appendix.

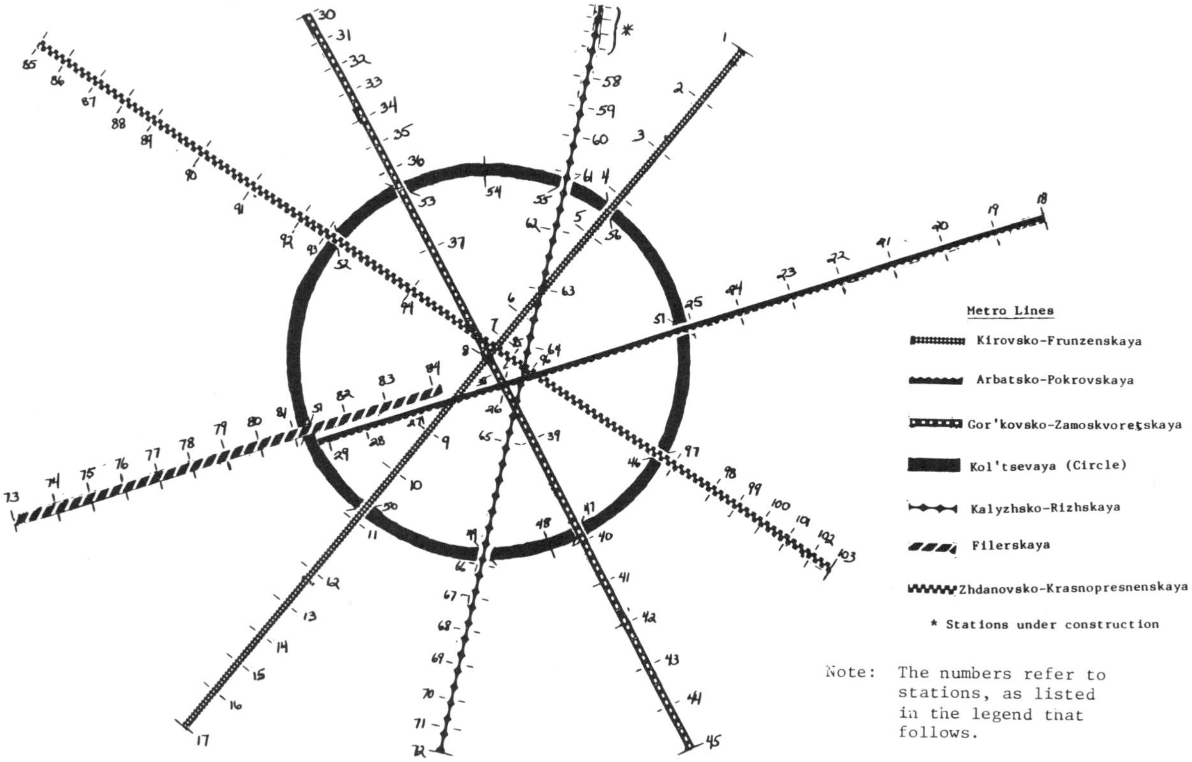

Metro Lines

Kirovsko-Frunzenskaya

Arbatsko-Pokrovskaya

Gor'kovsko-Zamoskvoretskaya

Kol'tsevaya (Circle)

Kaluzhsko-Rizhskaya

Filerskaya

Zhdanovsko-Krasnopresnenskaya

* Stations under construction

Note: The numbers refer to
stations, as listed
in the legend that
follows.

Table 7.21. Metro Operating Statistics, 1974

Route	150.8 kilometers
No. of stations	97
No. of transfer points	15
Daily passenger load	5.3 million
Annual passenger load	1.91 billion
Share of all public transit rides	36.5%
Share of all passenger-kilometers	55%
Total rolling stock	2,386 units
Total workers	20,500
In operations and service	17,000
In repair and maintenance	3,500
Fare (standard for all Metros in the Soviet Union)	5 kopeks

Surface Transport

There are two basic functions performed by the bus, trolley-bus, and tram route networks in Moscow. First, they feed into the Metro network, serving heavy demand areas where Metro construction has yet to take place, as well as areas of lighter demand where the large capital investments of the Metro are not warranted. Second, they provide local service along the Metro routes and along major arteries. This is required by the fact that Moscow Metro stations are spaced considerably farther apart than those in such cities as New York.

Capital purchase and construction costs for the period 1971-75 totaled 300 million rubles. The profitability of surface mass transit, like that of the Metro, has declined sharply owing to increasing costs, as shown in Table 7.23.

Contributing to this deficit has been the expansion of the city of Moscow itself. As new residential developments were constructed far from the center of the city, they outstripped the pace of Metro

Table 7.22. Profits from Metro Operations

	1966	1970	1975	1980
Revenue (in millions of rubles)	66.3	76.4	90	120
Operating expenses (in millions of rubles)	42.8	55	80	179
Profit (in millions of rubles)	23.5	21.4	10	49[a]

[a] Deficit.

Table 7.23. Profits from Surface Transit Operations

	1966	1969	1970	1971	1972
Surface transit payments to (from) the city budget (in millions of rubles)	28.7	4.9	(4.2)	(10.8)	(22.8)

expansion. Consequently, much longer and therefore less profitable surface routes have been designed, primarily for buses. Between 1971 and 1974 alone, there was an increase in passengers of 25 percent. This necessitated the creation of 60 new surface transit routes and 78 miles of new trolleybus lines. There are currently 420 surface routes, of which 310 are bus routes, including 78 express bus lines and 33 minibus or "route taxi" lines.

It should be noted also that revenue growth has been restricted because the fares of 5 kopeks for Metro and buses, 4 kopeks for trolleybus, and 3 kopeks for tram have not been revised in many years despite rising costs. Furthermore, the fare is the same regardless of the distance traveled.

Wages constitute a substantial portion of operating costs. On the average, a bus driver receives a monthly wage of 280 rubles compared with 190 for taxi drivers. The actual wage an individual receives depends upon several factors, including his classification as a first-, second-, or third-class driver, the type of vehicle he operates, and his performance record.

For the first 18 to 24 months on the job, a driver is classified as third class and operates a standard 75-passenger bus (including standees). If at the end of that period he has a good record, he receives additional training in other vehicles, takes a written examination, and may become a second-class driver, and after more training and examinations, he becomes a first-class driver.

As an example of the effect of other factors on a driver's wage, one who operates a 200-passenger articulated bus may receive a 50 percent higher wage than one of the same class who operates a standard vehicle. In addition, a 60 percent bonus over the base wage is available to drivers with a good on-time performance record.

On the whole, drivers receive by far the most attractive benefit package of the bus enterprise's employees. At some depots, a driver can expect a nearby and comfortable apartment to be made available (at the usual low rent) after 10 years of good service. On the other hand, mechanics earn some 50 to 60 percent less than bus drivers.

Freight Transport

Although not traditionally considered a municipal service in the United States, the transport of urban freight has been organized into one of the major agencies of the Moscow City Executive Committee. Glavmosavtotrans (Main Moscow Administration for Auto Transport) consists of 70 enterprises with over 37,000 vehicles and 96,000 employees. It was formed in 1955 to replace a system of over 3,000 individual trucking firms. By 1974, it had grown to an operation with revenues of 500 million rubles and a gross profit of 120 million rubles. The profit increased to 149 million rubles by 1976. About 40 percent of these profits is retained by the agency for capital investments, various incentive programs, and sociocultural activities for its workers. The average freight rate is 24 kopeks per kilometer for trips of more than 1,000 kilometers and 20 kopeks per kilometer for shorter trips. These rates are further adjusted depending upon the need for special equipment or auxiliary services.

Some figures will indicate the scope of the services provided by Glavmosavtotrans. It hauls more than 200 million tons per year, including 70 percent of the construction materials, 95 percent of the freight to railroads, airports, and riverports, 99 percent of goods sold in the municipal trade network, and 100 percent of the food and supplies needed by restaurants and cafes.

Glavmosavtotrans maintains a modern computing center that employs some 1,200 people. It is a general usage organization, self-supporting, which serves some 100 enterprises. It maintains 14 branch terminals at the major transportation facilities around the city, and turns over approximately 3.5 million rubles per year.

The main areas of work at the center include the following:

1. Development of optimal routing for various agencies, utilizing the center's computerized model of the Moscow road network and traffic constraints;
2. Development of pickup and delivery routes and daily schedules for the agency's own trucks, including integrated transport and assembly schedules for the Main Administration of (Housing) Construction;
3. Development and monitoring of the various plans for all constituent entities of Glavmosavtotrans;
4. Maintenance of all accounts for the agency, payroll, billing, truck and team performance, and so forth.

Traffic Control

Traffic control has become a growing problem in Moscow as the number of vehicles has increased rapidly in recent years. The city is still without any modern expressways other than the peripheral ring highway that forms its boundary with the surrounding Moscow oblast or province. At the present time, there are estimated to be approximately 300,000 private autos, 300,000 government-owned vehicles, and over 100,000 trucks registered in the city. In addition, large numbers of vehicles, primarily trucks, enter the city for business purposes from surrounding areas.

The approach that the city is taking to relieve the traffic problem has several elements. First, access to the central core of the city is restricted during working hours to those vehicles having necessary business in the area. Each vehicle entitled to enter the area carries a large permit on the windshield or on top of the dashboard.

Second, key radial and circular highways are being improved through the construction of pedestrian and vehicular underpasses.

Third, parking garages are beginning to be constructed on the periphery of the core so as to allow a "park-and-ride" type of movement into the core.

Fourth, a major computer-controlled traffic signal system is being developed for the principle arteries of the city. This system, called "Start," combines the principle of the "green" or "running" wave, which is widely used throughout the world for controlling traffic flow, with dynamic computer control and heavy emphasis on the feedback of visual information to the driver. The system improves upon the traditional "green-wave" method by making real-time adjustments to the length of the wave based on sensor data indicating traffic density and distribution on the road in question, as well as the demands of cross traffic. Furthermore, there are such visual aids as the traffic signals themselves, indicators that display the current speed at which the wave is moving along the road, and longitudinal displays mounted on the road median parallel to the street, which indicate by red or green lights whether a given car is currently within the green-wave segment, or whether it will be met by a red traffic signal at the next intersection. Construction of this system is now underway for trial on a limited basis.

Finally, a system of expressways is being contemplated and incorporated in the longer-range construction plans of the city.

Perhaps one of the more effective steps to control traffic congestion has recently been taken, with the doubling of the price of gasoline in the Soviet Union and accompanying increases in the cost of parts and service. This is clearly a manifestation of the official policy that private autos should be used only for recreation and that, with very few exceptions, mass transit should be used by urban residents to travel to work. [Note: Nevertheless, automobile-owning professionals appear to be no less addicted to driving to work than their U.S. counterparts.]

PUBLIC SERVICES

Organization

A single municipal administration is entrusted with the task of cleaning and maintaining streets and other public areas in Moscow. The Administration of Roads and Public Services is responsible for such services as street cleaning; the repair and maintenance of roads, bridges, elevated highways, tunnels, pedestrian underpasses, city ponds, and reservoirs; household refuse collection; and refuse disposal. Street cleaning and maintenance are performed in part by the city administration itself and in part by subordinate raion administrations of the same name. Household refuse collection is performed entirely by the raion administrations.

Administration of Roads and Public Services

The Administration of Roads and Public Services is subordinate both to the Moscow City Executive Committee and to the R.S. F.S.R. Ministry of Communal Services. Figure 7.13 illustrates the administrative organization of the agency.

The Production Technology Section develops productivity programs that are required elements of the service plans of each enterprise. The Technology and Cleaning Organization Section treats certain methodological questions regarding techniques for cleaning and service delivery. The Safety Section is concerned with the promulgation of safety regulations for the operation of the administration's special equipment. The Roads and Pavements Unit is responsible for the maintenance of the streets, sidewalks, and roadways of the city.

The complex of centrally administered enterprises and trusts as well as the functions of the raion administrations will be discussed below.

The administration has at its disposal the research output of the K. D. Pamfilov Academy of Communal Services. This branch of the R.S.F.S.R. Ministry of Communal Services is responsible for the development of new equipment and processes for use in municipal

Figure 7.13. Organizational Structure of the Moscow Administration of Roads and Public Services.

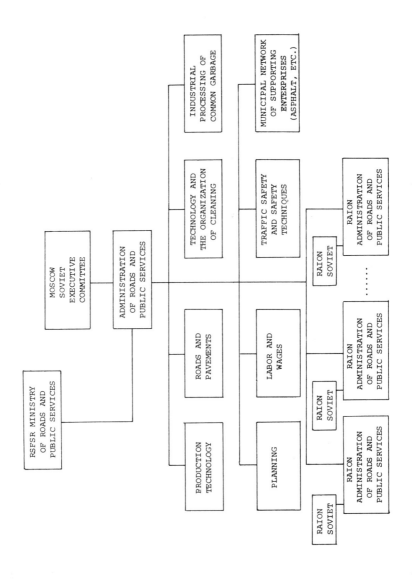

143

service delivery. With a 1971 budget of 218 million rubles, the academy conducts research in a wide variety of areas including service delivery norms, technology, improved chemicals to aid snow removal, the development of multipurpose vehicles and auxiliary equipment, and resource recovery from household refuse.

Subordinate to the administration is a complex of enterprises that provide that portion of the service administered centrally. Figure 7.14 illustrates the relationships of these enterprises and trusts to the city administration. The administration has 10,000 vehicles and 20,000 employees. Total capital investments by the administration for the year 1971 amounted to 67.33 million rubles.

The Hydrotechnology and Bridge Trust services all of the city's bridges, overpasses, pedestrian underpasses, tunnels, reservoirs, storm sewers, and other engineering installations.

The Moscow Belt Highway Division is a separate segment of the administration dedicated to the maintenance and repair of the ring highway that is the actual boundary of Moscow and completely encircles it.

The Asphalt and Concrete Trust provides the municipal and raion road maintenance enterprises with the necessary supply of these materials.

The Construction Materials Trust provides the administration with all other operational materials and supplies, but has no connection with the Main Administration for Construction Materials.

The Trust of Operating Production Enterprises includes the enterprises that operate the garbage disposal facilities.

The Test Design Bureau and the Experimental Mechanical Plant work together to design, construct, and test innovative experimental equipment, including garbage trucks, sand spreaders, etc. They frequently work in close contact with the Pamfilov Academy on various projects. The Experimental Mechanical Plant also carries out major capital repairs on older vehicles belonging to the administration.

The City Mechanical Trust (Gordormekhanizatsiya) is the key agency in the repair, maintenance, and winter and summer cleaning of the major thoroughfares of Moscow. Major roads and highways (excluding the Belt Highway) account for some 18 million square meters of the total street area of more than 68 million square meters. This network of over 500 streets is cleaned and maintained by the City Mechanical Trust.

Figure 7.14. Subordinate Enterprises of the Moscow Administration of Roads and Public Services.

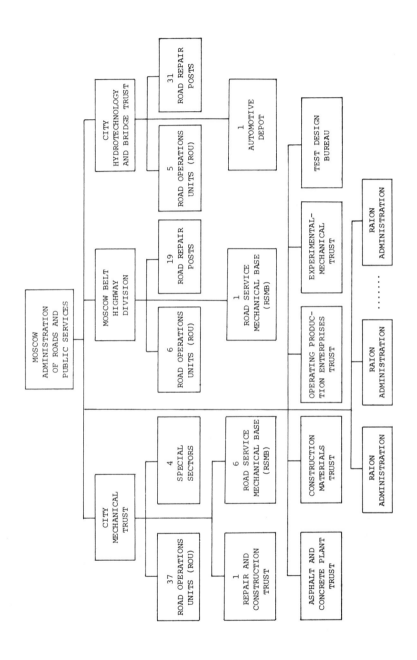

Secondary roads, amounting to approximately 40 million square meters in area, are maintained by individual enterprises of the raion administrations of roads and public services. The remaining roads, primarily interior streets within housing complexes or industrial areas, are maintained by their local housing offices and industrial enterprises responsible for their immediate surrounding area.

The City Mechanical Trust consists of 37 Road Operations Units (ROU), one Repair and Construction Unit (RCU), 6 Road Service Mechanical Bases (RSMB), and 4 Special Sectors. Each ROU is assigned a specific set of streets in the city for which its employees perform cleaning and repair operations. The average area served by a unit is 490,000 square meters.

The mechanized equipment used by the employees of the ROUs is maintained and repaired by the six Mechanical Bases. Each specializes in a particular type or group of vehicles. The more modern bases utilize conveyor belt or assembly line methods of equipment maintenance. The trust has 6,000 of the 10,000 vehicles in the administration.

The RCU is responsible for capital road construction and repair. The four Special Sections handle certain specific types of equipment and operations that do not fall into the domain of the ROUs or RSMBs.

Raion Administrations of Roads and Public Services

Each of the city's raion soviet executive committees has subordinate to it an administration of roads and public services. These agencies are responsible for the maintenance and repair of roads of raion subordination (approximately 40 million square meters), for their winter and summer cleaning, and for the collection of all household refuse.

In order to carry out these duties, each raion administration has several ROUs, an RCU, and an RSMB. Each ROU receives the street cleaning, snow removal, and road repair vehicles it requires from the RSMB. Refuse collection trucks are supplied also, together with drivers. As in the case of the City Mechanical Trust, there are some RSMBs that are quite modern and efficient in their maintenance duties. On the other hand, a significant number are obsolete and are the subject of criticism in the Party press. Moscow is in the midst of a major program to replace all existing outmoded equipment depots (garages). As of 1976, there were ten modern garages completed, six under construction, and seven more that had been designed and documented in preparation for construction. This would leave up to 9 garages requiring attention.

Housing Operation Offices (Zheks)

As described in the first section of this chapter, Housing Operations Officer are responsible for administering local clusters of residential buildings and their accompanying internal streets and grounds. There are over 600 such zheks in Moscow. It need only be recalled at this point that each zhek maintains and cleans its internal roads, contracting with the raion enterprises for any cleaning or repair work that requires machinery or special crews. Furthermore, whereas the raion budgets appropriate funds to support street maintenance and cleaning operations, refuse removal is funded through contracts drawn up with each zhek and institutions serviced by the raion administration. In the area of refuse collection, therefore, the zheks develop contracts for collection services in their areas, and organize the flow of refuse from individual households into centralized pickup areas.

Inspection Organizations

A number of central organizations monitor the performance of the service enterprises. They include the Administrative Inspectorate of the Moscow City Soviet Executive Committee, the various raion inspectorates, the sanitation-epidemiological stations, and the permanent commissions (of deputies) for roads and public services of the city and raion soviets.

These groups inspect streets, buildings, and courtyards in order to evaluate the work of municipal, raion, and zhek employees. Deficiencies are rectified through critical publicity, legislative action, and the imposition of penalties. In the first six months of 1971, the Administrative Inspectorate found a total of 25,000 infractions of all kinds, and imposed 8,500 administrative penalties.

Table 7.24. The Moscow Street and Public Works System

Total street length, 1970	3,462	kilometers
Total street area, 1970	68.277	million square meters
Total sidewalk area, 1970	31.124	million square meters
Total street area cleaned mechanically, 1970	8	million square meters
Total street area cleaned mechanically, 1975 goal	11	million square meters
No. of overpasses and bridges in city	247	
No. of other engineering structures	170	
Length of water system	2,480	kilometers
Length of utility manifolds maintained	167	kilometers
Area of reservoirs	170	hectares
Area of rivers and streams	260	hectares

Note: A hectare is 10,000 square meters, or 11,960 square yards, or 2.471 acres.

Road Cleaning and Maintenance

Service Structure

As mentioned above, street and sidewalk cleaning and maintenance operations are performed for the most part by the city and raion administrations for roads and public services, as well as by the zheks and industrial enterprises that maintain their own interior roads. As with the zheks, a large industrial complex may either maintain its roads with internal resources or contract with the local raion to have the work performed. Table 7.24 provides some data on the Moscow street and public works system. Tables 7.25 and 7.26 illustrate recent and planned levels of street service in the city.

Table 7.25. Recent and Planned Street Services

	1966	1970	1966-70	1971	1975	1971-75
Cost of street lighting (in millions of rubles)	6.4	8.7	40.4			
Cost of street cleaning (in millions of rubles)	12.6	19.3	71.6		20+	
Cost per square meter of cleaning (in kopeks)	48.4	41				
Capital investments in road services (in millions of rubles)			256[a]			378[b]
including						
Road improvements (in millions of square meters)			5			6.2
Intersections constructed (no.)			7			4
Overpasses constructed (no.)			8			9
Pedestrian underpasses constructed (no.)			56			37
Bridges constructed (no.)			2			5
Density of road network (in kilometers per square kilometer)			3.36			4.35

[a]The 256 million rubles was spent in the following manner: construction of engineering structures, 100 million; roads, 131 million; development of production base, 20 million.

[b]This figure includes 40 million rubles per year for road work.

Table 7.26. Work Measures for a Winter Quarter in Moscow, January to March 1978

Activity	Unit of Measure	Planned	Actual
Construction of new roads[a]	1,000 rubles	3,838	4,071
Industrial construction	1,000 rubles	2,442	2,579
Capital highway repairs	1,000 square meters	47	78
Current repairs	1,000 square meters	172	272

[a]By the City Mechanical Trust.

Table 7.27. Road Construction Material per 1,000 Square Meters of Paved Roads and Streets

			Type of Street or Road		
Type of Surface	Material Used in Each Layer	Unit of Measure	Highways and High-Speed Roads	Raion Roads	Local Roads
Cement	Cement	Cubic meter	250	200	160
Stone pavement	Paving blocks or slabs	Cubic meter	170	180	180
	Sand	Cubic meter	40	40	40
	Rubble mixed with astringent	Cubic meter	100	120	120
	Rubble	Cubic meter	250	330	330
Asphalt	Asphalt	Ton	140	120	100
	Rubble mixed with astringent	Ton	140	—	—
	Rubble	Cubic meter	350	430	360
Rubble mixed with astringent	Rubble mixed with astringent	Ton	140	110	140
	Rubble	Cubic meter	350	430	400

Note: Data do not include material used in lower levels

Road Repair and Transportation Indexes

Yearly expenditures for upkeep and repairs are calculated based on the following standardized data:

1. Expenditures on upkeep and routine repairs for 1,000 square meters of asphalt road surface will average 200 rubles.
2. The cost of capital repairs for 1,000 square meters of asphalt road surface will average 4,000 rubles.
3. The average length of time between repairs for asphalt surface is ten years. Therefore, the yearly expenditure on upkeep and repair for 1,000 square meters of surface is 200 + 4,000/10 = 600 rubles.

Tables 7.27 and 7.28 illustrate certain norms that have been set for the surfacing and repair of city streets.

Street-Cleaning Production Plan

The development of a street-cleaning plan is essential to the effective delivery of this service. There is a set of steps and planning norms that guide the development of the production plan:

1. Each year the Moscow City Executive Committee approves the list of streets to be cleaned mechanically, that is, by mechanized sweepers.
2. The City Administration of Roads and Public Services draws up lists of thoroughfares to be assigned to each agency subordinate to it.
3. Streets with a traffic density of greater than 1,000 vehicles per hour are washed once a day.
4. Gutters of these streets are also washed once daily and swept four times per day; secondary and tertiary streets receive correspondingly less service.
5. The enterprise must maximize vehicle utilization and labor efficiency.

Table 7.28. Standard Use of Materials for the Repair and Maintenance of 1,000 Square Meters of City Streets

Work	Materials
Changing or repaving any kind of surface with asphalt	Asphalt mixture—100 tons Bitumen—500 liters Other road construction materials— 10% of repair work
Repaving the upper layer with a hard surface	Bitumen—100 liters Dross (or sand)—5 cubic meters

Other types of repairs on all types of road surfaces	Asphalt mixture—10 tons
	Bitumen—1,000 liters
	Mineral dust—20% of a third of the
	  bitumen used in routine repairs
	  (by weight)
	Other materials—10% of repair work

Table 7.29 illustrates the planning calculations required to develop a production program for street and sidewalk cleaning.

Because of uncertainty about the weather, allowance must be made in the volume of work for time spent with workers and equipment on a standby status.

Examples of formulas for the number of vehicles needed by an enterprise for street cleaning in the winter are as follows for snow removal equipment:

$$M = \frac{P_1 K_1 K_2}{P_r K_{isp} V},$$

where M is the number of vehicles; P_1 is the area of the traveled part of the street to be mechanically cleared (1,000 square meters); K_1 is a coefficient that accounts for the part of the area P_1 to be processed by machines of the given type; K_2 is a coefficient that specifies the number of times the service is provided in a 24-hour period; P_r is the productivity of the vehicle (1,000 square meters per hour); V is the time allowed for each cleaning (hours); and K_{isp} is the coefficient of stock usage.

A separate formula is presented for the number of snow loaders and rotary snow removers, since their productivity is expressed in cubic meters per hour:

$$M = \frac{P_1 KS}{P_r V_r d K_u K_{isp}},$$

where M is the number of vehicles required; P_1 is the area of the traveled part of the street that is to be cleared mechanically (1,000 square meters); K is a coefficient that accounts for the removal of snow that is thrown from the roofs and cleared from courtyards; P_r is the productivity of the snow loader or rotary snow remover (cubic meters per hour); V_r is the duration of the presence of the vehicle on line (hours); d is the time allowed for each clearing (hours); K_u is a coefficient expressing the increase in the density of the snow between the time it falls and the time it is loaded; and K_{isp} is the coefficient of equipment usage.

Street-Cleaning Operations

In 1970, 19 million rubles was spent on summer and winter cleaning, including 14 million on snow removal, of which 11 million was spent to cart away the snow. In 1976, some 16 million cubic meters of snow was hauled. Table 7.30 lists the types of vehicles used by the city in its snow removal operations.

Table 7.29. Volume of Work for Street Cleaning

| Type of Operation | Area of Service in Square Meters | Mode of Operation | | Unit of Measure | Volume of Work (Equivalent Area) |
		Days	Times per day		
Winter Period					
Mechanized sweeping of streets during snowfall	750	84	7	Square meter	441,000
The same, without snowfall	750	82	1	Square meter	61,500
Mechanized sweeping of sidewalks during snowfall	85	84	7	Square meter	49,980
The same, without snowfall	85	82	1	Square meter	6,970
Spreading of sand on the streets	450	87	1	Square meter	39,150
The same, on sidewalks	51	87	1	Square meter	4,437
Carting of snow					
Mechanized loading	710	a		Cubic meter	426
Carting of snow to snow dumps by vehicles	710	—	—	Ton	292
Throwing of snow by rotary snow removers	270	a		Cubic meter	324
Time during which cleaning vehicles are on duty	—	—	—	Vehicle-hour	78
Summer Period					
Mechanized sweeping of streets	450	233	3	Square meter	314,550
The same, of sidewalks	85	233	3	Square meter	59,415
Washing of streets	1,000	196	1	Square meter	19,600

[a] Amount of snow, 0.6 cubic meter per square meter.

Source: A. I. Feinberg, *Ekonomika, Organizatsiya, i Planirovania Gorodskevo Khoziaistva*, Moscow, Izdatelstvo Literatury p stroitelstvu, 1969, p. 361.

Table 7.30. Types of Vehicles Used in Snow Removal

	1970	1971
Snowplows	920	983
Snow loaders	420	438
Sand spreaders	610	628
Rotary snow removers	125	124
Others (road graders, sand loaders, bulldozers, excavators, etc.)	NA	580

NA, not available.

Crews are on duty 24 hours a day during the winter to respond to emergencies. When snow begins to fall, the first phase of snow removal includes the shoveling and sweeping of the snow, the spreading of sand and chemicals to prevent the packing down of the snow and the formation of ice, and the parting of snowbanks at street crossings, city transportation stops, gates, etc. A sand-salt mixture or a mixture of chemicals (mostly chlorides) is spread on the streets at the beginning of the snowfall. After the snow has accumulated for three to five hours, it is swept or plowed. Sand spreaders follow the plows, and the process is repeated until the snowfall ends.

Generally, all of one side of a two-way street is cleared at one time. The first plow or brush moves down the middle of the street. It is usually driven by a veteran who knows the route and can set the speed and interval for the plows following. The interval is usually set at 15 to 20 meters between plows, with an overlap of the strip cleared of about 0.3 to 0.5 meter. The overlap may be greater on especially wide streets or during heavy snowfalls. In especially heavy snowfalls, a two-pass system may be used. During the second pass, brushes are used to remove the layer left.

The second phase of the snow removal operation is either to form a regularly shaped snowbank along the edge of the street or to throw the snow into adjacent vacant lots with rotary snow removers. The snowbanks are shaped, usually by a special vehicle, so that the snow can be loaded into dump trucks by a special snow-loading vehicle. A small gutter is left along the edge of the snowbank next to the sidewalk to allow water to run off when the snow melts and to help the snow loaders keep off the sidewalk. Gutters are cleaned after the snow is banked, and any packed snow or ice must be removed from the street.

As was noted above, the most expensive phase in snow removal is carting it to permanent disposal sites. In the winter of 1969-70, the snow was disposed of in the following ways: 17.6 million cubic meters was carried away by vehicles (to be dumped in rivers or vacant lots); 9.2 million cubic meters was moved by rotary snow removers (onto adjacent lots); and 0.76 million cubic meters was thrown into snow chambers connected to underground rivers.

Snow is dumped at points along the Yauza and Moscow Rivers. As of 1971, there were eight concrete snow-unloading piers on the Moscow River. The piers are equipped with fixed-screw propellers in the water that create a strong current in an area of about 40 by 7 meters. This helps to ensure that the river does not freeze near the pier and that the snow will melt and be carried away in the water. At that time, there were also 15 other snow-unloading points along the two rivers. At these points, the barriers are taken down from along the street above the river and are replaced by wooden beams to stop the trucks' wheels when they back up to the river. The river dumping points are becoming more and more important because vacant lots are becoming more scarce.

The enterprises have targets for snow removal. For snowfalls of less than 10 centimeters, all work should be completed in three days. Snow removal from sidewalks is the responsibility of the housing units or commercial enterprises.

Cleaning of the streets in summer has much in common with snow removal, in that the street-cleaning organizations are called upon to clean ever-increasing areas and to use increasing levels of mechanization. As was implied above, of 19 million rubles spent on street cleaning in 1970, only 5 million was spent on summer cleaning.

Summer street cleaning consists of washing and sweeping the streets. The washing is done in a fashion similar to the way plowing is done in the winter. On broad thoroughfares, several vehicles wash all of one side of a two-way street or all of a one-way street in one pass. They follow one after the other at intervals of 10 to 20 meters, each washing a strip of 5 to 6 meters with an overlap of 0.7 to 1.0 meter. Streets less than 12 meters wide are washed by a single vehicle. A special nozzle is attached to the vehicle that washes the gutter of the street to avoid throwing trash onto the sidewalk and greenery. Streets are usually washed between 11 p.m. and 6 a.m.

Only parts of the streets where litter actually accumulates are swept. These are usually the gutters and sometimes the middle of a street. Usually the strip to be swept can be covered by one vehicle, and columns of vehicles are an exception. Sweeping usually is done between 7 a.m. and 8 p.m.

Refuse Collection and Disposal

The raion administrations of roads and public services are responsible for the collection of household refuse. Three broad categories of refuse may be considered: industrial, construction, and demolition waste; food wastes from households and food service enterprises; and, finally, other household refuse.

Commercial, construction, and demolition waste amounts to approximately 2.5 million cubic meters annually in volume. It is collected and disposed of by a variety of construction, transportation, and other agencies. As this is not a municipal service, it will not be considered further here.

Food wastes are collected separately from other household refuse. A special office within the City Main Housing Administration, called the Procurement Office for Unplanned Feed, encourages and organizes the collection process. Working with the officials and staff of the zheks, this office arranges for the centralization within each housing unit of all food wastes and their removal by special crews of the local equipment depot (RSMB) of the raion administration. The material is subsequently sold to local farms for hog feed.

In addition to exhorting cooperation with this program, the Procurement Office distributes a portion of the revenues obtained from the sale of feed to certain zhek employees. For each ton of feed collected, 8 rubles is paid to the custodians and cleaning women, 1 ruble 20 kopeks is paid to the chief engineer, and 30 kopeks is paid to the zhek director.

In 1970, 1.7 million rubles was distributed for 176,000 tons of food waste. About 40 percent of the tonnage came from households, with the remainder produced by restaurants and other food service enterprises. By 1974, the total collected had grown to 220,000 tons.

Household refuse collection is carried out by employees of the ROU of the Raion Administration of Roads and Public Services, using trucks and drivers supplied by the raion equipment depot. Since this constitutes the major portion of the refuse collection activity in the city, its planning and operation will be considered in some detail.

Planning

Refuse is to be collected from all dwellings, schools, hospitals, and children's institutions. It must be collected according to a definite schedule and precise route. Generally, there is daily service, with certain buildings receiving twice-daily pickups.

The production plan for refuse collection, prepared annually, takes into consideration the number and types of vehicles available, the capacity and productivity of the vehicles, and the coefficient of utilization of the vehicle fleet (percentage of trucks available at any given time). The plan is based on certain norms and parameters:

1. Per capita refuse generation is 0.9 cubic meters per year (up from 0.4 cubic meters in 1969).
2. The refuse density is 0.2 metric ton per cubic meter (down from 0.4 metric ton per cubic meter in 1969).
3. Collection vehicles are to be used every day for an average of 1.5 shifts, or 11.6 hours per day.

Details of the subsequent calculations will not be given here. They are similar to those used in the street-cleaning production program illustrated above. Upon completion of the production plans, they become the key components of the annual planning activity for the enterprises. The completed enterprise plans are considered by the local administrative organs, in this case, the City Administration of Roads and Public Services. The administration, with Executive Committee approval, sends its draft plans to both the R.S.F.S.R. Gosplan and the R.S.F.S.R. Ministry of Communal Services. These central organs are primarily concerned with matching the local indicators for capital investment (principally the need for additional vehicles) with the output of plants producing this equipment and with preparing plans for material and technical supply.

Once the plan is approved by the central organs, it is returned to the city organs, the Executive Committee, and the Administration of Roads and Public Services. At this point, the most important element of the plan consists of a set of tasks expressed as indicators that are to be fulfilled during the plan year. The city organs make these tasks more detailed and precise while dividing them among subordinate organizations, e.g., the City Mechanical Trust and the raion administrations of roads and public services, and by adding additional tasks not specified by the central organs. The same process occurs at the trust and raion level. When an enterprise finally receives its plan, it must devise operating plans for shorter periods, usually of one month, and for each individual shop, service, or brigade within the enterprise. At this level, the plan must be very simple and concrete.

The final plan of each enterprise is made up of nine parts:

1. The basic quantitative goals, which include those approved by higher organizations (these are discussed below) and those set by the enterprise itself;

2. The production and sales plan, which considers the demand for and use of productive capacity;
3. The plan for increasing productive efficiency, which includes measures for the introduction of new technology and processes; organizational improvements; material, fuel, and energy savings; and quality improvements;
4. The capital construction plan, which includes additions to capacity and basic resources as well as capital investments and repairs;
5. The material-technical plan, which includes needs and sources for supplies;
6. The labor and wage plan, which includes the number of workers and their salaries and measures for improving labor productivity and training qualified personnel;
7. The cost plan, which includes product costs and operating expenditures;
8. The funds plan, which includes measures for the formation and distribution of economic stimulation funds, i.e., funds for material incentives (bonuses), for sociocultural measures (employee programs of various kinds), for housing construction, and for productive development;
9. The financial plan, which includes revenues and receipts, expenditures and deductions, profitability and the distribution of profits, interrelation with the budget, and credit interrelations.

There are seven plan indicators, alluded to above, which are approved by higher organs:

1. Total revenues from all products (services) according to existing tariffs;
2. Net profits;
3. Payments into the budget (transfers to higher organs) and allocations from the budget (receipts from higher organs);
4. Total wage fund;
5. Detailed plans to introduce new technology and technical processes, complex mechanisms, and automation, which are important for the given branch;
6. Volume of centralized capital investments, including capital repair;
7. Volume of supply of materials to the enterprise, of stockpiled materials, and of equipment and transportation resources required from higher organizations.

In the case of the refuse collection function of the raion administrations, the sources of revenue, the first indicator, are the housing organizations (zheks) that the administrations serve. Standard agreements that set the rate of payment must be established each year between the raion administrations and each of the zheks within the raion. Figure 7.15 illustrates the relationship of the organizations that provide and receive sanitation services in Moscow. The amount of payment is determined by calculating the cost of removing one cubic meter of refuse, taking into consideration the type of vehicle used and the distance the refuse must be carted. These parameters are translated into costs through application of the cost law. This cost (which ranges from 1.15 to 2.20 rubles per cubic meter) is then multiplied by the expected

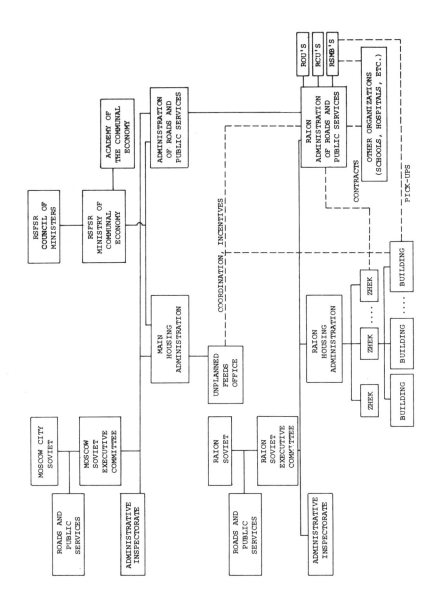

158

Table 7.31. Cost Structure of the Moscow Refuse Collection Enterprises

Article of Expenditure	Percentage of Total
Auxiliary materials and water	1.5
Fuel and lubricating materials	9.3
Amortization	10.8
Current repairs and maintenance of vehicles	14.3
Wage payments—basic and supplementary	42.5
Additions to wages	2
Shop, general operating, and overhead expenses	19.6
	100

Source: A. I. Feinberg, *Ekonomika, Organizatiya, i Planirovania Gorodskevo Khoziaistva,* Moscow, Izdatelstvo Piteratury p stoitelstvu, 1969, p. 380.

yearly refuse accumulation of the housing organization. Thus, the volume of refuse and distance carted make up the primary determinants of cost. The total cost for the city is more than 12 million rubles per year. The cost structure of the Moscow refuse collection enterprise is shown in Table 7.31.

A word should be said about the funds plan. The funds plan includes measures for the formation and distribution of economic stimulation funds. There are three such funds: (1) the material incentive fund; (2) the sociocultural and housing fund; and (3) the fund for the development of production. The reasons for the establishment of these as well as the methods of their formation and distribution are common to all Soviet industries. The fund for the development of production is simply one source of enterprise capital investment. The formation and distribution of the first two funds depend upon the fulfillment of indicators that vary greatly from industry to industry. They reflect the areas in which the state planning authorities believe workers can make improvements in each industry and thus the ones in which they are being encouraged to do so. The indicators for services as a whole are intended to augment the interest of workers in increasing the volume of services, improving the quality and nature of the services, bettering the city, and enlarging profits and profitability. Specific indicators, conditions, and sizes of awards for all types of nonmanagerial workers are set by the managing enterprises and organizations in agree-

Figure 7.15. Organizations That Provide and Receive Sanitation Services.

ment with the corresponding committees of the trade union. These managerial indicators include at least some of the basic indicators for the plan as a whole. The managers of refuse collection enterprises, for example, must fulfill the schedule for collection in order to qualify for an award.

The economic stimulation funds represent only one approach toward improving worker productivity and interest in and identification with the performance of the enterprise. Socialist competition is another program with the same goal. It apparently is not reflected in the plan, but should be discussed here along with the stimulation funds. Competition between collectives of workers is said to be a primary means of improving the operation of enterprises. There is competition between and within cities in maintaining the territory of households and streets in proper sanitary condition. The competition is with respect to the timely removal of refuse, its disposal in accordance with sanitary-technical standards, and the recovery of valuable materials from it.

Socialist competition is said to be widespread in the City Mechanical Trust. Thirty-three hundred of its workers take part in the Movement for Communist Labor. Of these, 1,590 have earned the title of "Shock Worker of Communist Labor." Sixty subdivisions are competing for the title of "Collective of Communist Labor." Seventy-two others have already earned this title. [One could infer from these figures that these titles are not especially difficult to earn, and thus may be of only marginal use as incentives.]

Operations

The first steps in the refuse collection process are taken by the tenants and workers of the zheks. It is their responsibility to see that garbage is preseparated into food wastes, refuse, and scrap paper, and that it is placed where it can be picked up. How this is done depends upon whether the building in question is equipped with refuse chutes or not. Generally, older and smaller buildings do not have them. In these buildings, it is the tenants' responsibility to separate their refuse into the three categories. Tenants deposit food wastes into containers kept in the hallways or right in the apartments. These containers are removed each day by housing workers of the building and either placed in temporary storage or emptied into larger receptacles. If the temporary storage location is not in the courtyard where it is accessible to collection trucks, then the housing workers must set the receptacles out to be picked up at the proper time. It is the responsibility of the housing workers to see that the receptacles are kept clean.

In buildings with chutes, the above system is still used for edible garbage. The chutes are used only for inedible refuse. It is the responsibility of the housing workers to see to it that the receptacles into which the refuse falls are not allowed to overflow and that they are moved out to the proper location for collection at the proper time.

Once the garbage has been sorted and placed out into the courtyards, the employees of the raion administrations of roads and public services pick it up and cart it away to disposal sites. Separate routes are maintained for the collection of food wastes and refuse. There are 150 routes in the city for the former and 860 for the latter.

There are at least four types of vehicles now used for refuse collection. Of the two oldest types, which apparently now collect less than 20 percent of the refuse, one is just a plain dump truck and the other is an enclosed truck similar to a dump truck that is equipped with a compacting mechanism. [Note: The compaction ratio is only 1.6, which is very low compared with that of the modern trucks used in the United States.] When these trucks are used, the receptacles must be small enough (80 to 100 liters) to be lifted by hand and dumped into the truck. They must then be washed by the housing workers of the building. The use of manual labor in carrying, lifting, and washing the receptacles is the main shortcoming of these vehicles.

The third type of vehicle used at the present time, which accounts for more than 80 percent of collection, uses containers. Basically, it consists of a flatbed truck mounted with a crane and a framework for holding eight rectangular containers. Upon reaching the area where a building's receptacles are stored, the crane is used to remove a clean, empty container from the truck and place it on the ground. A full container is then picked up by the crane and placed in the vacant place on the truck. All of the full containers are exchanged for empty ones in this way. The framework on the truck is such that it holds each container securely while the truck is in motion. When the truck reaches the place where the containers are to be emptied, the framework tips up in two halves toward the sides of the truck so that the containers, while still securely held, dump their loads on both sides of the truck. After the containers are emptied, they are washed mechanically and are ready for use again. The trucks are equipped to handle three sizes of containers varying from 0.5 to 0.75 cubic meter.

The container system is claimed to have the following advantages: less litter scattered about; no worker contact with the garbage; containers not washed in the vicinity of dwellings; full mechanization of loading and unloading; less metal needed for containers than for the old, smaller receptacles; less blocking of areas around dwellings; operation by a one-person crew.

The system, however, suffers from the lack of compaction. This will probably mean its replacement in the near future after a relatively short period of usage. As early as 1970, it was noted that the empty weight of the vehicle made up 70 to 75 percent of its total loaded weight. At that time, with the average density of inedible refuse being 0.4 metric ton per cubic meter, a truck loaded with eight large, full containers carried about 3.2 tons. The decline in density to 0.2 ton per cubic meter means that a full truck now carries only about 1.6 tons.

At least two alternatives to the present container system of collection are being tried. One is an attempt to eliminate the problems of the container system within the conventional system of garbage collection. A few trucks of Swedish design are now being tested in Moscow. This vehicle, the fourth of the types referred to above, has a capacity of 14 cubic meters and a compaction ratio of three to one, which means that it can carry 42 cubic meters of uncompacted refuse compared with the container truck's capacity of 6 cubic meters. [Note: This is similar to conventional refuse trucks.] The vehicle is also equipped to lift and dump a compatibly designed container automatically. Thus, the vehicle has some of the mechanization advantages of the container system. One problem that the Swedish vehicle does not solve is the mechanized cleaning of containers after they have been emptied into the truck. The Soviets have been trying to develop a vehicle of their own that would compact and carry up to 30 cubic meters of refuse and that would mechanically rinse the containers with disinfectant.

The other more radical solution to the refuse collection problem being tried is the use of a pneumatic system. The system is made up of two parts, one that moves garbage from a group of apartment buildings to a central collection point and another that moves the refuse from there to a disposal site. This system is being developed by several organizations together with the R.S.F.S.R. Academy of Communal Services, and an experimental model was built in Tbilisi during 1970-71.

One pneumatic system is planned for a new housing project in the Severnoe Chertanovo area of Moscow. This system is to be only the first half of the two-part system described above. The refuse will move to the collection point where it will be compacted and loaded onto trucks. In addition, a study was done on the costs that would be involved in installing a complete two-part pneumatic system in the new Lianozovo housing area. The distance from the collection point to a processing plant would be about three or four kilometers. Trains of three or four containers would be used. The capital costs were estimated to be 2.5 rubles per square meter of living space compared with 13 to 15 rubles per square meter for installing a sewer system in a city of 50,000 to 60,000 population. The operating costs estimated for the project were 2 rubles per cubic meter of refuse removed compared with 1.15 rubles per cubic meter using the present system in a similar area. It is argued that the higher costs are justified by the hygienic advantages of the new system and that these costs can be expected to decline with the increasing scale of operation and regular production of the system.

The complete two-part system would be most practical to install in a newly built housing area. However, the second part of the system could be installed in established areas. Trucks would collect the refuse as they do now, but rather than carrying the garbage 25 to 30 kilometers to disposal points, they would bring it to central collection points. There the refuse could be compacted and carried by pneumatic tube to the disposal site. Estimates made in the southeastern part of Moscow indicate that a ten-kilometer pipeline to the dumps in the Kuchinsky Raion (which would later go to the Lyuberetsky refuse-processing plant) would reduce operating costs from the present 2.2 to 1.56 rubles per cubic meter. The project would also release about 230 persons, saving a total of 500,000 rubles per year.

Collection is generally considered to be a simpler problem to solve than refuse disposal. Landfills are still the primary means of disposing of Moscow's garbage, but they give rise to several problems. At present, refuse must be carted 30 to 40 kilometers to landfills that pollute the land, water, and atmosphere around the city, and, if not properly covered, serve as breeding grounds for insects. In addition, the refuse disposed of in landfills contains valuable materials that could be recovered. The alternatives to landfills are plants of various types. Three types of plants are currently in operation in Moscow: refuse burning, refuse sorting, and refuse processing.

The simplest alternative is incineration, but this causes air pollution and requires the disposal of ashes that correspond to 30 to 40 percent of the intitial weight of material burned. Currently there is a plant in Beskudnikovo, which burns about 350,000 cubic meters per year.

Sorting plants also offer only a partial solution to disposal. A plant at Nogatin sorts iron, steel, paper, nonferrous metals, rags, leather,

Table 7.32. Refuse Collection Measures

Planning norm for solid waste generation, per capita, in 1974	0.9 cubic meter
Solid waste collected, 1970	6.5 million cubic meters
Solid waste collected, 1974	8.3 million cubic meters
Solid waste collected, 1976	9.7 million cubic meters
Recovered materials from refuse processing, 1975	
Paper	500,000 tons
Metal	50,000 tons
Textiles, polymer	100,000 tons
Total refuse handled by processing plant, 1977	950,000 cubic meters
Vehicles available for refuse collection, 1973	1,500
Cost of refuse collection, 1973	12 million rubles

etc., from about 400,000 cubic meters of refuse each year. What is left of the refuse after sorting must still be disposed of in landfills.

Processing plants combine incineration, sorting, and mechanical composting. A refuse-processing plant began operating in Korovin in 1972. It was designed to process 500,000 cubic meters of refuse each year. The first step in the process is the magnetic removal of ferrous metals. After being ground and crushed, the refuse is then put into revolving drums, the interior temperature and humidity of which are closely controlled. After three days, the material is removed from the drums. Oversized objects are sorted out by a screening process and are

Table 7.33. Illustrative Activity Measures for the Road and Public Service Administration, January to March 1975

Factor	Unit of Measure	Planned	Actual
Usage coefficient of the refuse collection and highway equipment[a]	—	0.64	0.65
Refuse transported	1,000 cubic meters	2,213	2,266
Food waste transported	Ton	59,380	55,875
Metal waste	Ton	2,725	2,798
Income	1,000 rubles	2,030	2,194

[a]Fraction of the norm that the average vehicle is used per day; the norm is 15 hours per day.

carried away to an adjoining burning plant. The remaining material is allowed to ripen in storage for at least two days before being usable as compost. The compost is used by agencies that are responsible for the city's greenery and horticulture. The city requires 400,000 tons of organic fertilizer each year, which could be provided by six or seven such plants.

It was originally planned that about 60 percent of the incoming garbage to the plant in Korovin would be composted, 30 percent burned, and about 5 percent metallic. Owing to changes in the composition of the refuse, the amounts composted and burned have been approximately reversed. This has led to problems with the capacities of the bunkers where the refuse and intermediate products of the plant are stored. There may have also been problems with incinerator capacity. [Note: The change in refuse composition, which required the prototypic plant to be reengineered, may also be the reason that the decision was made, after building one processing plant, to build only incinerators, at least until 1980.]

Workload

Table 7.32 lists some workload figures for refuse collection and disposal. Table 7.33 illustrates the collective activity of the administration during a recent winter quarter.

The material contained in this section was derived primarily from the original Soviet report for Subtopic I, "A Management Description of the Moscow City Government," and from personal interviews between U.S. authors and municipal officials of Moscow. Some additional data were obtained from the following sources:

James Frahm, *Solid Waste Management in Moscow*, Center for Government Studies, Columbia University, New York, 1977.

B. M. Frolic, "Soviet Urban Politics," Unpublished doctoral thesis, York University, Toronto, 1970.

B. A. Lifshits, "Za Samyi Chistyi Gorod (Towards a Most Clean City)," Moskovskii Rabochii, Moscow, 1973.

B. A. Lifshits, "Prochnaya Proizvodstvennaya Baza–Zalog Uspeshnoi Raboti (A Strong Industrial Base, the Guarantee of Successful Work)," *Gorodskoe Khozyaistvo Moskvu*, pp. 18-21, August 1977.

Yu. M. Safronov, "Upravlenie i Organizatsiya Rabot B Zhilishchnom Khozyaitsve (The Management and Organization of Work in Housing Services)," Stroiizdat, Moscow, 1976.

E. S. Savas, "The Department of Public Services in Moscow: Notes on a Visit," Center for Government Studies, Columbia University, New York, 1975.

F. A. Shevelev, "Rezervi Blagoustroistva (Reserves in the Organization of Public Services)," *Gorodskoe Khozyaistvo Moskvu*, pp. 15-18, December 1974.

Statistical Administration of the City of Moscow, "Moskva B Tsifrakh 1966-1970 (Moscow in Numbers 1966-1970)," Statistika, Moscow, 1971.

Statistical Administration of the City of Moscow, "Moskva B Tsifrakh 1971-1975 (Moscow in Numbers 1971-1975)," Statistica, Moscow, 1976.

F. I. Yangazin and A. H. Mavlenkov, "Mekhanizatsiya Dorozhnikh Rabot (The Mechanization of Road Work)," *Gorodskoe Khozyaistvo Moskvu*, pp. 18-21, December 1974.

WATER AND WASTE WATER

The direct supply of water to the population, city enterprises, and organizations is handled by the Administration of Water and Sewers of the Executive Committee. The administration includes the following trusts: Mosvodoprovod (Moscow Water Supply), Moschistovod (Moscow Water Cleaning), Mosvodokanalprod (Moscow Sewage Industry), and the Moscow Scientific and Research Institute for Water and Sewage. The total number of employees in this system is approximately 16,000, with some 50 employees at the central administration office. Figure 7.16 shows the organization of the administration.

Planning the city water supply and waste water treatment systems is the responsibility of the City Planning Commission, as indicated in Chapter 5. In order to give greater independence to the Water and Sewer Administration as well as to increase its responsibility, the City Soviet Executive Committee approves the annual plans only for a limited number of factors, e.g., the water supply to the network, the amount of waste water processed, the net cost of 1,000 cubic meters of water, the salary fund, capital investments, and new facilities.

Water Supply

In addition to the water supplied from distant sources, water is taken from the Vazuza River, a branch of the Volga. Furthermore, a number of enterprises obtain their own water, using recycling systems to reduce their needs.

At the present time, the average daily water supply amounts to approximately 4.5 million cubic meters. Water stations use 3 to 3.5 percent of the total volume for their local needs, such as cleaning filters.

Figure 7.16. Organizational Structure of the Administration of Water and Sewers.

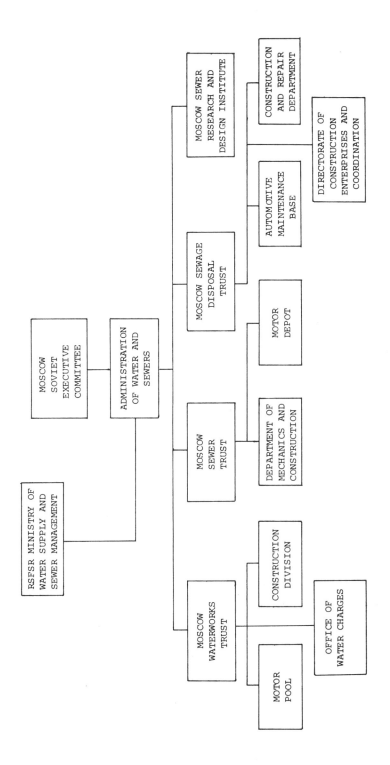

Water meters are used in industry, but there are no meters for individual apartments in residential areas. A charge of 45 kopeks per month per person is included in the rent to cover both water supply and sewage services.

The General Plan for the development of Moscow sets the following long-range goals: daily water supply capacity, 8.1 million cubic meters; utility allowance per capita, 550 liters; daily industrial-grade water supply, 1.3 million cubic meters. The industrial system will use predominantly surface sources and aeration water purification stations;

Table 7.34. Moscow Water Supply System, 1970

Index	All Departments	Administration of Water Supply and Sewage
Water mains, primary (in kilometers)	530.5	525.0
Street pipeline network (in kilometers)	3,936.9	3,867.8
No. of street water outlets (booths, hydrants, taps)	2,021	2,021
Water supply, annual (in thousands of cubic meters)	1,451,705	1,445,670
Average daily water supply to the network (in thousands of cubic meters)	3,960.7	3,960.7
Water passed through the processing facilities (as a percentage of the water in the network)	98.9	98.9
Water for all consumers, annual (in thousands of cubic meters)	1,340,450	1,334,415
Water for utility needs of the population and the enterprises, annual (in thousands of cubic meters)	947,282	941,247
The above (as a percentage of the total amount)	70.5	70.5
Average daily amount per citizen (in liters)	557	557
Operating income from user charges (in rubles)	75,089,000	75,089,000
Operating expenditures (in rubles)	39,925,000	39,925,000
Average income per cubic meter (in kopeks)	5.6	5.6
Average expenditure per cubic meter (in kopeks)	3.1	3.1

circulating (recycling) water supply systems will be used for enterprises requiring large amounts of water.

Basic operating data for the enterprises of the Administration of Water and Sewers and for other organizations whose planning is within the authority of Gorplan are listed in Table 7.34.

Waste Water Treatment

Between 1966 and 1970, the Southeast, Novobratsevskaya, Pokrovsko-glebovskaya, Vihinskaya, and other sewer stations were constructed.

During the 1971-75 period, the construction of the second block of the Novo-Kurianovska aeration station continued. The construction of an aeration station on the Pakhra River has been scheduled. In the future, this station will receive sewage not only from Moscow, but also from the protective forest belt and a number of cities and settlements of the Moscow region.

By 1976, the total length of the sewer network increased to 403 kilometers, and the capacity of the purification facilities reached 5.145 million cubic meters per day. In recent years, the aeration sta-

Table 7.35. Moscow Waste Water Treatment System, 1970

Index	All Departments	Administration of Water Supply and Sewage
Major collecting lines (in kilometers)	102.9	95.9
Sewage network (in kilometers)	2,660.6	2,609.3
Waste water, annual (in thousands of cubic meters)	1,302,488	1,300,389
Average daily amount of waste water (in thousands of cubic meters)	3,562.7	3,562.7
Waste water passed annually through the sewer plants (in thousands of cubic meters)	1,292,294	1,291,805
The above (as percentage of the total)	99.3	99.3
Annual operating income (in rubles)	55,793,000	55,793,000
Annual operating expenditures (in rubles)	31,477,000	31,477,000
Average income per cubic meter of waste water (in kopeks)	4.3	4.3
Average expenditure per cubic meter of waste water (in kopeks)	2.4	2.4

Table 7.36. Growth of Water Supply and Waste Water Systems in Moscow (as percentages)

	(1965 = 100%)			
Measure	1970	1975	1976	1977
Pipeline network	116	129	132	134
Total water supplied	112	132	135	139
Residential water supplied	125	149	153	163
Sewer network	121	133	134	136
Waste water handled	119	143	150	155

tions Lubretskaya and Lublinskaya were substantially expanded and improved. Treated sewage released into the rivers went up to 95 percent of all sewage.

The basic 1970 operating data on the state of the sewage network of all ministries and enterprises of Moscow are listed in Table 7.35. Table 7.36 illustrates the dynamic growth of the water supply and waste water treatment services in the city.

PARKS

There are 16,000 hectares of parks and gardens in Moscow. Of these, 3,400 hectares are city parks, 1,300 are raion parks, squares, and boulevard lanes, 3,100 are nurseries, orchards, and protective belts, and 7,800 are forests. About 70 percent of the green area is located on the periphery of the city.

Responsibility for the parks and green areas in and around Moscow is divided among a number of agencies.

The forest belt that surrounds the city is managed by two agencies of the Moscow oblast or regional (provincial) government, Forest Parks and Forest Trees.

Most large parks in the city (Parks of Culture and Rest) are managed by the Main Administration for Culture of the Moscow City Executive Committee, though a few are under the jurisdiction of the

---

The material contained in this section was derived primarily from the original Soviet report for Subtopic 1, "A Management Description of the Moscow City Government," and from personal interviews between the U.S. authors and municipal officials of Moscow.

Department of Education (Mosgorno) and its Division of Parks. Smaller parks are managed by the raion administrations of culture. The organizational chart of the Main Administration of Culture is shown in Figure 7.17.

Other areas of greenery not formally designated "Park of Culture and Rest" together with street trees and shrubs are under the jurisdiction of the city or raion departments of forests and parks, depending upon their size and usage. Green areas around residential buildings are the responsibility of the zheks that manage the buildings.

Figure 7.17. Organization of the Moscow Main Administration of Culture.

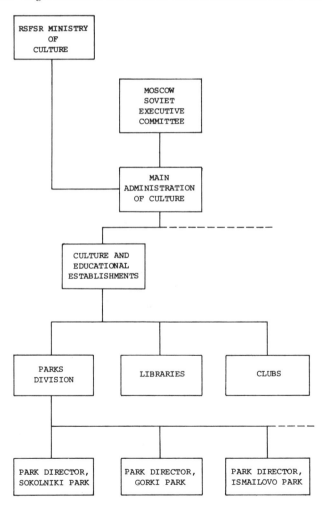

Table 7.37. The Moscow Park System

Employees of the City Forests and Parks Administration, 1976	5,000	
including		
Management and administrative personnel	609	
Budget of the City Forests and Parks Administration, 1975	15.016	million rubles
including		
Salaries (63%)	9.5	million rubles
Amortization and capital investment (5%)	800,000	rubles
Capital repair (4%)	602,000	rubles
1980 per capita goal for green space		
City parks	15	square meters
Raion parks and greenery	10	square meters
1969 per capita water surface in city and forest belt	6	square meters
1980 per capita goal for water surface in city and forest belt	15	square meters

In a similar fashion, recreational facilities are managed by various levels of government, depending on their size and usage. Major stadiums and pools come under the city Department of Physical Culture. Athletic facilities within the raion parks are operated by the raion, whereas local sports fields and playgrounds are operated by the zhek.

In general, the maintenance work performed by the zheks is of an unsophisticated nature, using volunteer labor and simple equipment. Only one-third of the zheks employed specialist gardeners as of December 1974. Should major work be necessary, such as tree replacement, the zhek will pay the Raion Department of Forests and Parks to perform the service.

There are very strict laws regarding fines for damaging trees, shrubbery, and flowers. These may be levied upon individuals (up to half a person's monthly salary) or organizations such as the zheks. The fine may be up to ten times the replacement cost of the damaged plant.

The Moscow City Administration of Forests and Parks was formed in 1964. It deals with the preservation, restoration, improvement, and expansion of green areas as well as the improvement of their

Figure 7.18. Organization of the Moscow Administration of Forests and Parks.

Table 7.39. The Moscow Emergency Ambulance System, 1975

Norm (state law) for no. of ambulances	1 per 10,000 population
Total no. of ambulances	approx. 750
Average no. of ambulances available on a typical day	approx. 350
No. of ambulance stations	27
No. of stations projected for 1980	48
Average no. of calls received per year	1 million
Average no. of ambulance runs per year	800,000
Average no. of calls received on a typical weekday	3,500
Norm for maximum distance of a point from an ambulance station	5 kilometers

The three most common causes for ambulance calls are cardiac arrest, surgical emergency (primarily appendicitis), and neurological disorders. A typical station includes a 24-hour dispatch post and a dispensary, and serves as the base for approximately 15 ambulances. The staff, headed by a director, includes a pediatrician, a specialist in automobile accidents, two obstetricians, a senior doctor, a senior paramedic, and perhaps 40 doctors and 60 paramedics plus drivers. The 15 vehicles are typically available as follows:

Hours of duty	*No. of ambulances*
24 hours	7 (including specialists)
8:00 a.m. - 10:00 p.m.	4
9:00 a.m. - 11:00 p.m.	3
9:30 a.m. - 11:30 p.m.	1

All data pertaining to the receipt of calls, the dispatch of ambulances, the rendering of first aid, and possible hospitalization are keypunched and fed into the department's computer. Analyses are subsequently performed with the aim of improving the management of the system.

TRADE AND PUBLIC FOOD SERVICES

One of the most important factors in the national standard of living is retail trade activity—the sale of food and industrial goods to the population. In 1971, product sales amounted to 10.237 billion rubles. This had risen to 12.7 billion rubles by 1974, and to 15.33 billion rubles by 1977. There are 10,324 trade companies in Moscow.

The structure of trade in Moscow is the following: retail sales establishments, 92.2 percent; public eating places, 7.8 percent.

The sale of industrial products is conducted by 71 commercial organizations. The major one is the Main Administration of Trade of the Moscow City Executive Committee. It covers 96 percent of the trade of industrial products in the city. There also is a cooperative that handles sales from cooperative producers.

Public catering or food service activity is conducted by more than 100 organizations. The major one is the Main Administration of Public Food Services. It handles about 85 percent of prepared food sales.

The development of the trade network and the network of public eating places is planned by the Department of Trade and Food Services of the City Planning Commission. The department consists of 12 people: the department head, 2 deputies, and 9 economic engineers. The work of this department, like that of all other departments, is guided by the laws of the Soviet Union and the R.S.F.S.R., Party resolutions, state resolutions, directives of the State Planning Commissions of the Soviet Union and the R.S.F.S.R., orders of the Ministries of Trade of the Soviet Union and the R.S.F.S.R., decisions and rulings of the Moscow City Executive Committee, decisions of the permanent committees of deputies of the Moscow Soviet, and the working plans and orders of the City Planning Commission.

Organizational Structure

The work of the Main Administration of Trade and the Main Administration of Public Food Services is planned by the Department of Trade and Public Food Services of Gorplan.

The Main Administration of Trade (Glavtorg) organizes work to improve services to the population, to develop the trade networks, and to implement progressive trade methods. Its directives pertaining to trade organization are obligatory for all city trade enterprises. Glavtorg includes specialized departments for industrial and food trade, transportation and storage of vegetables and fruit, and market management.

In the raions, there are raion departments of food trade (raipishtorg). They are managed by the executive committees of the raion soviets and Glavtorg; i.e., they are under double subordination.

Glavtorg submits to Gorplan proposed plans for retail trade activity, available funds, further development of the trade network, capital construction, and the transportation and winter storage of potatoes, vegetables, and fruit. Gorplan considers these proposals from the viewpoint of coordinating them with the income of the population, the construction capacity of the trade enterprises, and the improvement of trade services. The proposals of Glavtorg, approved by Gorplan, are submitted to the Ministry of Trade of the R.S.F.S.R.

The Main Administration of Public Food Services (Glavobshepit) manages the organization of the system of food services in the city. It includes the raion catering trusts, the city restaurant trust, and all

Figure 7.19. Organizational Structure of the Trade and Public Food Service System in Moscow.

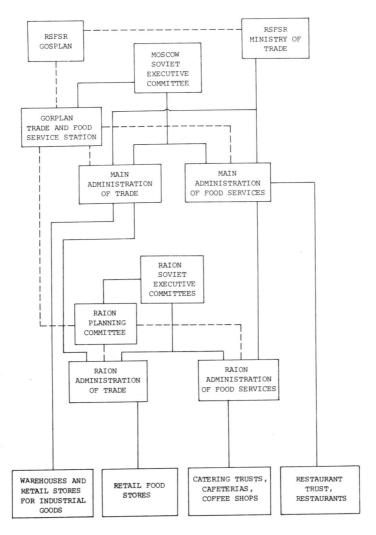

– – – FLOW OF PLANNING INFORMATION

city restaurants (with the exception of those in the railway stations). Glavobshepit submits to Gorplan proposals for trade activity, local products, expansion of the network of public eating places, and capital construction. Figure 7.19 illustrates the organizational structure of the food and trade planning system.

According to the data of the City Statistical Administration, the employees of trade and the public food services for 1970 amounted to 300,000, with 100,000 working for the latter. The planned salary fund for 1970 amounted to 350 million rubles, of which 111.5 million was for the public food services. The average worker's salary was 1,167 rubles per annum, whereas in trade alone it was 1,208 rubles per annum and in public food services it was 1,090 rubles per annum.

Planning

The Gorplan Department of Trade and Public Food Services performs planning functions in the area of operations and in design and capital construction.

Operations

The Department of Trade and Public Food Services performs the following:

1. Plans the distribution of industrial goods and food annually, for five years, and for the long term;
2. Plans the salary fund annually, for five years, and for the long term;
3. Supervises support for trade and public food services;
4. Plans the transport and storage of potatoes and vegetables, as follows:
   • calculates the rate of transport and storage;
   • prepares proposals on the potato and vegetable supply of Moscow (operational and planning);
   • prepares directives;
   • reports on the availability of physical facilities for the storage of potatoes and vegetables;
5. Plans the activities and initiation of production of local enterprises of trade and public food services of the Moscow Executive Committee on an annual basis;
6. Plans and distributes the investments of local industry and other available funds;
7. Plans the development of the industrial trade and public food service networks;
8. Reports and controls the development of trade and the public food services within the cultural-public service network;
9. Balances the income and expenditures of the population through cash and credit plans.

Design and Capital Construction

The General Plan for the Development of Moscow established the following norms for trade services to the population by 1980 (per thousand citizens): 15 employees in stores and 150 seats in public eating places. These requirements are used as a point of departure for the development of five-year and annual plans for trade network growth, which include design work, capital construction, lists of construction sites, distribution of capital investments from the state plan, distribution of local and government capital investments, operational reports on the course of construction and accounts of expenditures, requests for agricultural machines, fertilizers, or other resources by the city enterprises and by the Main Administration of Public Food Services, and accounting for food expenditures.

The Gorplan Department of Trade and Public Food Services develops five-year plans for retail sales volume, for acquiring trade goods, and for the development of trade and warehouse networks.

The total turnover (volume of goods received and passed on) of the food service enterprises of Moscow is calculated and determined from the individual turnover of the food enterprises and local production.

For the determination of turnover, the following factors are considered:

1. The stipulated growth in the number of workers and employees; the number of students in the schools, universities, and technical schools; projected changes in the population structure;
2. The increase of market funds for food; the growth of the proportionate share of food in the total amount of goods for public distribution;
3. The increased income of workers, the growing involvement of women in production, and the decrease of poorly paid work categories, all that lead to an increased share of public food services in total food sales.

The information for the annual and the five-year plans is gathered through the following report documents from the City Statistical Administration and the main administrations of trade and public food services:

1. Report on goods received, sales, and remainders;
2. Report on public food services performed;
3. Report on the existing trade network and its development;
4. Report on the enterprises of public food services and their development;
5. Report on the implementation of the work plan for trade;
6. Report on available facilities for refrigeration, trade, mechanical equipment, hoisting, and transportation equipment;
7. The conjuncture reference, which is a document showing an analysis of market demand;
8. Report on the cash plan (trade profits).

Planning is based on the purchasing power of the population. Purchase funds for the period are determined using the income and expenditure balance of the population, according to a formula approved by the R.S.F.S.R. Gosplan.

The turnover plan also uses data reported in previous plan periods for trade enterprises according to the following factors:

1. Turnover in the city as a whole and rates of annual growth;
2. Turnover in the trade network and rates of annual growth;
3. Turnover in public food service network and rates of annual growth;
4. Local production, annual growth rate, and share of total sales;
5. Sales per citizen for trade and for public food services;
6. Structure of sales (food and nonfood goods);
7. Balance of income and expenditure, and the growth rate of the net income of the population;
8. Development of the networks of trade and public food services;
9. Population of Moscow.

The annual sales plan is based on the annual plans of the main administrations of trade and food services and other trade enterprises. Growth rates based on recent sales, changes in public income, and other planning factors serve as a methodological basis for projecting goods turnover during the succeeding five years.

The coordination of these supply and demand factors is achieved by the development of a system of balances and other calculations as follows:

1. General needs for the goods;
2. Structure of goods turnover (separately for food and other goods);
3. Average sales prices;
4. Summing up of goods procurement.

The general need for goods exceeds sales. The difference depends (in part) on price variation during the plan period in accordance with the Party and government policy of improving the standard of living.

The plan for goods procurement is developed according to the requests of the trade organizations. The plan stipulates resources (funds) in the following forms: (1) funds received from direct sales to the public; and (2) funds received for supplying government agencies.

On the basis of the total goods procurement plan, detailed calculations of the needs for the individual goods are developed.

The Ministry of Trade of the R.S.F.S.R. informs Gorplan of Moscow (City Planning) of the funds available for 16 food and 22 nonfood types of goods, which represent 50 percent of the entire turnover procurement. The rest of the goods do not have strictly specified funds.

Physical Facilities

The retail trade facilities consist of the stores and enterprises of the retail trade, the public food service enterprises, the storehouses for industrial goods, the fruit and vegetable storehouses, the associated trade and food enterprises, the farm markets, and all the equipment belonging to these organizations.

A number of new trade centers are being planned and constructed in the city. These centers are either in new buildings (separate trade centers and stores on the first floors of apartment houses and office buildings) or in reconstructed and expanded existing buildings.

Furthermore, the capacity of the trade enterprises is increasing owing to the implementation of new retailing methods such as specialized shops (dairy, fruit, etc.), more self-service stores, the sale of products through catalogue shops that display samples, prepacked sales, automation, etc.

According to the plan for the detailed development of the microraions, a list of trade and food enterprises with their addresses is approved annually for initial operation in the new and old sections of the city.

The distribution of trade and public food service enterprises among the raions of Moscow as of January 1, 1978, is listed in Table 7.40. Table 7.41 gives some data on refrigeration, hoisting, transportation, and miscellaneous equipment used in the trade system (in warehouses, etc.). Tables 7.42 to 7.44 indicate the growth of the trade and food service system in recent years.

Service Norms and Capital Investments

The existing norms for public service by the trade and food enterprises are the starting point for the planning of the trade network. According to data of the General Plan for the Development of Moscow, the following norms apply to the development of the trade network over the next 15 years:

Employees per 100-square meter trade area (industrial goods)	4.65
Sales persons per 1,000 city inhabitants (industrial goods)	9
Employees per 100-square meter area (food services)	5
Seats per 1,000 city inhabitants (food services)	150
Employees per 1,000 city inhabitants (food services)	6

Table 7.40. Trade and Food Enterprises in Moscow

Raion	No. of Retail Trade Enterprises	No. of Public Food Service Enterprises
Babushkin	203	269
Bauman	151	307
Volgograd	157	204
Voroshilov	137	127
Gagarin	138	191
Dzerdjin	185	265
Zhdanov	131	275
Zheleznodorozhni	109	101
Kalinin	165	309
Kiev	234	275
Kirov	177	242
Krasnogvardeisky	127	149
Krasnopresnesensky	169	277
Kuibishev	175	257
Kuntsevo	168	180
Leningrad	178	302
Lenin	145	305
Lublin	134	181
Moskvorets	160	297
Oktyabr	227	346
Pervomaisky	261	322
Perovo	169	227
Proletarsky	177	291
Sverdlov	208	327
Sevastopol	138	161
Soviet	158	148
Sokolnitchesky	139	555
Timiriazevsky	182	223
Tushino	109	128
Frunzensky	206	315
Tcheriomushinsky	116	199
Zelenograd City	43	76
Not considered within a particular raion	31	71
Total	5,207	7,902

Table 7.41. Data on Equipment Used in the Retail System (1970 data, except as noted)

Items	Quantity
Refrigerators, 1977	14,024
Refrigeration equipment, 1977	55,773
Vending machines	7,589
Production lines	68
Hoisting and transportation equipment	27,883
Cash registers	23,670
Weighing machines	90,466
Machines and equipment for the selling and the preparation of nonalcoholic beverages	1,496
Equipment of the supply trade enterprises	3,728
Wrapping and packaging equipment	281
Miscellaneous trade equipment	3,413

Source: The Moscow City Statistical Department.

Table 7.42. Growth of Retail Trade Turnover (as a percentage of 1956 volume, at constant prices)

	1966	1967	1968	1969	1970
Total retail goods turnover	108	117	127	138	148
Food	104	109	116	126	134
Nonfood	112	127	140	152	166
Turnover per worker	107	114	120	125	131
Turnover per capita	106	114	122	130	137
Turnover per capita—food	102	105	111	118	123
Turnover per capita—nonfood	110	123	134	143	153

Table 7.43. Growth of Turnover in Public Eating Places (as a percentage of 1965 volume, at constant prices)

	1966	1967	1968	1969	1970
Total goods	105	111	122	133	137
Products of internal production	106	113	124	136	144
Purchased goods	102	109	117	126	122
Per individual worker	103	106	110	114	115
Per capita, population	104	109	117	125	127

Table 7.44. Growth of the Trade and Food Service System

	Growth in 1966-70	Growth in 1971-75
Retail stores constructed	NA	1,000
Retail stores constructed (sales positions)	13,700	16,000
Restaurants constructed (seats)	175,000	155,000
Vegetable warehouses (metric tons of storage)	334,000	274,000

NA, not available.

The following sources supplied capital investments for the development of facilities for trade and public food services during the five-year period 1971-75 (in millions of rubles):

State (centralized) capital investments for trade	125
State (centralized) capital investments in the form of 5 percent deductions from housing construction funds	77
Capital investments from noncentralized sources, i.e., through reinvested enterprise profits	142
Capital investments from centralized and noncentralized sources, spent by other ministries and departments for the construction of trade and food centers	71
Total for the development of facilities for the Moscow trade and public food network	415

In accordance with expected turnover increases owing to the growth of the trade network and the development of public food enterprises, expanded warehouse facilities for enterprises are planned. The creation of major centralized warehouse centers with underground railways is anticipated.

The methodology for determining the storage space demand is specified in the methodological directives for the development of the state plan for the national economy issued by Gosplan.

Problems in Determining Demand

The development of sales and the improvement of retail services for the public require the constant availability of operational data on the production and demand for goods. Demand can be actual, evolving, or unsatisfied. Actual demand is determined by analyzing the quantity of goods delivered and sold.

The basic purpose of a study of unsatisfied demand is to determine the reasons behind it. Such a study uses all sorts of public inquiries and questionnaires about the existing system.

The structure of demand in industrial and agricultural trade is formed dynamically by a large number of factors, including the total income of the population after all taxes and deductions, the costs of all products for public use, and the size of the population.

In summary, one should note that the development of trade as a whole depends on the following:

1. Social factors:
   • the social structure of the population;
   • the cultural development level;
   • national and ethnic characteristics;
   • consumers' habits.
2. Economic factors:
   • the level of material production and the degree of diversification of the work, product resources, and trends in trade;
   • income and its distribution among separate population groups;
   • the levels and the relations between the price of products and services for the population;
   • the degree of saturation of the population with durable goods, etc.
3. Demographic factors:
   • the size of the population;
   • the population's sex and age group structure;
   • variations in average family size and structure;
   • migration.

EVERYDAY AND COMMUNAL SERVICES

Everyday services constitute a separate branch of the national economy. At present, the enterprises and centers for everyday services perform a variety of services (about 600 types) for the population. They serve millions of people, making their lives easier by providing them with time for leisure, study, and cultural improvement.

In spite of their great variety, the services can be partitioned into two types of activities: the so-called "productive services," which imply some sort of resultant product, and the "nonproductive services," i.e., services in the conventional sense of the word.

Productive services include the repair of appliances, utility equipment and machinery, and private vehicles, the repair and production of custom furniture, fabric production, custom tailoring, cloth repair, the repair of natural and synthetic leather products, the custom tailoring of leather clothing, shoe repair, the repair and custom production of jewelry items, dry cleaning and dyeing, and the maintenance and repair of apartments. (These last are "extra" maintenance services ordered by the resident, above and beyond those supplied by the housing organization. The work might include installing partitions, painting, and laying parquet floors, for example, and is paid for directly by the resident.)

Nonproductive services include enterprises and organizations that provide everyday services for the population, for instance, public baths and showers, hair cutting, photography and movie labs, apartment cleaning, laundry, the rental of utensils, and multiple service establishments that include a number of services under one roof.

Management Structure of the Service System

The Moscow Executive Committee directs 19 departments and administrations dealing with everyday services. Two of them (the Everyday Service Administration and the Repair and Custom Tailoring Administration) are responsible for approximately 85 percent of all everyday services delivered to the public.

In addition to the 19 municipal agencies mentioned above, there are a number of networks in the city that are attached to ministries and other agencies not managed by the Executive Committee. The most important administrations, ministries, and departments having their own enterprise networks for service to the general public are listed below (note that some have been discussed in detail earlier in this chapter):

1. Everyday and Communal Service Administration of the Moscow Executive Committee;
2. Repair and Custom Tailoring Administration of the Moscow Executive Committee;
3. Television Trust of the Ministry of Everyday Services of the R.S.F.S.R. (TV repair);
4. Central Experimental and Technological Tailoring Laboratory;
5. Main Administration of Housing of the City Executive Committee;
6. High-Rise and Hotel Administration of the Executive Committee;
7. Main Administration of Trade of the Executive Committee;
8. Main Transportation Administration of the Executive Committee;
9. Cultural Administration of the Executive Committee;
10. Pharmacy Administration of the Executive Committee;
11. Administration for the Accounting and Allocation of Housing;
12. Committee for Sports and Physical Culture of the Moscow Executive Committee;

13. Main Scientific Research Administration of the R.S.F.S.R. Ministry of Light Industry;
14. Economics Administration of the Council of Ministers of the R.S.F.S.R.;
15. Economics Administration of the Government Committee to the Council of Ministers of the R.S.F.S.R. for Material and Technical Supply;
16. Central Union of Consumer Associations (maintains special markets in various products purchased from decentralized sources, e.g., pelts, honey);
17. Central Soviet Trade Union Department;
18. Music Fund of the Soviet Union;
19. Literature Fund of the Soviet Union;
20. Everyday Service Combinat, Administration for General Affairs of the Academy of Science of the Soviet Union;
21. Administration of the Labor Supply of the Moscow River Shipping Department of the River Shipping Ministry of the R.S.F.S.R.;
22. Everyday Service Combinat, Economics Administration of the River Shipping Ministry of the R.S.F.S.R.;
23. Main Administration of the Prosthetics Industry of the Ministry of Social Security of the R.S.F.S.R.;
24. Administration of the all-Union stock company "Intourist;"
25. The "Likhachera" Dry Cleaning Plant;
26. Administration of the Enterprises Affiliated with the Economics Department of the Ministry of Interior of the Soviet Union;
27. Administration of Services for the Diplomatic Corps of the Ministry of Interior of the Soviet Union [Note: Interesting. The police agency services foreign diplomats.];
28. Combinat for Applied Art of the Moscow Branch of the R.S.F.S.R. Art Fund;
29. Production Combinat of the Russian Choir Society;
30. Russian Theatre Society;
31. Central Sports Productions of the Central Council of the Sports Societies and Organizations of the Soviet Union;
32. Miscellaneous other organizations.

The structure of the management of the Everyday Service Administration of the city is shown in Figure 7.20. A number of factors determine whether an enterprise is of city or raion subordination. Basically, if the raion budget has financed its construction, it is a raion enterprise, whereas if it has been built with funds from the city budget, it belongs to the city. Thus, larger and more elaborate enterprises will tend to be subordinate to the city since necessary capital funds are more readily available at the city level.

In the newer residential raions, many establishments are of city subordination because available space and high population densities made it desirable to construct large, expensive, multiservice establishments. In the older raions, however, space exists only for smaller shops, and the raions generally finance these.

Figure 7.20. Organizational Structure of Everyday Services in Moscow.

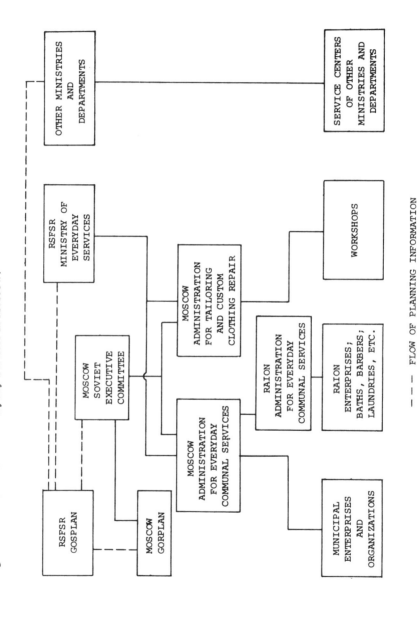

190

Figure 7.21.   The System of Planning for the Everyday Services of Moscow.

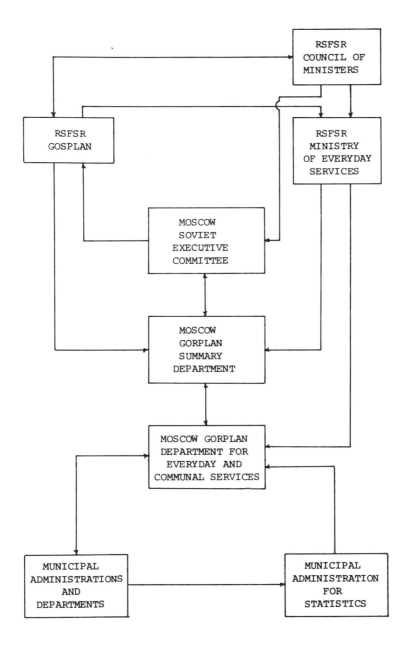

Planning and Management of the Everyday Services

The Everyday and Communal Service Department of the City Planning Commission (Gorplan) is organized according to a general structure approved by the Moscow Executive Committee. It plans the activities of the service enterprises.

The structure and the scope of the department are determined by the staffing norms. The department consists of five people: the director, three senior engineers, and one engineer. The director of the department is responsible to the vice-chairman of Gorplan.

The department adjusts the plans of the Everyday Service Administration of the Moscow Executive Committee and the 18 other agencies subordinate to the committee; it coordinates the service plans for all everyday service-delivering agencies in Moscow; it adjusts the capacity calculations and the work volumes of the service enterprises, the net prices and the profits, and the service volume in terms of money; and it plans the actual work of the administration for custom tailoring and clothing repair and its 17 enterprises. Furthermore, it handles reports, planning, and control for the further development of the service enterprise network in Moscow.

The process of developing the service plan is similar to the one described in Chapter 5.

The plan for the development of the service enterprise network is approved by a decision of the Moscow Executive Committee and includes the scheduled opening of new service centers and five-year and annual plans for the development of the service network.

The flow of documents during the development of the plan is shown in Figure 7.21.

The basic factors in the calculations of the service plans are the following:

1. Total volume of the everyday services for the public, by type;
2. Capacity and volume of the service enterprises;
3. Size of the population;
4. Volume of capital investments and new enterprises;
5. List of the most important service projects of the national economy.

Figure 7.22 illustrates part of the analysis that is involved in the planning of the operations of a municipal laundry. Such calculations are used to improve labor productivity and enterprise efficiency.

As an example, the number of workers, W, in a laundry is 42; the number of workers engaged in mechanized work (washing machine operators, dryer operators, roller operators, pressers), W_m, is 29. The

Figure 7.22. Labor Time of Workers in Different Sections of a Laundry Enterprise.

Elements of Work Time	Time Spent							
	Sorters		Washing Section		Drying-Ironing Section		Laundry Collection Section	
	min.	percent	min.	percent	min.	percent	min.	percent
1. Preparation-Conclusion Time receiving the work and	847	2.8	1,815	3.6	7,968	4.0	624	1.3
equipment	544	1.8	605	1.2	2,789	1.4	432	0.9
handing in work and equipment	303	1.0	1,210	2.4	5,179	2.6	192	0.4
2. Operating Time:	22,105	73.1	33,214	65.9	134,261	67.4	35,904	74.8
Sorting dirty laundry, making up loads depending on the volume of the washing machines, writing out a ticket for each load indicating where it is to go	22,105	73.1						
Washing the laundry, including loading the machine, setting and starting the machine, making sure the machine functions properly, operating water, detergent, and steam valves			33,214	65.9				
Ironing the laundry, placing it in the machine and removing it, folding the laundry					134,261	67.4		

193

Figure 7.22. (*continued*)

				Time Spent				
	Sorters		Washing Section		Drying-Ironing Section		Laundry Collection Section	
Elements of Work Time	min.	percent	min.	percent	min.	percent	min.	percent
Delivering the clean laundry according to the tickets written at the point of collection, packaging the laundry							35,904	74.8
3. Servicing the Work Area	968	3.2	2,750	5.1	10,956	5.5	3,502	7.3
Getting the laundry to the work area	575	1.9	1,109	2.2	2,988	1.5	1,486	3.1
Removing finished laundry from the work area	393	1.3	554	1.1	1,992	1.0	2,016	4.2
Care for equipment (cleaning the washing machine, changing the cloth on the drying-ironing machine)			907	1.8	5,976	3.0		
4. Time wasted by worker	1,875	6.5	2,167	4.3	7,968	4.0	1,968	4.1
Personal needs	666	2.2	1,109	2.2	4,382	2.2	1,056	2.2
Incidental conversations	363	1.2			1,992	1.0	384	0.8
Absence from place of work	302	1.1					192	0.4
Arriving late to work or from the lunch break	242	0.8	857	1.7				
Leaving work early or to the lunch break	302	1.0	201	0.4	1,594	0.8	336	0.7

5. Time lost but not due to the worker	4,445	14.7	10,433	20.7	37,051	18.6	6,000	12.5
By the shop	3,568	11.8	8,820	17.5	30,278	15.2	5,328	11.1
The absence of laundry: because of late delivery from the points of collection	2,963	9.8	3,074	6.1	10,159	5.1	4,752	9.9
Because of the disproportion between the productivity of washing and drying-ironing equipment					6,754	3.3		
Waiting for a cart	605	2.0			1,394	0.7	576	1.2
Waiting for equipment repair			3,427	6.8	5,976	3.0		
Equipment repair			2,066	4.1	6,175	3.1		
Lack of water pressure			253	0.5				
6. Time lost but not due to the shop	876	2.9	1,613	3.2	6,773	3.4	672	1.4
Lack of electricity			806	1.6	3,187	1.6		
Lack of steam			151	0.3	996	0.5		
Lack of laundry (caused by a laundry's service organization's refusal to serve)	876	2.9	656	1.3	2,590	1.3	672	1.4
7. Work outside of designated functions					996	0.5		
Preparation of detergent	201		201	0.4	996	0.5		
Shaking out laundry	201		201	0.4	996	0.5		
Total	30,240	100	50,400	100	199,200	100	48,000	100

time spent on manual operations is T_{man}, and the time spent on mechanized labor is T_{mec}. The level of mechanization of the production processes in a laundry is defined by the percentage of workers engaged in mechanized labor:

$$L_m = \frac{W_m}{W} \times 100 = \frac{29}{42} = 69\%.$$

The level of mechanized labor in terms of time spent in the washing and rinsing section is:

$$L_m = \frac{T_{mec}}{T} \times 100 = \frac{39.2}{56.8} \times 100 = 69\%.$$

The level in the drying-ironing section is:

$$L_m = \frac{11.2}{54.2} \times 100 = 20.7\%.$$

Scope and Output of the Everyday Service System

In 1970, the everyday services employed 92,200 people, 9,500 of which were graduates of universities and technical schools. By the end of 1975, the number of employees increased to 102,300, for an average annual growth rate of 3 percent, which is 1 percent greater than the average growth rate of the entire city economy. (By 1977, the administration had been split into the Administration for Everyday Services, with about 50,000 employees, and the Administration for Communal Services, with about 53,000 employees. In addition, the central administration offices contained about 200 to 250 people each.)

Neither in this nor in other fields are salary data available. Different enterprises under different ministries have their own salary scales. The national average salary of all workers is 150 rubles per month, though this is higher in Moscow.

Data on the number of enterprises in the service network and the volume of their work are listed in Table 7.45.

In 1975, the value of the everyday services delivered was 350 million rubles. The following types of services experienced the greatest expansion:

1. Consumer-ordered housing repair was planned at a value of 13.7 million rubles.
2. Home appliance repair services were planned at a value of 36.5 million rubles.
3. Dry cleaning was planned at a value of 29 million rubles, or 27.7 thousand tons; per citizen, this represents 3.7 items as opposed to 2.5 in 1970.

Table 7.45. The Moscow Service Network and Its Output

Type of Service	No. of Enterprises in 1970	No. of Intake Centers Separate from the Service Enterprise Itself in 1970	Volume of the Work in Thousands of Rubles	
			1970	1977
Shoe repair and custom shoe production	460	39	16,345	19,600
Cloth, leather, hats, and lingerie repair and custom tailoring of clothes	641	133	57,348	70,600
Repair of service machinery and utensils, repair and production of metalware, and repair and service of private autos	435	94	25,253	39,500
Furniture repair and production	83	8	8,013	4,500
Dry cleaning and dyeing	42	463	18,268	24,500
Laundries	81	650	28,288	38,300
Repair and custom production of knitted fabrics	8	80	2,010	2,500
Photo shops and labs	132	20	5,446	8,400
House repairs on personal request	25	–	3,857	4,100
Baths and shower rooms	98	–	3,839	3,500
Barbers	677	–	27,372	31,700
Labor centers	109	–	1,964	3,500
Miscellaneous services	696	27	31,208	50,200
Total	3,487	1,514	299,211	300,900

4. Linen washing was planned at a value of 39.4 million rubles, or 173 thousand tons; per citizen, this represents 23 kilograms per annum as opposed to 17.4 in 1970.

The total amount of the everyday services paid for by one citizen in 1975 was 38 rubles, 48 kopeks, as opposed to 30 rubles, 95 kopeks in 1970, and 13 rubles, 20 kopeks in 1965.

During 1971-75, the construction of everyday service centers was to amount to 92.8 million rubles, or 1.5 times more than in the previous five-year period.

It should be noted that the price lists for everyday services of the centers are approved by the Moscow Executive Committee according to a standardized work list, taking into account the recommended norms for the work and for material expenditures.

APPENDIX: Moscow Metro Stations

Kirovsko-Frunzenskaya Line

1. Preobrazhenskaya Ploshchad'
2. Sokol'niki
3. Krasnocel'skaya
4. Komsomol'skaya
5. Lermontovskaya
6. Kirovskaya
7. Dzerzhinskaya
8. Prospekt Marksa
9. Arbatskaya
10. Kropotkinskaya
11. Park Kulturi
12. Frunzenskaya
13. Sportivnaya
14. Leninskie Gor'y
15. Universitet
16. Prospekt Vernadskovo
17. Yugo-Zapadnaya

Arbatsko-Pokrovskaya Line

18. Shchelkovskaya
19. Pervomaiskaya
20. Izmailovskaya
21. Izmailovskaya Park
22. Semenovskaya
23. Elektrozavodskaya
24. Baumanskaya
25. Kurskaya
26. Ploshchad' Revoliutsii
27. Arbatskaya
28. Smolenskaya
29. Kievskaya

Gor'Kovsko-Zamoskvoretskaya Line

30. Rechnoi Vokzal
31. Vodnii Stadion

32. Voikovskaya
33. Sokol
34. Aeroport
35. Dinamo
36. Belorusskaya
37. Mayakovskaya
38. Ploshchad' Sverdlova
39. Novokyznetskaya
40. Paveletskaya
41. Avtozavodskaya
42. Kolomenskaya
43. Kashirskaya
44. Varshavskaya
45. Kakhovskaya

Kol'Tsevaya (Circle) Line

46. Taganskaya
47. Paveletskaya
48. Dobrininskaya
49. Oktyabr'skaya
50. Park Kulturi
51. Kievskaya
52. Krasnopresnenskaya
53. Belorusskaya
54. Novoslobodskaya
55. Prospekt Mira
56. Komsomolskaya
57. Kurskaya

Kaluzhsko-Rizhskaya Line

58. VDNKh (Exhibition Grounds)
59. Shcherbakovskaya
60. Rizhskaya
61. Prospekt Mira
62. Kolkhoznaya
63. Turgenevskaya
64. Ploshchad' Nogina
65. Biblioteka Lenina
66. Oktyabr'skaya
67. Leninskii Prospekt
68. Akademicheskaya
69. Profsoyuznaya
70. Novie Cheremushki
71. Kalyzhskaya
72. Belyaevo

Filevskaya Line

73. Molodezhnaya
74. Kunsevskaya

75. Pionirskaya
76. Filevskii Park
77. Bagrationovskaya
78. Fili
79. Kytuzovskaya
80. Studensheskaya
81. Kievskaya
82. Smolenskaya
83. Arbatskaya
84. Kalininskaya

Zhdanovskaya-Krasnopresnenskaya Line

85. Planernaya
86. Skhodnenskaya
87. Tushinskaya
88. Shchukinskaya
89. Oktyabr'skoe Pole
90. Polezhaevskaya
91. Begovaya
92. Ulitsa 1905
93. Barrikadnaya
94. Pushkinskaya
95. Kuznetskii Most
96. Ploshchad' Nogina
97. Taganskaya
98. Proletarskaya
99. Volgogradskii Prospekt
100. Tekstil'shchiki
101. Kuz'minki
102. Ryazanskii Prospekt
103. Zhdanovskaya

BIBLIOGRAPHY

SOVIET GOVERNMENT PUBLICATIONS

Main Scientific Research and Computing Center of the Moscow City Soviet. *Characteristics of Municipal Data Processing Applications in Moscow.* Moscow, Soviet Union, 1975.

————. *A Description of the Management System of the City of Moscow.* Moscow, Soviet Union, 1979.

Poliak, G. B., and E. V. Sofronova. *The General Plan and Budget of Moscow.* Translated by N. Szalzvitz and J. Kaiser. New York: Center for Business and Government Studies, Columbia University, 1976.

OTHER PUBLICATIONS

Cattell, David. *Leningrad: A Case Study of Soviet Urban Government.* New York: Praeger, 1968.

Frahm, James. *Solid Waste Management in Moscow.* New York: Center for Business and Government Studies, Columbia University, 1977.

Frolich, B. M. Soviet Urban Politics. Unpublished doctoral thesis. Toronto: York University, 1970.

Kaiser, J. A. *The Use of Computer Systems by Local Governments in the Soviet Union.* New York: Center for Business and Government Studies, Columbia University, 1976.

Lewis, Carol W., and Stephen Sternheimer. *Soviet Urban Management: With Comparison to the United States.* New York: Praeger, 1979.

Savas, E. S. *Municipal Data Systems in the Soviet Union.* Government Data Systems, November/December 1973, New York.

Taubman, William. *Governing Soviet Cities: Bureaucratic Politics and Urban Development in the U.S.S.R.* New York: Praeger, 1973.

PERIODICALS

Biulletin' Ispolnitel'novo Kommiteta Moskovskovo Gorodskovo Sovieta Deputatov Trudyashchikhsya. Bulletin of the Executive Committee of the Moscow City Soviet. Moscow, Soviet Union.

The Current Digest of the Soviet Press. The American Association for the Advancement of Slavic Studies. Columbus, Ohio, U.S.A.

Gorodskoye Khosyaistvo Moskvi. Journal of the Executive Committee of the Moscow City Soviet. Moscow, Soviet Union.

INDEX

Administration of Roads and Public Services, 142-46

Administration of Taxi and Automobile Transport, 132-33

Administrative Inspectorate, 147

Asphalt and Concrete Trust, 144

ASU Glavmosstroi, 82

ASU Moskva, 82

ASUs: additional, 84; Branch, 83-84; definition of, 80; and dispatch centers, 107; examples of, 82-83; future of, 82; and housing facilities, 100; Interbranch, 83-84; levels of, 81-82

automatic (computerized) systems (*See* ASUs)

Budget Committee, 61-62

budget expenditures: for bridge and highway construction, 78; capital, 71-72; for cleaning and lighting city, 77; for cultural centers, 78; for education, 75; for garbage collection, 77; for health care, 73-74; for housing, 72-73; increases in, 71; for libraries, 78; for national economy, 71-72; for parks, 77; for raions, 71; for recreation areas, 78; for sewage treatment, 79; for social security, 74; for sociocultural development, 74; for sports facilities, 78-79; for transportation, 76-77; for water supply, 79

budgeting: and city revenues, 67-71; expenditures (*See* budget expenditures); and modern management efforts, 79-84; procedures, 60-65; and raion revenues, 67-71; and revenue sources, 65-67

Central Dispatch System, 107-8

city: boundaries of, 2-3; definition of, 2; functions associated with, 1-2; modern management techniques of, 80; problems in development of, 3-4; revenues, 67-71

City Executive Committee, 118

city government: and city soviets, 36; and City Raion Executive Committee (*See* City Raion Executive Committee); and Communist Party, 47-48; and deputies, 45-46; and deputy groups, 46; and district government structure, 34, 36; legal basis for, 19-22; and local soviets, 22-28; and municipal government structure, 28-29, 34; powers of, 22-28; and public organizations, 46-47; and raion soviets, 36; rights of, 22-28; and standing committees, 44-45

City Mechanical Trust, 144, 146

City Planning Commission: and education, 123; and everyday services, 192; and health care system, 115-16, 118; as planning organ of Moscow, 54; and revisions of plans, 56; and schedules for stages of planning, 56; and stages of planning, 55-56

City Raion Executive Committee: basic sections of, 38-41; and control and inspection, 41-44; functions of, 36-38; problems handled by, 34, 36; structure of, 34

city soviets, 19-20, 36, 62

climate, 6

coefficient of labor cooperation, 88

Communist Party, 1, 47-48, 70

computers (*See* ASUs; RYAD computers)

Constitution of the Soviet Union, 19, 22-23, 60

Construction Materials Trust, 144

Control Group, 41-42

demography (*See* population)

Department of Education and Health Protection, 115

Department of Municipal Passenger Transportation, 132

Department of Trade and Public Food Services, 180-81

deputies, 45-46

deputy groups, 46

202

Deputy Status Law, 45-46
Division of Parks, 171

economic development: basic planning procedure for, 54-56, and municipal development, 56-59
economy, 11-13 (*See also* economic development)
education: budget expenditures for, 75; and
construction of schools, 125-26; description of, 16-17; and extended daily schedule, 123; and location of educational institutions, 123, and Mosgorno, 121, 123-24;
and number of schools, 125-26; organization of, 121, 123; and preschool children's
institutions, 127-30; and RONOs, 123;
statistics, 125; and vocational school network, 123, 125
Emergency Ambulance Service, 176-77
everyday services: management of, 192-196;
output of, 196-98; planning of, 192-96;
scope of, 196-98; structure of, 188-92;
types of, 187-88
Everyday Service Administration, 189-90
Executive Committee: agencies of, 29; authority over, 21; and budgeting, 63-64;
election of, 28; and everyday services,
188; organization of, 28, 32-33; and system of administration, 34; units under, 29
Experimental Mechanical Plant, 144

"Finances," 82
Fire Protection Service, 175-76
Five-Year Plan, 69

General Department, 43
General Plan for Municipal Development:
current, 56-59; design of, 54; deviations
from, 59; and food services, 180-81; and
housing, 58; and metro, 136; post-war,
56; and transportation, 58; and water
supply, 168
geography: physical, 5-6; political, 6, 8
Glavapu, 94, 96
Glavgorzdrav, 118
Glavmosavtotrans, 98, 132, 134, 140
"Glavmosavtotrans," 83
Glavmosingstroi, 94, 96
Glavmospromstroimaterialu, 96
Glavmosstroi, 82, 94, 96, 98
"Glavmosstroi," 82-83
Glavmoszhilupravlenie, 96
Glavobshepit, 178-80
Glavtorg, 178-80

Glavuks, 94, 96
Gordormekhanizatsiya, 144, 146
Gorfin, 62-63
Gorplan (*See* City Planning Commission)
"Gorplan," 82
Government Automobile Inspectorate, 132
Great Circular Railway, 13
Great Moscow Principality, 5

health care: budget expenditures for, 73-74;
and hospital centers, 118; system of, 115-
16, 118, 121
history, 5
housing: administration, 98-100; agencies,
94, 96-97; assignment of, 99-100; budget expenditures for, 72-73; and capital
repairs, 112-14; as concern of city government, 92; construction, 93-98; and
current repairs, 109-12, description of,
14-15; expenditures, 108-9; and General
Plan for Municipal Development, 58; income, 108-9; management, 100-1, 103,
105-8; statistics, 92-93
Housing Operation Offices (*See* zhek)
Hydrotechnology and Bridge Trust, 144

K. D. Pamfilov Academy of Communal
Services, 142, 144
KGB, 174
"Kurs," 83, 100

labor, shortages of, 59, 79 (*See also* personnel)

Main Administration for Architecture and
Planning, 94, 96
Main Administration for Capital Construc-
tion, 94, 96
Main Administration for Construction Mater-
ials, 96
Main Administration for (Housing) Construc-
tion, 82, 94, 96, 98
Main Administration for Internal Affairs, 174
Main Administration for the Construction
of Engineering Projects, 94, 96
Main Administration of Culture, 171
Main Administration of Public Education of
Moscow, 121, 123-24, 171
Main Administration of Public Food Serv-
ices, 178-80
Main Administration of Trade, 178-80
Main Housing Administration, 96, 100
Main Moscow Administration of Auto Trans-
port, 98, 132, 134, 140
Main Public Health Administration, 118-19

Main Scientific Research Computing Center, 42, 80-81
"Material Technical Supply," 82
mechanized work, 192-96
Metro Administration, 130
metropolitan area, 3
militia, 174-75
Moscow: administration of, 19; budgeting for (See budgeting); climate of, 6; and connections with other cities, 22; demography of, 8-11, 57-58; economy of, 11-13; education in (See education); environmental protection of, 17; government of (See city government); health services in, 122 (See also Health care); history of, 5; hospital centers in, 117, 121; housing in (See housing); labor resources in, 59, 79 (See also personnel); life expectancy in, 121; long-term planning for (See economic development); municipal services in (See Municipal services); parks in (See parks); physical features of, 5-6; planning structure of, 57-58; political geography of, 6, 8; problems of, 4; production activity of, 3, 12; raions of, 7-8; recreation in, 17-18; short-term planning for (See budgeting); urban zones of, 57; utilities in, 14-15
Moscow Administration for the Accounting and Allocation of Housing, 98-99
Moscow Belt Highway Division, 144
Moscow Canal, 14, 18
Moscow City Administration of Forests and Parks, 172-74
Moscow city agglomeration, 6
Moscow City Executive Committee (See Executive Committee)
Moscow City Finance Administration, 62-63
Moscow City Party Committee, 47-48
Moscow City Party Conference, 47
Moscow City Soviet: authority over, 21; and budgeting, 62; power of, 22-28; rights of, 23-28
Moscow Metro, 136-38
Moscow River, 5-6, 18
Moscow Soviet Executive Committee (See Raion Executive Committee)
Moscow Soviet of the Workers' Deputies, 28, 30
Moscow Soviet Executive Committee, 49-51
MosGorIspolCom (See Executive Committee)
Mosgorno: and parks, 171; responsibilities of, 121, 123; structure of, 123-24

"Mossoviet," 83
municipal services: education (See education); parks, 170-74; preschool children's institutions, 127-30; public food services (See public food services); public safety, 174-77; public services (See Public services); waste water, 166-70; water supply, 166-70

national secret police, 174

"On the City and Municipal Raion Soviets of People's Deputies of the R.S.F.S.R.," 19
"On the Introduction of Amendments and Additions to the Decree of the U.S.S.R. Supreme Soviet entitled 'Basic Rights and Obligations of the City and the Municipal Raion Councils of Workers Deputies'," 19

parks: budget expenditures for, 77; classifications of, 170; damage to, 172; description of, 17-18; management of, 170-72; and Moscow City Administration of Forests and Parks, 172-74; system of, 172
Passenger Transport Administration, 130-32
personnel: administration for, 87-89; evaluation of specialists and technical managers, 90-91; number of employees in, 85-87
police, 174-75
population: age of, 9; changes in, 11; educational level of, 16; increase in, 8; as labor force, 9-11; male, 8-9; and migration, 11; of urban zones, 57-58
"Population and Labor Resources," 83
Production Technology Section, 142
public food services: capital investments in, 183, 186; growth of, 186; physical facilities of, 183; planning of, 180-83; and problems in determining demand, 186-87; service norms of, 183, 186; structure of, 177-80
public organizations, 46-47
public safety: ambulance service, 176-77; fire service, 175-76; police, 174-75
public services: organization of, 142-47; refuse collection and disposal (See refuse collection and disposal); road cleaning and maintenance (See road maintenance)

R.S.F.S.R., 6, 19, 60
Raion Administration of Housing Services, 101

Raion City Executive Committee, 23, 64-65
raion departments of public education, 123, 127
raions: and budgeting, 61-63; and City Raion Executive Committee, 23, 64-65; financing for, 63; functions of, 36; importance of, 19-20; list of, 7-8; revenues of, 67-71; and roads, 146-47; structure of, 34-36
Raion Soviet Executive Committee, 98
Raion Soviet of Workers' Deputies, 34, 52-53
raion soviets, rights of, 23-28
RCCs, 98
RCU, 146
refuse collection and disposal: operations, 160-65; planning, 155-60; workload, 165
Repair and Construction Unit, 146
Residential Construction Combinats, 98
road maintenance: and operations of street cleaning, 151-55; and production plan of street cleaning, 150-51; and repair, 148-50; and service structure, 147-48; and transportation indexes, 148-50
Road Operations Units, 146
RONOs, 123, 127
ROU, 146
RSMB, 146
Russia (*See* Soviet Union)
Russian Soviet Federated Socialist Republic, 6, 19, 60
RYAD computers, 80

sanitary-epidemologic station, 120
"Signal," 83
6 Road Service Mechanical Bases, 146
Soviet Union: Constitution of, 19, 22-23, 60; and intracity passenger transportation, 130; urban development in, 1-4 (*See also* city; Moscow)
St. Petersburg, 5
standing committees, 44-45
"Start," 84, 141

State Construction Committee, 2
street cleaning, formulas for, 151 (*See also* road maintenance)
Supreme Soviet, 21-22

taxes: bachelor, 67, 71; deductions from, 66-67; on enterprise, 65-66; income, 66, 70-71; local, 66, 70; personal, 67; state, 66; turnover, 66-67, 70-71
Test Design Bureau, 144
trade (*See* public food services)
traffic control, 132, 140-42
transportation: budget expenditures for, 76-77; description of, 13-14; freight, 140; and General Plan for Municipal Development, 58; growth, 135; operations, 135-36, 138-42; organization of, 130, 132; planning of, 130, 132; surface, 138-39; and traffic control, 132, 140-42
Trust of Operating Production Enterprises, 144

Union of South Socialist Republics, 6
urban development, in Soviet Union, 1-4 (*See also* city; Moscow)
utilities, 14-15

waste water treatment, 79, 169-70
water supply, 79, 166-69

zhek: and Central Dispatch System, 107-8; description of, 105; directors of, 100; expenditures of, 105; and housing repairs, 113; maintenance staff of, 105; operation of, 103; organization of, 103; and parks, 172; responsibilities of, 105-6; revenues for, 105; services provided to, 105; strengthening of, 106-7; work of, 103
Zhilishehno-Ekspluatsionnie Kontori (*See* zhek)

ABOUT THE AUTHORS

John A. Kaiser is the Associate Director of the Center for International Business Cycle Research at the Columbia University Graduate School of Business. Born in Brooklyn, N.Y., Mr. Kaiser worked for ten years as a specialist in public sector management for the federal, New York State, and New York City governments before coming to Columbia in 1975.

From 1975 through 1983 he was project director of the US-USSR Cooperative Agreement on the Use of Computers in Urban Management, during which time he made eight research trips to the Soviet Union. He is the editor and translator of numerous articles on the Soviet economy and public service system.

Mr. Kaiser has extensive consulting experience with local government agencies in the areas of management reform, labor relations, and productivity improvement. He lives with his wife Kay and their four children in Chatham, New Jersey.

E.S. Savas is professor of management at the City University of New York. He served as Assistant Secretary of Housing and Urban Development in the Reagan Administration, and as First Deputy City Administrator of New York under Mayor Lindsay. In the 1970's, under a bilateral agreement between the U.S. and the Soviet Union, Professor Savas served as the American director of a joint U.S.-U.S.S.R. project on the management of large cities. In this capacity he visited and studied eight major cities throughout the Soviet Union and interviewed mayors and other local officials. This book is a result of that project.